Introduction

Repairing an old piece of furniture, a rug, a plate, or some other cherished antique, can be a highly satisfying activity. There is not only the thought that you might well have saved yourself the often considerable expense of having it done professionally, there is also the pleasure of having performed the job yourself and of having seen a piece be restored to its former glory in your hands. While a certain degree of wear and tear is necessary to give an old piece the required patina of age, it only wants the wear and tear to have been taken too far and instead of looking aged, the piece is damaged, and much of its charm disappears. But it does not necessarily require special skills or complex instruction to carry out the repair that will restore the former beauty of the piece.

This book will be of value to those who wish to learn the basic skills of repairing wooden or upholstered furniture, ceramics and china, rugs and carpets and antique metalware. It will be useful to collectors of antiques, who may have in their collection damaged pieces which they would like to see recover their original beauty, and to the serious student who wishes to learn restoration up to a high standard.

None of these crafts can be rushed; patience will avoid errors, and ultimately produce the most satisfactory results. Apart from the simplest jobs, you cannot expect to finish in one session. However, none of the tasks described in this book is excessively time-consuming either; even the longest only takes four or five sessions of work, with time in between to allow glues to set or surfaces to dry.

Careful choice of materials is an essential prerequisite of proper restoration. Although it is neither practical nor desirable to avoid modern materials altogether, this book generally emphasizes using the older methods and materials where possible, as these will give the most authentic-looking repairs to an ancient object. Materials that will not be seen, such as glues, do not create much of a problem, providing that they work well with the object, but whenever restorers replace missing parts they should ask themselves if they are like the originals.

The same is also true of the finish applied to a piece. Polyurethane varnish, for instance, is a modern material, and has no place in restoration work. The restorer who uses traditional tools and techniques, with an understanding of the methods of the old craftsman, can rest assured that his or her work will gradually blend with the original piece.

None of the topics covered in this book need prove expensive hobbies. Indeed, you will probably find that you have many of the items listed in the tools and materials pages of each section of the book in your kitchen or toolbox already. Occasionally, costly tools are recommended, but they are usually optional and can often be hired or borrowed, rather than bought. Nor do you need to set up a special workspace, although you may wish to do so.

There is also the cost advantage for the person who wants to make a hobby out of antique repair, as opposed to the person who just has some damaged

This beautiful pine chiffonier was in a sorry state, with missing handles, broken door and drawers, and a badly marked surface. Careful repair and painstaking finishing have transformed it into a delight. Major jobs like this take time, but are very satisfying.

pieces and wants to repair them, in that damaged antiques are easily available and can be remarkably cheap. Sometimes, applying some simple techniques, such as stain removal and filling, can increase the value of a piece as well as making it far more pleasing to the eye. Nor is this fraudulent if one wants to sell the piece on; our museums and art galleries are filled with works of art that have been restored and repaired to make good the damage of centuries. It would only be wrong if you pretended that a piece had not been repaired or restored and was still in its original state. But apart from the morality of this, it is unnecessary as a well-restored piece will generally be worth more than one still untouched but in a poor state.

To be a good restorer, you need some knowledge of the basic skills of the original craftsman. For example, there are few constructional differences between oriental rugs, but the variety of textures, colour and design is never-ending. It is these differences which surround the oriental rug with magic and mystique, and at the same time help the expert to establish the date and country of origin for each piece. For the good restorer the subtleties of colour and texture are important for the challenge they create to achieving the perfect repair, rather than for what they say about the rug's history, but without the sort of love and fascination for oriental rugs that prompts one to learn as much as possible about them a restorer is unlikely to achieve the high standards set by the original weavers.

Likewise, with wooden and upholstered furniture, the more you know about the history of furniture-making, and how pieces were originally constructed, the better guided will be your decisions on choosing replacement parts or applying authentic finishes.

Much of this book is organized into specific projects. The aim of this is not to show only how to tackle those types of objects, but to teach the techniques through practical example. The projects have been carefully chosen to cover between them all the techniques that the average restorer is likely to need and in a form that easily relates to the particular jobs that he or she is likely to come across. The simpler tasks are given first in each section, and these give the basic techniques that are necessary for all types of repair work in that medium. Once you have mastered them, you are equipped to tackle the more complex and challenging jobs such as are described in the later projects.

This old-world workshop holds no inaccessible secrets; basic to all wood finishing and polishing techniques are patience, and a feel for the materials.

1

WOODFRAME FURNITURE

Furniture restoration means different things to different people but the ordinary furniture craftsman, who is working for his own pleasure, should attempt to preserve the beauty and usefulness of his possessions, but avoid alterations which conflict with the original use and appearance of the piece.

Skill alone does not make a good restorer. In order to improve his work the restorer should learn something about the history of furniture and furniture-making. This will help when making decisions about the correct form of replacement parts, and in creating an authentic period finish. The most valuable tools in the restorer's kit are the eyes. 'Eyes first, hands last' is a good general rule, and an hour or two spent looking really closely at a piece of furniture can help immensely when it comes to deciding what is to be done. Keep a record of what you do in a notebook; over a few projects this will build up into a file of useful information for future reference. In this way, you can profit from your mistakes, and not repeat them.

The tools of the trade

Most restoration work can be done in the home without an extensive toolkit or elaborate facilities, but warm surroundings and good light are important. If you lack space, a folding bench and vice (vise) will do. Tools, whether old or new, are expensive, but treated well they will last almost indefinitely.

Regular woodworking tools – most of which you will probably already have – are the basis of the restorer's kit: a panel and a fine tenon saw; a coping saw and a small hacksaw; a hand or electric drill with variable speed; a carpenter's brace; two screwdrivers, one of the long slim electrician's type and one middle-sized; a jack plane; a small block plane; a shoulder plane; a set of bevel-edge chisels; a cross peen hammer; and a wooden mallet comprise the basic toolkit.

The problems of the restorer are often different from those of the cabinet-maker, and to tackle restoration effectively, you will need some special tools. Many of these can be made simply at home.

Spring clamps can be cut from old upholstery springs with a small hacksaw. Cut various sizes from a full circle to just over half a circle. They can be used in various ways as clamping aids.

Rubber webbing is a powerful way of holding awkward items while you are gluing them. Thin strips can be cut from old auto inner-tubes by slicing round in a spiral pattern with a sharp knife. Rings cut to make large bands will also be useful. Alternatively, buy some large rubber bands. Webbing is wound over the parts to be joined and pulled tighter with each turn. A few turns will exert a powerful pressure without leaving scars on the surface.

Folding wedges are a lightweight alternative to sash cramps. Simple to make, they are used for all kinds of bigger cramping jobs, like rejointing table tops. In use, the bottom rail is set to a handy length and the wedges are tapped in to increase the pressure.

The scratch-stock is used to make mouldings, or for cutting small grooves. The two handles are made to a comfortable shape, and cutters are filed as required from scrap steel.

A veneer hammer is used when you are re-laying larger pieces of veneer. Its size and shape are not critical, but make the blade from a smooth-surfaced strip of brass.

Sash and g-cramps (clamps) are very useful. If you plan to buy some, get the lighter types, since many joiner's cramps are too heavy for delicate items.

A gluepot, for hot animal (scotch) glue, can be improvised from an ovenware jar, and an old pan. A good small brush will be needed for applying glue. Animal glue is the best for restoration work, and well worth the trouble of preparing it. Details of how to mix animal glue are given on p. 15.

Miscellaneous tools, most of which are in the handyman's toolkit already, will also be needed on occasions. Files, pincers, and electrician's pliers and cutters are useful. A sturdy old screwdriver will help lift tacks, and a few old chisels will protect fine tools from damage where you suspect old nails might be hidden.

Clamps like these are expensive but vital aids to repair and reassembly. Cheaper wooden cramps are sometimes available.

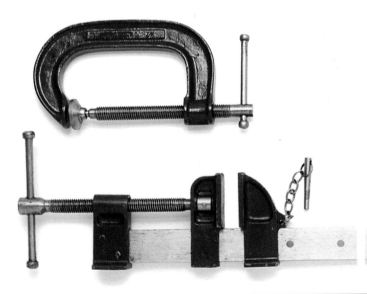

Materials

Glues and fillers

Animal (scotch) glue is the professional restorer's first choice for all wood to wood joints, and is also used for hand veneering, and bone and shell inlay.

PVA (yellow) glue is a good second-best to animal glue. If you use this, remove all traces of old animal glue, since the two do not mix well.

Resin glues can be used where strength is at a premium (for example, on chair back repairs).

Two-part epoxy glues stick almost anything, but may make problems for future restorers, since they are difficult to remove.

Cyanoacrylates are suitable for small repairs to inlay and moulding, *not* for structural work.

Starch paste, *not* the modern 'cellulose' type, is good for laying baize, leather, and paper linings.

'Clam' is a modern paperhanging paste. It is expensive but a strong substitute for starch.

Contact (impact) glues can be useful for lining work but are not 'sympathetic' materials for restoration.

Beaumontage or hard stopping is a mix of beeswax, resin and shellac. See p. 16 for details on use.

Clay-based fillers, a mix of clay, glue and water, are good for *small* splits or dents.

Cellulose wax is a modern synthetic wax material suitable for use under all kinds of finishing material.

Beeswax, the traditional filler for all small blemishes, is not suitable for use under varnish or cellulose, unless it is sealed with french polish (shellac).

Polishes and waxes

Beeswax polish is a mix of beeswax and Mexican turpentine, and may be modified with other waxes. Use it with a duster for routine cleaning (not more than four times a year) or with steel wool for refinishing.

Silicone wax polish should be avoided for old furniture. Under certain conditions of temperature and humidity, it can deteriorate. This 'bloom' is best treated with a reviving solution (see p. 37).

French polish or shellac solution is a mixture of shellac resin and methylated spirit (wood alcohol) and is available in many grades (see pp. 89-93).

Shellac or 'spirit' varnishes are a variety of french polish mixed so as to be suitable for application with a brush. They can give good results if *carefully* used.

Copal varnish is the traditional material for finishing some American furniture.

Polyurethane varnish is modern and tough and should only be used where pieces are given hard daily use.

Cleaning materials

Steel wool can be used with wax for polishing wood, or with a little olive oil on corroded metal parts. Use only the very finest (0000) grade.

Pumice powder is mildly abrasive and can be used to remove paint stains and so on from polished surfaces, and also for dulling glossy french polish.

Jeweller's rouge is mixed to a paste with olive oil, and used for polishing fine metals of all kinds.

Real soap flakes and warm water are the best and most gentle cleaning medium for all types of surface. Rinse off all traces of soap after use.

Best quality furniture wax, fine, soft steel wool, and old cotton cloth give the best results when polishing.

Basic techniques

Damage repairs

Restoration often involves dismantling, and the art of success here is to be methodical. Beware of nails, which were put into joints in the past. This problem is common, and trying to open a joint with a nail in can do a lot of damage. If a part feels rigid, glue is probably holding it firm. The safest way to open a good glued joint is to render the glue useless by washing it out, or melting it. Both modern PVA (yellow) glue, and animal (scotch) glue, soften when hot. Use boiling water, or after wetting the surface well, a gas torch. Be patient as wood is a poor conductor. If you have a workbench with a tail vice (vise), use the vice to prise (pry) apart chair and door frames. Fit the vice dogs inside the frame, and wind the jaws apart. The steady pull will open stubborn joints.

Another common problem which many people find difficult to deal with is opening up secret wedged tenon joints. Wedging may be used by restorers as a method of improving loose joints. The tenon is slotted and one or more small wedges put in. When the joint is reassembled, the wedges hit the base of the mortise, and are forced into the tenon, spreading it apart. This makes it difficult to take the joint apart again. The best method is to open the joint as far as possible, and cut the tenon. The cut should go into one of the slots, and you should be able to pull out the reduced width tenon, leaving the wedge and part of the tenon inside the mortise. The tenon can be glued back normally when you are reassembling.

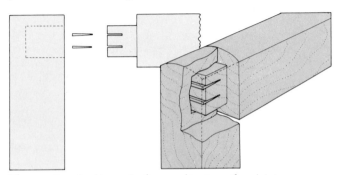

The secret wedged tenon is often used to strengthen joints.

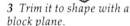

Strengthening with dowels

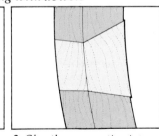

1 Cut a replacement section in suitable timber.

2 Glue the new section into place.

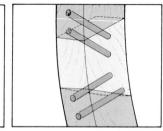

3 Trim it to shape with a block plane.

4 Strengthen with dowels inserted at an angle.

Strengthening methods

Large cracks give restorers difficult problems. Filling large splits with stopping will not be successful; the job may last a while, but the filling will eventually fall out, because the sides of the crack move independently. Lock the edges together with a dowel, then fill the split and repolish the surface.

Where panels are too thin to dowel, apply two layers of veneer to the back of the panel. The grain of each layer should run at right angles to its neighbour, and the three-ply sandwich you create should reduce the tendency of the panel to warp. Trim the veneer, then fill and polish the part.

Splits in cabinet ends and tops can sometimes be squeezed shut with a couple of strong clamps. The secret is to apply a very slight pressure over a long period. In these circumstances the glued joints in the piece gradually creep, and the split closes. Tighten the clamps twice a day, but don't hurry this part. When the split has closed, slacken off the clamps, glue the cleaned crack, and reclamp until the glue has set.

Replacing cloth and leather

Desks and tables covered with leather, or a type of fine felt cloth called baize, became fashionable in the eighteenth century. This type of surface was quieter and kinder than wood, and more suitable for fine glasses, card playing, or writing. At first linings were made from fairly heavy hides, but morocco leathers, glazed and beautifully coloured, soon became popular.

Removing the old cover is fairly straightforward. Lift up a corner, and simply tear it off. This will leave a residue of glue and fibres beneath that can be washed off with hot water. Allow the water to soak into the old paste for a few moments and then wipe it off.

Like veneer (see p. 78), leather should be laid on a sound base, so this is the time to attend to holes or loose knots. Since repairs on defects here are unlikely to be seen, you can use a strong durable filler like autobody repair paste. This has the advantage that it is easy to rub down flat – remember that the slightest bump will be seen through the new cover.

The old method of fixing leather tops, with starch paste, has yet to be bettered. Modern contact glues can be used, but an inadvertent crease put into the surface as you lay it is impossible to remove, and any splash of adhesive on to a polished part of the work will destroy

This Victorian desk has a plain leather top without a border, the simplest kind to lay and trim.

Replacing a leather top

1 Clean off and repair the area to be covered.

2 Coat the ground evenly with paste.

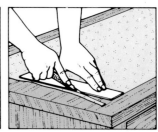

3 Unroll the leather on to the surface.

4 Trim off any excess with a sharp knife.

the finish. You should also consider the problems of following generations of restorers, who will find contact glue hard to shift.

You can make your own paste by adding enough tepid water to a cup of flour to make a thick, smooth sauce. Add about 500ml (1 pint) of boiling water, stirring as you go. The result should be translucent lump-free paste. Leather skivers (tops) are best ordered from a specialist supplier, who will add a tooled border if you wish.

Coat the ground evenly with paste – two thin coats are best – then lay the leather by unrolling it on to the surface. (Cloth is laid in the same way.) Take care to keep the roll straight, though the paste will allow for some adjustment. Use an iron, cool enough to bear on the palm of the hand, to press it down. Where the covering fits into a groove, you can push it firmly down with the rounded end of a steel rule. Trim off any surplus with a razor-sharp craft knife.

Finally, when you are laying cloth, keep the paste to a minimum because any excess will penetrate through and spoil the surface.

Project 1: Windsor chair

Solid wooden chairs

Country-made chairs with turned legs and backs, and shaped solid wooden seats, are found all over the world. One type of country chair, produced and sold in Britain in various styles for over three hundred years, is the Windsor chair. These chairs were also exported to the USA, where they influenced the development of American Windsor chairs. These, in turn, were the inspiration for the very similar Boston rocking chair. The seat was generally made from a single piece of elm, and the other parts from beech, ash, or occasionally, yew. All the jointed parts of the chair were turned on a crude foot-operated pole lathe and legs, arms, and back-sticks were fitted into holes bored with an auger.

Diagnosing faults

With simple items, many of the faults are immediately obvious, but nevertheless, the restorer should look carefully at every part of the piece for signs of damage, old repairs, and to ensure that the item is authentic. Search for nails or screws in the joints, worm damage, and loose parts. These must all be attended to, since a chair is more highly stressed than other pieces of furniture, and must be sound if it is to be used regularly. One or other of the turned parts may be missing, or may perhaps have been replaced with a similar, but not identical, part. New parts can be turned on a simple power-drill lathe attachment.

The chair illustrated had a broken leg, and almost all the joints were loose and creaking. The only way to fix failed chair joints properly is to take the chair apart, but we should emphasize here that complete dismantling is only called for when most of the chair joints have failed. Single joints can often be repaired without major surgery, by injecting fresh glue, or in the case of wedged joints, by cutting out the loose wedge and gluing and knocking a larger one into the slot.

Sometimes, the whole back frame will still be sound, in which case it may be possible to leave this in one piece and dismantle only the seat board and front legs. Windsor chairs, however, have no back frame, and the rear legs and the chair back are completely separate.

Left: *Produced in a variety of styles for over three hundred years, the Windsor chair is valued for its simple elegance and sturdy construction.*

Dismantling techniques

Dismantling old chairs is a nerve-racking job until you have had some practice. Clear a space to work in before you begin – it will help if you have a workbench big enough to lay the chair on. The best technique for the home restorer is to use a wooden mallet to drive the joints apart. The surface of the chair must be protected from bruising, so keep an old blanket or rug between the chair and bench and fix a scrap of carpet to the mallet with masking tape to soften the blows. If you take care to strike firmly and in the correct direction to open the joint, few joints will resist for long.

Removing chair legs

It is usually simplest when you are dismantling a chair to remove the legs first, since this gives better access to the underneath of the seat, where the more difficult arm-rest supports may be wedged in position. Lay the chair on its back, grasp one of the legs firmly in one hand and strike the underside of the seat smartly with the mallet. After a couple of blows, the leg ought to come out of its socket. It can then be separated from the

Removing wedges

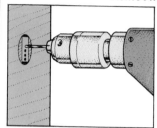

1 Drill a row of holes along the wedge with a small bit.

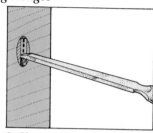

2 Clean out the wood between them with a 3mm (⅛ in.) chisel.

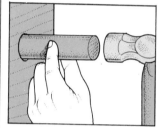

3 Knock out the part with a hammer and wooden rod.

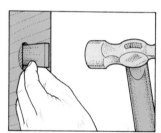

4 Glue and tap in a new wedge during reassembly.

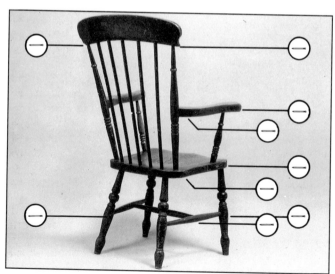

Any joint which fails to come apart after a couple of firm mallet blows is probably held together with a nail or dowel driven sideways through the joint. The photograph shows the most likely places to find nails in a chair.

stretchers that join it to the other legs, and laid aside. Work round the chair, removing each leg in turn.

It is a good idea, particularly when you first start, to put paper tape labels on each part so that you know where they come from. If any joint fails to come apart, examine it carefully, since this is a sign that it may be fastened together with a nail. This must be removed before the joint will part. Use a pair of sharp-nosed electrical cutters to get a grip on the nail; it may help to tap them into the surrounding wood with a hammer.

Removing the back and arms

The back and arms usually protrude through holes drilled right through the seat. When the chairs are made, the timber is slit with a saw up to the point where it enters the hole, and a small wedge knocked into the slit from beneath the seat. This wedge opens the slit out, effectively locking the parts together, and makes a very firm joint, which remains strong even after the glue has perished. The wedges, however, must be removed before the parts can be separated.

Cleaning the joints

Clean joint faces will contribute a great deal to a successful repair. If your chair has never been mended before, the glue in the joints will be the original animal (scotch) glue, which can easily be removed with hot water and a coarse cloth. Animal glue can be recognized by its brown toffee-like appearance and highly soluble nature. Chairs that have modern repairs may have been glued with PVA (yellow) resin, which can be identified by its semi-transparent, white colour and cheesy feel. You can use hot water or methylated spirits (wood alcohol) to remove PVA, but remember that spirit will also dissolve french polish from surfaces which show. The worst kind of glues to find in a repaired chair are the resin adhesives. These set like cement, by chemical reaction, are glass-hard and proof against all solvents. The only way in which they can be removed is by scraping or filing the glue from the joint surfaces.

Making a new leg

Windsor chairs have turned legs, and to make a new one you will need a lathe although for simple work the type sold as a power-drill attachment is adequate. You will also need a piece of beech, a little longer, thicker and wider than the biggest dimension of the original leg. Take the measurements of the surviving leg, or if both are missing, find a similar chair and copy the legs from that – about 500 × 50 × 50mm (20 × 2 × 2 in.) will usually be about right. Turn the wood to a smooth cylinder, by pressing the tool against the wood so that it brings off a steady stream of shavings.

Measure the main features from your pattern piece, and make bold lines with the lathe running. The small round features (called beads) are made with a skew-chisel. Always work so that the tool cuts from the larger diameter to the smaller. Working 'downhill' like this will result in a smoother surface. The larger vase-shaped details can be cut with the gouge, once again working downhill. Deep grooves at the top and bottom of the leg can be cut with a small gouge. When the work is finished, you can remove the waste at these points with a saw. Sand the work in the running lathe, using a long strip of sandpaper held firmly, and finish by burnishing it with a small stick of wood, pressed firmly against the spinning leg.

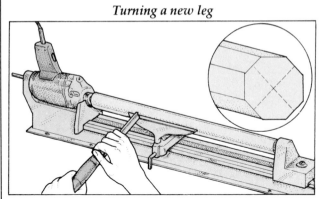

Turning a new leg

1 *Mark the centre of the wood and plane off the corners. Then, using a gouge, turn the wood to a smooth cylinder.*

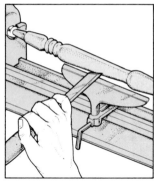

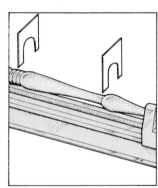

2 *Mark the details on the leg with a skew-chisel.*

3 *Check the size at several points with plywood gauges.*

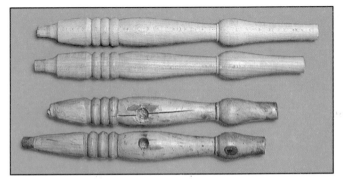

Turned with care, a new leg will match the size and shape of the old one perfectly.

Preparing glue

When the repairs are complete, the chair can be put together again. Animal glue is the most suitable adhesive for restoration work, but it will need to be prepared. Glue of this kind is always best when first made, so only make up a little at a time; for the average chair about 110g (4oz.) should be plenty. If you have bought cake glue, break up the lumps by putting them into a strong plastic bag and hammering it. (This will prevent the fragments flying in all directions.) Put the glue beads or broken lumps into a small container – a jam jar is the right size – and just cover them with cold water. Ideally, you should then leave the mixture to soak overnight. Stand the glue mixture in its container in a small saucepan half-full of cold water. Heat the pan gently, until the water is too hot to touch, but not boiling, and keep the water at this temperature. A small hotplate containing a spirit heater (alcohol lamp) or candle is ideal for this. When the glue has turned to an even brown soup, about the consistency of single (thin) cream, it is ready to use. You can buy special glue brushes, but if you do not have one, you can use a stiff bristle paintbrush to spread it with.

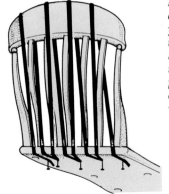

It is difficult to use sash-cramps on a chair back unless you make a saddle to hold them, so use rubber webbing to hold the pieces together while the glue dries. Knock some panel pins into the underside of the seat and wrap the webbing around them.

Reassembling the chair

It is difficult to make firm rules about reassembling chairs, since the details of their construction vary so much. Most chairs with arms are best put together from the top down, so if you dismantled the back, begin by regluing the back-slats and centre splat into the crest rail. Animal glue only works well when it is hot, so work quickly. Warming the parts briefly in the blast from a fan heater will give you more time to fit them together. When all the back is assembled, glue it into the seat-board. Lay this flat on the bench, and put a generous brushful of glue into the sockets. Take the back assembly and push the uprights into the seat. If you have difficulty with some of the slats, wrap a wad of carpet over the crest rail, and tap the back home with mallet blows. Still working as quickly as possible, insert the arm supports, without gluing them into the seat, and fit the unglued arm-rests into position – this will help to ensure the back is in the correct position.

The back will need clamping up tight, to ensure that all the parts are fully home. When you have clamped the back together, lay it on the bench and glue new hardwood wedges into the slots in the bottom of the main uprights. Examine the chair carefully to make sure everything is straight and set it aside for 24 hours.

The legs are fitted in much the same way as the back. Glue the stretchers in place first, and then insert pairs of freshly glued legs into the seat. Pull the whole assembly hard together with rubber straps. This final clamping should be done with the chair standing on a level floor to ensure that it does not dry out with a built-in twist.

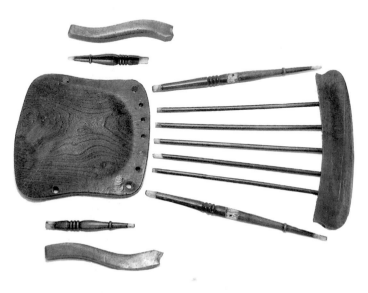

Speed is essential if you are using animal glue, so lay out all the pieces in order before you begin reassembling the chair.

Final touches

Beauty is skin deep' is an expression the restorer should remember. Most of our judgements about the quality or looks of a piece of furniture are based on its surface appearance. For this reason, restorers always consider carefully the finish they give to their work. Indiscriminate stripping of the surface is not recommended, unless it has deteriorated due to damp or neglect, or in cases where a piece has been refinished with paint or varnish that is definitely not original. This may require research. Eighteenth-century Windsor chairs found in Britain, for example, were originally waxed or spirit varnished, while contemporary exports, for assembly in the USA, were usually painted black or green with line decoration.

Minor surface repairs

Whichever method of finishing you choose, surface damage will have to be made good. The ways of doing this are much the same, whether you are going to polish or paint the piece. The traditional filling material used for small holes – old nail or screw holes, for example – is hard stopping, or beaumontage, which is made from equal parts of beeswax and resin, and available from finishing specialists in a wide variety of colours. Make sure that the hole to be filled is free from dirt and grease before you start.

Small dents on exposed surfaces can often be repaired by wetting the surface of the dent and pressing the tip of a hot iron against it. The steam produced swells the wood fibres, and the dent may almost disappear. Larger cracks and holes should be repaired with an insert of wood, as described on p. 24. Splits at the edge of a seat or table top will need reinforcing; the easiest way to do this is to bore a hole in the edge of the split part, and glue a dowel into it to unite the two parts as described on p. 10. This stops the crack from spreading and helps keep the filler in place.

Wax polishing

All furniture needs a finish of some sort and wax polishing is a simple technique appropriate for country-style furniture. Wash the piece down with a mixture of equal parts of turpentine and methylated

Hard stopping

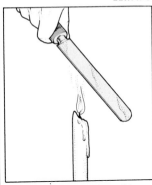

1 Heat the blade of an old table knife over a candle.

2 Press the hard stopping against the blade until it melts.

3 Let the stopping run into the hole or crack.

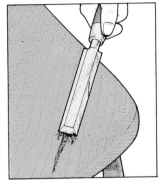

4 When it has cooled, pare off any excess with a chisel.

spirits, to remove old polish and grease. Any remaining polished parts have probably been finished with oil varnish, which can only be removed with paint stripper. When the surface is clean and dry, sand it smooth with 240 grit paper. It is now ready for wax polishing. You can buy special wax from finishing suppliers, or you can make your own, as described on p. 37. The wax is best applied with a clean, soft shoebrush. When the whole piece has been coated, rub it hard with a small pad of finest grade (0000) steel wool. A final burnish with a soft cloth will finish the job.

Waxing can be repeated as often as you like, but you should take care to avoid a build-up of sticky wax on the surface.

Project 2: Scrub-top table

The farmhouse table

The country-made table, with square or turned legs, has a history almost as long as that of the Windsor chair. British examples were generally made from pine, or more rarely, oak, while maple, or a mix of other local woods, were more common in America. The tops were usually made from a light wood. Such tables were used for the preparation of food, and proud cooks would scrub the top with hot water and lye soap until it was snowy-white. The legs were often painted, or stained and polished to a dark gloss.

Genuine old tables of this kind are still plentiful, and relatively inexpensive. However, strong interest in country furniture, and the simple structure of this kind of table, has led to many imitations. Regularly spaced nail marks are a sign that a top may have been made from old floorboards. Another guide is the thickness of the wood used to make the underframe; view wood thinner than 25mm (1in.) with suspicion.

Diagnosing faults

As these tables are of fairly standard construction, the same faults are common to them all. First, many have been painted at some time, and a good part of this may remain. If this is the case, paint stripping is the first task. Usually, the table top will be made up of at least four boards, and these will probably have shrunk apart, leaving gaps that may have been filled with plaster or putty. The best method of repair is to remove and refit the whole top. As the boards are often merely nailed to the frame this is not too difficult and, if the legs are loose or broken, the top will probably need to be removed in any case. Because this type of table was made for heavy use, the underframe is usually fairly sturdy, but the legs will probably have suffered damage, caused by the table being dragged around on floor-wash day. Frayed feet, and a worn look around the base of the legs, are usual. Finally, the drawer bottom, or the drawer supports, called runners, may be badly worn or missing. This job can be safely left until last.

Left: *Two variations of the farmhouse table, valued for its sturdy simplicity. The plain styling* (top) *is typical of American Shaker furniture. A drawer to hold the cook's tools* (bottom) *is common – and likely to be one of the restorer's major problem areas.*

Paint stripping

Stripping off old paint and polish is sometimes necessary, but should be done only when you are sure the surface is not original.

There are many different paint strippers on the market for home use, and most are suitable for restoration work; the important thing is to select the right one for the job at hand. Broadly speaking, there are two main types of liquid stripper – those which are washed off after use with water and those which are removed with white spirit (paint thinner). Both are suitable for solid timber furniture, but the spirit-washable kind is best for delicate articles, and wood-veneered or inlaid surfaces since water will soften the animal (scotch) glue used to lay the decoration. Commercial paint-stripping firms have proliferated in recent years. They usually strip paint by dipping the item in a large tank of hot caustic soda solution (lye water). While very effective, this is far too drastic for all but the sturdiest items. It is also unlikely that your furniture will get the same care as you would give it.

A stiff nylon-bristle brush can be used to remove water-soluble paint stripper.

Stripping techniques

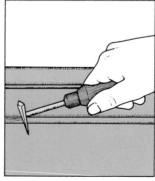

1 *Strip paint off mouldings with a multi-edge scraper.*

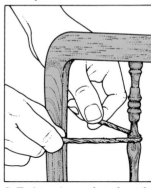

2 *Twist string and steel wool together for awkward shapes.*

3 *Wrap steel wool around a thin stick for carvings.*

4 *Remove debris with a soft wire brush.*

The best place to strip paint is outdoors, preferably in cool weather to prevent the stripper drying out too quickly. If space or the weather are against you, work in a well-ventilated room, without any form of heating, keep the window open and do not smoke. Cover the floor with plenty of old newspapers, and wear old clothes, gloves, and goggles. Follow the manufacturer's instructions carefully, and pay special attention to cleaning out all the awkward grooves and corners. Two or more applications of stripper may be needed for stubborn or thick paint, so ensure that you have plenty of materials, and cotton rags at hand. When you have finished, remove all traces of stripper from the piece – any residue will affect the quality of new polish.

Repairing the top

Unlike polished furniture, which would have been protected from harm, the scrub-top table was made to stand hard use. Hot water, grease, meat juices and kitchen tools will all have left their mark on the surface. One of the commonest results of this wear is that large gaps appear between the boards. The top may be held on by screws, or buttons, but the usual thing with country tables is for the top to be fixed down with old-style flat nails, called cut nails.

To remove a nailed top, tap a wide wood chisel into the small gap between the underside of the top, and the frame members. When the chisel has gone in about 25mm (1in.), pull steadily downwards on the handle, to separate top and frame. You can buy a special tool for separating boards, called a flooring bolster (pry-bar), if you would rather not try this with your favourite wood chisel. By working around the frame, prising (prying) the boards up inch-by-inch, you should be able to remove the whole top without damaging it. The old cut nails usually pull through the back of the top boards and remain in the framework of the table. They can easily be removed with pincers.

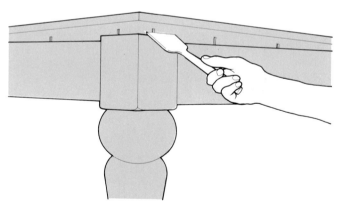

Work a flooring bolster into the joint and prise the board up.

Although some table tops are joined with tongue-and-groove joints, or more rarely, wooden dowel pins, the boards will usually come apart quite easily. Pour boiling water over stubborn joints before you prise them apart. Work from the back to avoid bruising the table face.

Improving the fit

If the boards have shrunk apart, but the tongue is a tight fit, plane the tongue down to improve the appearance.

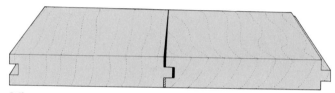

Where the tight spot is underneath the boards, cut away the surplus with a shoulder plane.

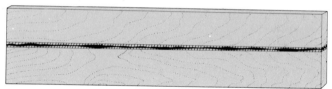

Dress along the edges of plain-edged boards with a sharp plane, set to take off fine shavings.

If the table-top boards are fastened together with pegs or tongue-and-groove joints, improving the fit of the parts is a fairly skilled task. With a tongue-and-groove jointed top, you must carefully clean out the groove, which may have filled with dust and food crumbs over the years. Test-fit the boards back together in the correct order, and pull them tightly together with at least three clamps. If the boards will still not close up, you will have to plane away the lower edge of the groove. Plain-edged boards without joints should be dressed along the edges with a sharp plane. Remove only a little wood at a time and test the fit of the boards as you work. Undercutting the edges slightly will improve the surface fit.

If your table has a dowel-jointed top, treat it in the same way; the only difference is that you will have to remove the dowels and replace them after you have dressed the edges. If the table needs no other attention, nail the top back in position, using old nails if possible.

Fixing the frame

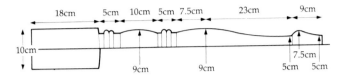

A measured sketch for a replacement leg. 'Hairline precision' is not vital; the eye will accept slight differences in legs more than 60cm (2ft) apart.

One or more of the legs of your table may be missing, or damaged beyond repair. Whole legs can be turned on a small lathe, as described on p. 14, but for an item of this size it is better to make a measured sketch of the leg, and find a woodturner with a bigger machine. The Yellow Pages or local craft associations are good places to look. If the glue has simply failed, but the joint parts are still intact, all you need to do is clean up the joint faces with hot water, coat them with hot animal glue (see p. 15) and reassemble. A convenient way of supporting the table is to lay it on its back, on top of a pair of trestles (saw horses), or across the workbench. The leg must be straight after gluing, so sight carefully along the frame and pull the leg upright before the glue sets. You can cure persistent leaning by propping up the leg with a length of scrap wood while the glue sets.

If the leg has split around the joint area, remove it, and clean the joint faces. Clamp the leg in a vice (vise), so that you can get at the splits easily. You have to get as much glue as possible deep inside the cracks, and then force the damaged parts together until they set. Animal glue cools and thickens too quickly to be of use here, but ordinary PVA (yellow) woodworking glue, thinned with 25 per cent volume of water, will usually do the job. Force the split apart with a chisel or screwdriver and push as much glue as you can into the joint with a paintbrush. Then bind the crack up tightly with rubber strips or hold it shut with screw clamps. Wipe away any surplus glue while it is still wet, or remove it with methylated spirits (wood alcohol).

The simplest way to repair a broken tenon on the end of the frame is to cut the damaged stub of the tenon off, make a new one and let it into a notch in the end of the

frame. Use well-seasoned old wood for this job, and measure and mark the shape of the replacement tenon carefully. Cut the joint faces with a saw, and pare them to fit with a sharp chisel. When the part repairs are complete, reassemble the frame, making sure that the whole assembly is not twisted out of shape.

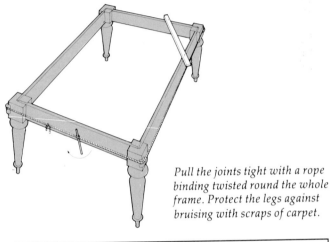

Pull the joints tight with a rope binding twisted round the whole frame. Protect the legs against bruising with scraps of carpet.

Fitting a false tenon

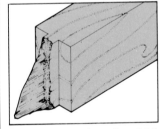

1 *Cut a slot in the rail as thick as the broken tenon.*

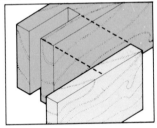

2 *Make the false tenon twice the length of the original.*

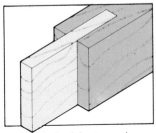

3 *Check the false tenon is a snug fit then glue it.*

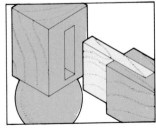

4 *Reassemble the joint and clamp the table tightly.*

Drawer repairs

Most traditional kitchen tables were fitted with drawers to hold the cook's tools and, since many of these were heavy, the drawer or the runners that support it eventually break. If the parts have not been lost, it is relatively easy to glue them back in place, but, if too much is missing, you will have to make a complete drawer.

Making traditional drawers

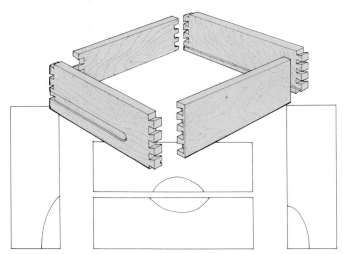

An exploded view of the parts to cut to make a new drawer. Label each before you start, to avoid confusion later.

Your drawer will look better if you can use old wood, and if you have an old chest drawer that can be altered to fit your table, it will save you some work. If you must make the drawer from new timber, use 22mm (⅞in.) thick for the front, of a type to match the rest of the table frame. Cut the sides and back from 10mm (⅜in.) boards and the bottom from 6mm (¼in.); this may be hard to find ready-made, so ask the lumber yard to prepare it. The sides, back, and bottom can be made from oak or high-grade joinery pine. Cut the drawer front, which should be a very tight fit in the frame, first. Make the sides the same width as the front and work out their length from the old runners, which will show signs of wear along the length of the original drawer. Cut the back exactly the same length as the front and around 20mm (¾in.) narrower.

Cutting the joints

The traditional joint used in drawer parts is the dovetail, for which you will need a marking gauge, a fine handsaw, and two chisels, one 6mm (¼in.), the other 10mm (⅜in.). To avoid confusion at the joint-cutting stage, mark each piece of wood before you begin. Set the gauge point to around 12mm (½in.) and, working from the inside face of the drawer front, scribe a line along each end of the drawer front. This line marks the 'lap', or amount that the drawer sides are let into the front. Without altering the gauge, scribe a line all round the front end of the sides. Now set the gauge to the exact thickness of the drawer sides and mark a line all round the back end of each drawer side, and round both ends of the drawer back. Set out the dovetails as illustrated below. When you have a complete set of parts, glue them together. The drawer bottom should be inserted into a groove, and note that the grain runs from side to side. Finally, plane the drawer sides until the drawer runs smoothly in and out.

Making a dovetail joint

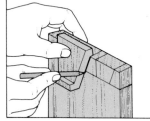

1 Mark the dovetail on the drawer side down to the lap.

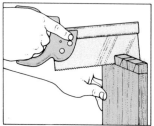

2 Saw carefully down the lines with a fine dovetail saw.

3 Chisel out the sockets with a sharp chisel and mallet.

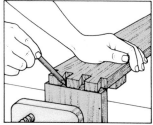

4 Use the side as a template for the back and front.

Project 3: Blanket chest

Types of chest

Wooden chests and boxes have always been popular items of furniture, made by generation after generation of craftsmen, who either followed the fashion of the day, or imitated the taste of their forebears. There was a strong tradition in mainland Europe of giving a bride her trousseau in a stout chest, and in many poor homes such an item was the main piece of furniture, serving as table, wardrobe, linen store and seat. Many were taken to America by European immigrants, and a large number were built in the United States by the early settlers. Also found in the US are the smaller and usually more highly decorated Bible boxes. These share many features with their bigger cousins, and can be regarded as the same for restoration purposes.

The most common kinds of chest are the framed – the best, since its more complicated construction resists damp or very dry conditions better – and the 'country', which is made from plain wide boards, nailed up to form a box, and is less resistant to damage of all kinds. Inside both types there may be drawers, or a fixed inner tray with a lift-up lid. These chests were usually lined although the original lining may be missing.

Diagnosing faults

The parts of a chest most vulnerable to damage are the base and the lid. The base may be a simple skirting, sometimes called a plinth, or, less commonly, the chest may sit on four turned feet. Another alternative is that the end boards of a solid chest may sweep down below the box bottom and have been cut to form two legs at each end. This type of foot is a sign of an early piece. The most common problems with bases are that any decorative moulding may have been lost and will have to be replaced, and that the blocks which strengthen the skirting may have become loose.

The lids of almost all chests are made from solid boards, fixed together to form a single piece. The excessive dry heat of central heating causes the boards to twist or split and this, along with breaks around the lock or hinges, is the most common form of lid damage.

Left: *This framed blanket box* (top) *with its carved and moulded skirting is based on a traditional design. Once renovated, these boxes can enhance any room.*

Removing linings

In simple chests, you may find a decorated paper lining, often on top of a layer of newspaper, which can give some idea of when the piece was manufactured. Panelled boxes were usually lined with cloth pinned on to the inside. If the lining is in poor condition, or you are going to be doing major work on the box, you will have to remove it. The best way to do this with paper linings is to soak them off, rather as if you were stripping wallpaper. Cloth linings were generally pinned in place, but may also have been glued around the edges.

If the linings are original, you should keep them and re-attach them when you have finished all the structural work. In this case, it is essential to take great care when you are removing them. Old fabric can be strengthened before replacement by bonding fine calico (muslin) to the back. Heat beeswax in a waterbath as described for animal (scotch) glue on p. 15, and brush a thin film on to the calico, then press the old fabric on to the waxy surface with a warm iron.

The best way to strengthen paper linings is to attach them to well-washed cotton sheeting with a thin coating of ordinary wallpaper paste.

Base repairs

If the base of your chest is of the simple skirting type, you should clean any old glue off the surfaces with water and a scraper and then simply reglue the loose parts in place.

Missing parts are more difficult to deal with because although the overall shape may be easy to make, there will probably be moulded or carved detail on the edges or front face. Short lengths of moulding are best made with a scratch-stock, which is discussed on p. 9. In order to use this to make a custom moulding, you will need to file a small piece of sheet steel to the right shape. The best way to do this is to keep filing away at the steel, fitting it to the shape of the remaining moulding as you work. When this cutter is the right shape, mount it in the stock.

Clamp the replacement piece of skirting in the vice (vise), grasp the scratch-stock firmly in both hands, and push it along the edge of the board. Press the side of the stock against the face of the board, keeping the moulding straight; the horizontal leg will limit its depth. The

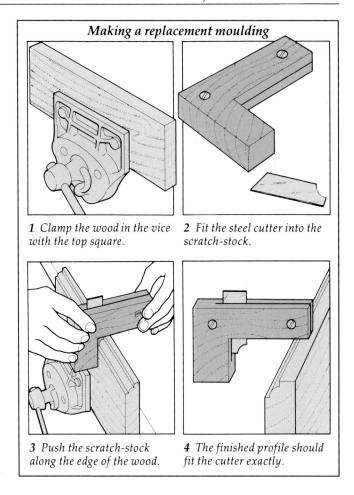

Making a replacement moulding

1 Clamp the wood in the vice with the top square.

2 Fit the steel cutter into the scratch-stock.

3 Push the scratch-stock along the edge of the wood.

4 The finished profile should fit the cutter exactly.

steel cutter will gradually scrape away the surplus timber until the moulding is the finished shape. When this is done, trim and mitre the new piece of skirting, then glue it in place.

Skirtings are often strengthened behind with rows of small wooden blocks glued into place with animal glue. These often work loose and are lost, so if you need to replace them, cut lengths of wood about 50-100mm (2-4in.) long. Turn the chest upside-down, then coat the blocks with hot animal glue and press them firmly into place. Remember that with animal glue you must work quickly. A slight rubbing motion will help to squeeze out any excess glue, and make the block firm without any need for clamps or pins (nails).

Lid repairs

Box lids are often damaged by being opened too far, which strains the hinges, and sometimes pulls the screws out of the wood. As well as causing strain, and perhaps bending the hinges, this enlarges the screw holes and loosens the grip of the woodscrew threads. The best remedy is to take the hinges off completely, and carefully bend the leaves straight again. The enlarged holes in the lid can then be plugged with slivers of wood dipped in glue. These chests were fitted with many different types of hinges; the most common were tee hinges, made from iron, or more rarely, brass, but you might also find butt or leaf hinges, good-quality examples of which are made from cast brass. Although not common, wooden hinges are sometimes found on old chests, and are usually broken when found. In this type of hinge the only metal parts are the pins that run through the wooden hinge segments. The only good way to repair these is to let in new timber pieces and recarve the broken segments. With a little care this can be done in such a way that most of the new wood is concealed beneath the old surface.

Sometimes ordinary hinges damage the chest so much where they screw into it that you will have to glue in similar pieces of wood to mount the hinges on. Cut a suitable piece of old wood to the size and shape of the required insert, but leave it thicker than necessary. Place the shaped insert over the spot that it is to go in, and mark around it. With a saw and sharp chisel, chop out the cavity, shaving it smooth on the bottom, so that the insert beds down well. A wedge shape is best for these simple inserts since they will fit tightly when you

These black enamelled iron tee hinges and brass butt hinges are the ones you are most likely to come across in renovating old furniture.

push them into the gap. Spread a brushful of animal glue into the recess and insert the block immediately. Clamp it into position while the glue dries. After 24 hours, trim the block down flush with the surface using a sharp plane, set to take off a fine shaving, and refit the hinge. This is also a good way to repair damaged woodwork around locks.

Another common problem with chest lids is warping (curling) of the timber. There is no guaranteed cure for this problem, but it sometimes helps to veneer the convex side of the lid with some matching wood veneer. As this dries it will shrink and should pull the curl out of the top. More details on hinges are given on p. 35 and on veneering on p. 78.

Making a simple wooden insert

1 Cut a scrap of matching wood, bigger than you need.

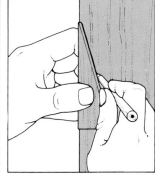

2 Trace a line round it with a sharp pencil.

3 Chop out the cavity with a chisel.

4 Glue the insert and clamp it until the glue is dry.

Project 4: Pine chest of drawers

Furniture for everyone

At the turn of the twentieth century, the great manufacturing centres of London and Philadelphia produced vast amounts of furniture, much of it solid and middle-class to suit the widening prosperity of the age. The increasing use of machinery concentrated production into ever bigger factories, and began to squeeze out the small workshops who had catered for this market. Many survived by producing for the city workers inexpensive versions of the mahogany and cherrywood pieces made for the better-off. The chest of drawers illustrated is a perfect example of this kind of furniture. Made from white pine, but polished (finished) to look like the more costly mahogany, the chest's sides and top are cut from single wide boards, and the sides are let into grooves beneath the top. Drawer supports are nailed straight on to the sides, and the front rails – the parts in between the drawers – are fixed in with mortise and tenon joints. The drawers themselves are dovetailed. Everything in the piece was done for simplicity and cheapness, but the overall effect is pleasing, and it has stood the test of time fairly well.

Diagnosing faults

A preliminary examination of the chest reveals that the back-boards are damaged, and all the drawer bottoms have shrunk, so that they have pulled out of the drawer-front grooves. The stops that prevent the drawers being pushed in too far are broken, or missing, and two of the drawer runners have broken away from their mountings. The surface, made of a softer wood than most furniture, is dented and cut here and there, and the polish has discoloured to a livid purply-red. As always, it is important for the restorer to decide in advance the order in which to tackle the problems. If the carcase (case) is badly damaged, that should be your first priority. Next, repair the drawers themselves, then tackle the rest of the carcase work. The surface can then be re-polished. Leaving this until last will give you a chance to blend in new parts or patches.

Left: *An incomplete attempt to strip this chest, and broken drawer runners and stops made it a sorry sight* (top). *Basic restoration and gentle stripping of the old polish have improved its appearance enormously.*

Repairing the back

Damaged or missing back-boards are common on old furniture, because the wood used for those parts that did not show, like the back and the dustboards fitted between each layer of drawers, was of the poorest quality. Backs usually consist of two or more boards, nailed on and fitted between strengthening uprights called muntins (stiles). These dividers, which stiffen large, thin panels, are also found in doors and on the bottoms of large drawers. Muntins may have grooves along each edge, or have a step-shaped reduction in the edge thickness, called a rebate or rabbet. Panels are either tapered to slip into the groove or, on cheaper work, are trapped under the edge of the rabbet when the muntins are fixed to the carcase.

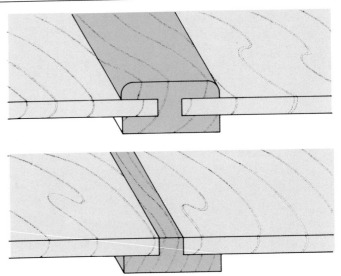

There are several types of muntin, but two of the most common are the grooved, which is usual in the bottoms of large drawers, and the rebated, more usual on cabinet backs.

The thin wood used for chest backs is easily damaged. If you can't cannibalize old work for replacements, try using the dustboards; they were often made from a similar wood.

The back panels and muntins of our chest are made from white pine. Better-class British pieces may have backs of oak, or, if they were made in the early twentieth century, of soft, greenish canary wood (poplar). Replacing the back panels will be difficult, unless you have access to old work that can be cannibalized for spare wood. The chief problem is that it is difficult to find wide, thin boards of any quality. There are two possible solutions you can adopt. The first is to replace the back-boards with plywood panels. Cut them to the same width as the old boards, then slip them between the muntins and nail them home.

The alternative is to look inside the chest for dustboards. These are protected from the hazards of moving house, and so on, and often survive intact. The dustboards are also, usually, cut from the same, or very similar, timber as the back panels. Remove the dustboards and recut them to make new back panels. Replace them with plywood panels, cut to size and fitted into the dustboard grooves inside the chest.

Remember that you should only adopt these solutions if you are certain that your piece is not a 'classic' (and, therefore, valuable) antique. Pieces of distinction should always be restored using completely authentic materials, or a considerable loss in value will result.

Repairing drawers

As long as all the parts are intact, most drawer repairs are fairly easy. Basic instructions on how to make replacement drawers are given on p. 21. In furniture made before the twentieth century, drawer bottoms are usually of solid timber, rather than plywood. Since natural timber changes in size with varying humidity, there was always some movement of the drawer parts through the seasons. Central heating and air conditioning reduced this effect to a certain extent, but have brought a new problem. Modern homes are excessively dry, and since our antiques were built to live in a more natural environment, actual harm is caused by shrinkage of all the parts. Indeed, in some cases valuable pieces have been ruined almost beyond repair by modern hot, dry conditions.

Drawer bottoms

Drawer bottoms tend to shrink in width, that is, at right angles to the grain; timber shrinks only minutely along the grain lines. They are never glued, but slide into grooves at the front and sides of the drawer and, with time, they are pulled out of the groove at the front. This means that the drawer bottoms are unsupported and prone to damage during use. To repair this fault, remove the nails or screws holding the bottom to the back of the drawer, and push the drawer bottom firmly back into its slot – there is usually enough spare timber at the back of the drawer to do this – and then replace the fastenings along the back.

Shrinkage often causes drawer bottoms to pull out of the groove on the drawer front.

Drawer runner repairs

With the passage of time, the constant opening and closing of drawers results in the wooden runners which support the drawers becoming deeply grooved. This often causes the drawer fronts to sag out of line with the front of the piece. Similarly, the drawer sides also tend to wear along the rubbing surfaces. The best way to cure this is to level the affected parts with a plane, and once the surface is flat, to build it up to the right height with a slip of wood.

While the work is in progress, check constantly that you are keeping the surface flat. The edge of a steel rule is an ideal guide for this.

Repairing drawer runners

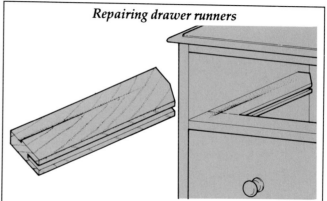

1 The original smooth surface and thickness of the drawer runner is often damaged by constant rubbing.

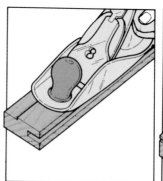

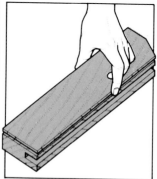

2 Plane down the runner to give a level surface.

3 Restore its size and surface with a thin sheet of wood.

Carcase repairs

When the drawers are running smoothly again and all the major structural problems have been attended to, minor repairs to the body of the chest, or carcase, can begin. Most old chests tend to lose the small wooden drawer stops, which are glued and pinned to the front rails and prevent the drawer from being pushed right back into the chest. You can make replacements from scraps of wood about 4-6mm (³⁄₁₆-¼in.) thick, shaped as shown below. When you are replacing them, take care to set the stops in the right position, so that the drawers line up well when they are closed.

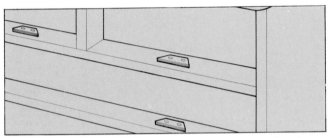

Take care when you position replacement drawer stops that the distance from the front of the chest to the stop is exactly the same as the width of the drawer front.

Repairing mouldings

Mouldings on chests are usually found around the top, around the base, or around or on the drawer fronts. There are two kinds of top and base moulds, worked mouldings – which are made on the edges of a large solid piece – and stuck mouldings, which as their name suggests are made separately and then stuck on. Mouldings on or around the drawer fronts are generally stuck. All these can be of almost any shape, though some types were associated with particular periods. You should look closely to see whether the mouldings are cut from cross-grained wood or not. Cross-grain walnut was used principally on high-class furniture of the late-seventeenth century, and you should treat any piece bearing this type of moulding as being of high potential value. The usual problem with cross-grain moulds is cracking or looseness, which you can fix by carefully gluing the mould in place, and filling the cracks with slips of matching timber.

The simplest method of repair for ordinary moulds of all kinds is to cut away any badly damaged portion and insert a block of new wood. Glue and clamp the block into place, and when it has set firm, roughly trim it to shape with a small plane. The final work of shaping and smoothing can be done with carving tools or the scratch-stock (see p. 8). Where mouldings are missing or badly damaged, it is best to replace the whole lot with a length of ready-made moulding from a cabinet-making or picture-framing specialist. The tiny half-round mouldings, called cock-beads, used around drawers are hard to make, and should also be bought.

Finally, you might be lucky enough to find old-style wooden moulding planes, which will help you to make a really authentic repair.

A simple moulding (top) *can be shaped in position with planes and sandpaper. More complex moulds* (bottom) *are best made with the scratch-stock.*

Blending old and new

When all the structural repairs are done, and everything is running smoothly again, you should make good any surface defects. Bear in mind that the sheen or patina of old furniture is built up over many years of wear and, if you have had to strip a surface, or fill in cracks in a large piece like a chest of drawers, you cannot hope to achieve this appearance of age and loving care immediately. Be patient, and let time, exposure to light, and regular dusting finish what you have started.

Trade techniques

Contrary to what many people think, wood polishers (finishers) do not achieve their results with wood dyes and polish alone. In fact, this is seldom the case, and most craftsmen use pigment as well as dye in order to match parts. A list of the most useful restorers' polishing materials is given on p. 9. Many of these are difficult to obtain, and you will probably have to look through craft magazines for sources of supply.

Colour matching

Wood colours are based on combinations of red and black, with the addition of yellow, and sometimes green. By using dyes of these basic colours, perhaps with the addition of paint pigment, you can match any surface shade, although it will take time, so be patient. Try to work in good natural light only, and begin with a mix that is lighter than you need and darken it gradually until it matches. Water stains, based on cloth dyes, are very good for a foundation colour. Follow this with spirit (alcohol-soluble) colours, and when that layer is dry, overpaint it with pigments, or artist's water colours to achieve the correct appearance. An advantage of using this progressive system is that, if you make a mistake, you can remove the last layer without disturbing the one beneath. Use the appropriate solvent to remove any layer which is not right. Lines to imitate the grain of wood surrounding a patch can be added with water colour and a fine brush. After your surface repairs, seal the wood with a coat of french polish, diluted with an equal volume of methylated spirits (wood alcohol). Use a soft cotton pad and apply the solution as quickly as you can.

Repairing a damaged surface

1 Stick on and shape the new wood.

2 Stain it to the same basic colour, and seal.

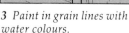

3 Paint in grain lines with water colours.

4 Seal the surface with a coat of french polish.

The surface of this piece has many marks, but patination like this adds charm.

Project 5: Sabre leg chair

Egypt and Trafalgar

Thomas Hope, a notable influence on art and architecture, is credited with the introduction in Britain of flat-sided chairs, which are based on illustrations in ancient Egyptian records. The interest in classical arts was such that the design soon became very fashionable, and many variations on the basic structure were produced. The version illustrated opposite is an early Victorian chair. Its simple appearance conceals precise and complicated internal joints. Brass lines and inlay patterns are also common on chairs of this type, originally made to celebrate Nelson's victory at Trafalgar.

The structure of these chairs was radically different from anything that had gone before, and reflects the enthusiasm for bold and uncluttered lines so typical of the Regency. The apparently simple construction is not without its drawbacks, however. The sweeping curves of the sabre legs mean that almost inevitably some of the parts were cut from wood with the grain lines running across, rather than along them. This makes these parts liable to break under pressure. The rope mouldings, also, are fragile and cane seats, common on this type of chair, are also prone to damage – they usually sag or split. Caning seats is really outside the scope of this book, indeed many professional restorers have this work done by people who are themselves experts. We will, however, consider the most usual types of fracture, and how to treat them, and also explain how to carve a replacement for the curved back rail.

Before you begin any major repair work, try to determine what wood the chair is made from. Mahogany, walnut and rosewood were the most common materials used for these chairs, although cheaper types were sometimes made in beech. The rarer American variants may be in cherry or maple. Recognizing the type of timber used is often difficult but as a general guide, mahogany of this period will be dark reddish-brown, with tiny white flecks in the cut surface. Walnut is pale golden-brown, and often strongly patterned; rosewood is heavy, oily, and a rich purplish-brown; cherry is faintly marked, and a warm mid-brown; both beech and maple are paler creamy woods. If your chair is maple, it is probably American.

Left: *This Victorian version of the flush-sided chair has sturdier front legs, but the weak back has damaged the seat frame* (inset).

Front leg repairs

As we have seen, classic flush-sided chairs have some weaknesses 'built-in', as a result of their design. Later examples of flush-sided chairs have turned front legs like the one illustrated. These are usually stronger than sabre legs, since they are made from straight-grained timber. Breaks in turned legs usually occur just below the joint (the joint at the top of the leg rarely breaks).

Turned leg repairs

Chair legs must be dowelled together wherever possible, for strength and safety. The most difficult part of the job is aligning drilled holes for a dowel to fit into. The best way round this problem is to drill deep into the broken-off part of the leg, then saw neatly through the leg at a convenient point near the break. Glue the sawn-off section back on to the chair, and, when the glue has set, use it to guide the drill into the chair frame. When a dowel is glued into place, it will strengthen and align all three pieces perfectly.

Knee joints

Earlier chairs, with sabre legs front and back, also have a more fragile joint between the leg and seat frame, often called the knee joint. Knee joints are tricky items to deal with. A tidy repair can often be made merely by gluing the parts together again, but this will leave the chair dangerously weak. In severe cases, the only remedy is to make a new upper leg and knee.

Most knee joints are variations on the mortise and tenon. The tenon is usually undamaged, but you should clean off the old glue, then use the damaged part of the leg as a pattern to make a new section. Graft this on to the old leg as described on p. 32. Cut the mortise holes after you have joined the old and new sections; take the sizes and angles of the joint parts from the old pieces. Work slowly – this is a skilled job.

Mark out with a gauge, or sharp knife, to give a thin clear line. Chop the mortises with a strong narrow chisel. Start in the middle, and work towards the ends, squaring the hole up as you go – drilling out the waste saves time and effort. Glue on and clamp the complete leg, carefully aligning it with its companion.

Repairing a turned leg

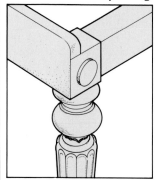

1 Breaks in turned legs usually occur near the joint.

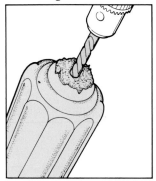

2 Drill deeply into the broken-off part of the leg.

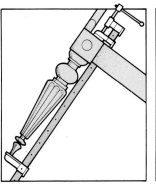

3 Saw across the broken piece below the break.

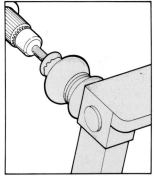

4 Glue to the frame; use as a guide for drilling.

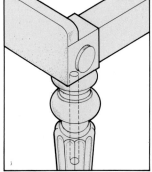

5 Clamp the pieces together while the glue dries.

6 A dowel holds all three pieces together.

Broken backs

The sweeping sabre curves of this type of chair may lead to problems with the rear frame members. The most usual fault is splitting or failure of the lower section of the legs, often caused, like so many problems with chairs, by them being dragged across carpets or tipped back while someone is seated. The break is generally a long one when it occurs here and can often be rejoined with glue. As always, clean the surfaces carefully before you start gluing. Rubber lashings will hold the parts still while the glue is setting.

Since the results of a sudden failure of a repair of this type can be dangerous for sitter and seat alike, many restorers like to reinforce the glued joint with dowels or pegs. This is best done after the two parts have been joined. One very good method is to use slim dowels made from split cane. The thin pieces of bamboo sold for garden use will provide hundreds of very strong dowels at low cost. These should be inserted at an angle to increase the strength of the joint – the downward force will tend to push the two parts more closely together. More complex breaks in the back frame may have to be dealt with by inserting a new section, in the same way as described for knees on p. 31.

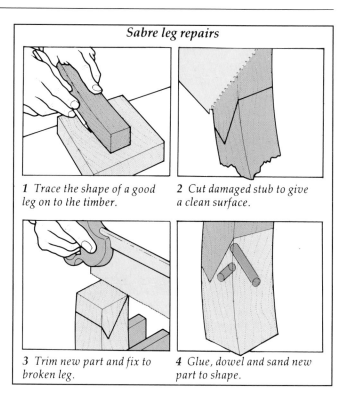

Sabre leg repairs

1 Trace the shape of a good leg on to the timber.

2 Cut damaged stub to give a clean surface.

3 Trim new part and fix to broken leg.

4 Glue, dowel and sand new part to shape.

A loose joint between the crest rail and the back upright has resulted in wood flaking away round the joint. The repair involves cutting a smooth wedge-shaped slice away from the damaged portion, then gluing in and carving an insert to shape.

Broken back rails

The curved cross rails on the upper back of typical flush-sided chairs are a challenge for the restorer. Often they are so badly damaged that complete new parts must be made. If repair seems possible, then follow the methods described on pp. 28 and 34. If you need to make a new part, put a large square of wood off-centre in the lathe and, turning it very slowly, work the pins that fix the rail in the chair frame, and the small bobbin ornaments at each end. Techniques for turning are given on p. 14. When these are done, mark the curved shape of the rail between the turned portions, and cut away the waste with a bandsaw or coping saw. Then, roughly shape the curved part with a rasp, or carving tools. If there is carved detail, you will have to add it by hand, after rough shaping. Many workers find it convenient to hold work of this kind in the lathe where it can be rotated by hand. This ensures easy access to all sides.

Project 6: Pennsylvania Dutch dresser

The Germans of America

The first German colonists arrived in Pennsylvania in 1683, soon after the founding of the colony. These early settlers were relatively wealthy people, who brought with them their own belongings from the Rhinelands. The poorer 'Redemptioners' who came later were bonded labourers, and created their own homes with a grant of land and tools, given after they had discharged their obligations. These were all people who concentrated primarily on their homes and farms, and many of them became prosperous. The craftsmen developed a typical style of furniture, based on native German work, which was distinguished by elaborate painting and graining of the wood, and the use of intricate fret-cut scrolls. This type of furniture is usually called Pennsylvania Dutch, a corruption of *Deutsch*.

While eighteenth-century furniture of this kind is rare and expensive, good later examples are sometimes found, and the general principles of construction and restoration of this type of work apply to country furniture of all types.

Diagnosing problems

Made for everyday use in simple homes, most country furniture was extremely sturdy. The common failings are the results of ordinary wear and tear, and the excessive shrinkage caused by air-conditioning and central heating.

This type of furniture was often decorated with fretwork or scrollwork. Much of this was delicate and, naturally, in time pieces are broken off and some are lost completely. We will look at the ways to replace this work. Door damage is also very common on dressers. In some cases, the doors themselves split or crack, and sometimes the hinges break. Fixing hinges is not difficult, and we will examine the techniques involved. Finally, because this type of furniture was made for everyday use, surfaces often deteriorate, so we will consider ways of reviving finishes.

Left: *This handsome Pennsylvania Dutch dresser is now a valuable museum piece. Note the many small dents and scratches which the restorer aims to reproduce when 'distressing'. Simpler country pieces* (inset) *are still to be found at bargain prices. In this piece the doors have sagged a little, due to worn hinges.*

Repairing fretwork

There are two basic types of fretwork decoration on country furniture. The first, and most common, is properly called scrollwork, and consists of boards of 6mm (¼in.) thickness or more, scalloped on the edges and sometimes pierced through with decorated shapes. This type of work is found mainly on the tops and bases of all kinds of cabinet work, in varying degrees of complexity. Since it was often done in thin timber to reduce the labour of cutting, pieces tend to break off, and if the piece is old, inevitably some are lost. The best way to deal with this is to graft a new section on to the damaged frieze, and re-create its original form. If all of the shaped part is missing, you will have to look for similar pieces, and use patterns drawn from them to make a completely new replacement. Careful research will give a piece that will look harmonious with the whole and pass unnoticed by all but experts. The best way to graft a new piece on is to prepare a board of similar timber to the correct thickness, but allow extra on the length and width. The amount of this allowance will depend on the shape of the part to be replaced. Remove the old frieze, clamp the new board firmly behind the damaged part, and cut away the broken edge of the old part. It will not matter if the line is straight since the saw will also pierce the new board. This double-cut method will ensure a good fit when the new part is glued to the old. When the glue has set, mark the shape on to the new part, and cut it with a coping saw, an electric jigsaw or, if you are a real traditionalist, a bow-saw.

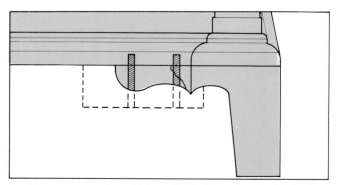

Grafting on a new piece of frieze: the double-cut method helps to ensure a good fit.

Ornamental fretwork

You may find thin plywood or solid timber fretwork, usually about 3mm (⅛in.) thick, stuck or pinned over a solid surface, or in dainty pieces, left unsupported and used to form gallery rails, decorative shelf edging or corner brackets. Cut new parts from thin plywood, which you can make from layers of decorative veneers.

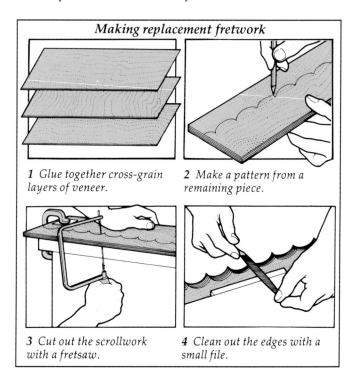

Making replacement fretwork

1 *Glue together cross-grain layers of veneer.*

2 *Make a pattern from a remaining piece.*

3 *Cut out the scrollwork with a fretsaw.*

4 *Clean out the edges with a small file.*

This cornice has applied fretwork, made from thin wood.

Fixing broken turnings

On p. 14, we considered ways of making new turned parts. The repair of turnings is possible without the use of a lathe, however, so long as you have the main parts. The most satisfactory method of repair is to dowel the broken pieces together, in the same way as described for turned chair legs on p. 31. For extra strength, use metal dowel, which is easily cut to the required length from carpentry nails of different sizes.

Hinge repairs

Broken door hinges and hinge fastenings are found repeatedly on cabinet furniture of all types and periods. There are many varying patterns of hinge but two basic types are found most often on country furniture. The particular kind favoured by makers of Dutch furniture is the surface-mounted hinge, which is generally made from iron or, more rarely, brass. The two leaves, or flaps, are cut into ornamental shapes along the margin. Damage to hinges usually consists of a broken or missing leaf, or a badly worn pin, which makes the hinge slack. This slackness makes the door droop, and causes further damage to both door and cabinet. Anyone with access to a metalwork shop can turn a new pin, but you can make sound repairs without access to expensive machinery.

If the hinge is intact, you will have to remove one leaf. Brass leaves should be softened by heating with a blowtorch, and plunging into cold water before you attempt this. The pin will be fixed into one leaf, and it is the other, 'loose leaf', that you should remove. This can be done by opening the rolled part with a screwdriver blade, until the two hinge leaves come apart. The worn pin will now be exposed, and can be built up with wire and plumber's solder. Use brass wire for brass hinges, and soft iron florist's wire for iron. Clean the wire and the pin carefully with emery paper, and then wrap the wire around the pin in a tight spiral. When the spiral is complete, hold the piece in tongs, and use liquid flux and plumber's solder to both bond the wires together, and bond them to the pin inside. Set it aside to cool and then file it to shape. The hard wire will resist wear for a long time. When the pin has been reshaped, replace the other side of the hinge and tap the 'wrap' shut with a small hammer.

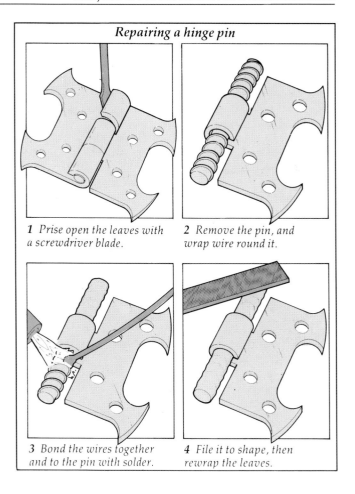

Repairing a hinge pin

1 *Prise open the leaves with a screwdriver blade.*

2 *Remove the pin, and wrap wire round it.*

3 *Bond the wires together and to the pin with solder.*

4 *File it to shape, then rewrap the leaves.*

Missing leaves are more difficult to fix, one of the problems being obtaining the right material to make the new part from. Old-fashioned ironbox locks, of the kind once used for house doors are a good source of soft iron sheet, and old brass may be found in the mechanisms of broken mantel-clocks of the 1950s. Make a pattern for the new leaf in card, and cut out the part with a small piercing saw. The wrap that goes round the pin can be partly formed by hammering around a nail, and finished in the same way as described for the pin repair.

The more carefully engineered butt hinges are more difficult to repair, and you should look for a replacement, or seek help from an expert.

Door repairs

Broken hinges often lead to problems with doors. There are many potential sources of trouble here, but we will examine the most common. Breaks around the hinges are caused by excessive weight on the door. Small children are often at fault here, leaning heavily on the top of the door as they bend to peek inside. Where the hinge screws have simply pulled out, plug the holes with slivers of wood dipped in glue, and refix the hinges. Sometimes, the strain will break away a long strip of the wood. If the break is not too severe, simply reglue the wood, and strengthen it with small dowel rods (see p. 10) after the glue has set. If the part is very badly broken, or missing, you must replace it.

The problem of finding timber to match the door can be overcome by cutting a square strip of material from the inside edge of the door with a tenon saw. Glue a piece of material, which need be only an indifferent match, into this rebate, and use the sawn strip as a source of exactly matching timber to replace the missing piece. This method can also be used to provide timber to build up the bottom of doors, where slack hinges have resulted in abnormal wear.

The only remedy for loose door joints, which cause the whole door to sag, is to dismantle the door, clean the joint surfaces, and reassemble it with fresh glue. Where the tenons are a loose fit into the corresponding mortise, spread them slightly with slim wedges let into saw-slots. Sometimes the secret wedged tenon (see p. 10) will be a good method of stiffening joints, but try to avoid doing this, since modern restoration practice is not to do anything which is liable to cause problems for future generations.

Replacing door panels

Sometimes, you will need to make a whole new door panel. Most doors on country furniture have simple fielded panels and, if you need to make one of these, a suitable piece of old furniture timber is almost essential, since new wood will rarely look 'at home'. Making fielded panels is a job where a spindle moulder or router comes in handy, although you can get good results by hand. Use a small shoulder plane to make the sloped fielding, and run it along a fence clamped to the work.

Repairing damage to doors

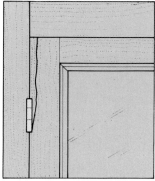

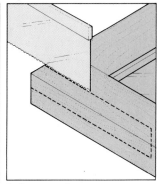

1 *Loose hinges often result in door damage.*

2 *Saw a replacement strip from inside the door.*

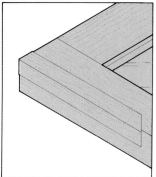

3 *Glue the matching insert into place.*

4 *Plane it smooth, then refit the hinges.*

This classic type of door has a fielded panel retained by a thin moulding, making it easy to remove.

Cleaning and reviving paint and polish

Painted and polished surfaces are often renewed quite unnecessarily, reducing the value of a piece in the process, since much of the patina that gives old things their beauty is lost. Careful cleaning can render refinishing totally pointless. Try the remedies here carefully and choose an unobtrusive spot to begin work, since the great variety of old finishes means that results can vary.

Metal fittings can usually be cleaned in position, but you should remove them for heavy cleaning. Final buffing of polished surfaces and metalwork demands soft, clean cloths – cotton are best.

Dirty paint

A gentle method for cleaning light grime is to dissolve 50g (2oz.) of common soda (baking soda) in 500ml (1 pint) of hot water. Dip a soft cloth in the mixture and squeeze it almost dry, then use it to wipe the surface over. Repeat this treatment with a cloth dipped in warm water with a little wine vinegar. Once again, keep the cloth almost dry. Leave the finish for two hours, then polish it with a soft, dry, cloth.

A more vigorous cleaner is made from equal parts of dishwashing liquid and white spirit (paint thinner). Shake well and set it aside until the mixture sets to a firm jelly, then rub it into the surface, and wipe it off with a clean damp cloth as you go. Do not leave it in contact too long, since it may soften some paints.

French polish

More common on British furniture, french polish looks like a thin glassy-smooth varnish. To make a reviver, mix 1 part shredded beeswax with 3 parts Mexican turpentine, 3 parts unboiled linseed oil, and 3 parts methylated spirits (wood alcohol). Stand this in a bowl of warm water, and shake it until the mixture is smooth. Apply it frugally with a soft polishing pad.

All-purpose cleaner

This mixture will remove old sticky wax and most other built-up dirt from all kinds of surface, and is particularly good for American varnish finishes. In a screw-top bottle mix one cupful of wine vinegar, one cupful of Mexican turpentine, one cup of boiled linseed oil, a quarter cup of methylated spirits, and a teaspoonful of strong ammonia. Apply with a soft paintbrush, and wipe off any excess with tissue or cloth.

Cleaning metal fittings

Commercial metal polishes are far too harsh to use routinely for cleaning old brass and iron fittings. By far the best material to use is jeweller's rouge. This is a fine red powder, and should be mixed for use with a little olive oil. Apply the paste with a pad, and remove it with a clean cloth. Severe corrosion can be removed with grade 0000 steel wool dipped in turpentine.

2

RE-UPHOLSTERY TECHNIQUES

The pieces for the projects in this section of the book have been chosen to cover as many techniques of traditional upholstery as possible so that with thought and careful note-taking you will be able to tackle other items not covered here. If you are about to begin your first piece of upholstery do not attempt an armchair; you may lose heart simply by the length of time it takes. To give some idea of the time involved, the first project may take almost a whole day, and the second could take you two or three days.

Read the projects right through several times before you start work so that you have some understanding of what you are aiming for. Remember that you are in charge and can take out something you do not like – such as a row of stitching – and begin again; aim for perfection but do not give up if your first attempts are not too good. It is a good plan to do several similar items one after another before you move on to more complicated work. No matter how tempted you may be to start work on your grandmother's button-back chair, wait until you know you can solve the problems you may come across.

Tools and equipment

For consistency, throughout we have given sizes and measurements in metric, with their imperial equivalents in brackets. Many of these items, however, are sold in standard imperial measures.

Upholsterer's hammers are available with various different combinations of face, but you should have one with one plain face, about 12mm (½in.) in diameter. It does not matter if the other end has a claw or is magnetic.

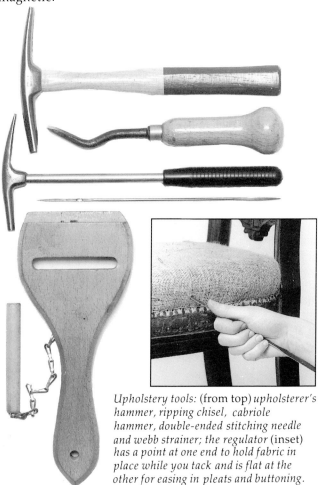

Upholstery tools: (from top) upholsterer's hammer, ripping chisel, cabriole hammer, double-ended stitching needle and webb strainer; the regulator (inset) has a point at one end to hold fabric in place while you tack and is flat at the other for easing in pleats and buttoning.

The cabriole hammer has an extra small face, about 8mm (⁵⁄₁₆in.) in diameter, and is useful when you are tacking close to polished show-wood or carving.

A ripping chisel is essential, inexpensive and used for ripping out old upholstery. It looks rather like a screwdriver with a hardened edge to the blade, and is available with either a cranked or straight shaft.

The webb strainer enables you to pull webbing more tightly than would otherwise be possible. The 'bat' type is the most common and inexpensive.

A regulator is used mainly for moving the stuffing about within the scrim ('regulating') and is essential. Of the various lengths and gauges, 23 or 25cm (9 or 10in.) and a fairly light gauge is the most useful.

Buttoning and stitching needles are double-ended. There are two types, round-pointed for buttoning work and bayonet- (triangular) pointed for stitching. They are available in various lengths and gauges, but 25cm (10in.) and fairly heavy gauge is best to begin with.

The spring needle is a curved needle with a flattened point used for stitching springs to webbing and inserting bridle ties.

Semi-circular needles are available in various sizes and gauges from 25mm (1in.) to 15cm (6in.). The smaller sizes are used for slip-stitching, the larger ones where it would be difficult to use a straight needle.

A wooden mallet is used with the ripping chisel for removing old tacks and upholstery, so it should be fairly large.

Shears should be good quality and stay sharp right to the points for snipping. Any good scissors can be used, but 20 or 23cm (8 or 9in.) is the most useful size.

Upholstery skewers (pins) are often used to hold hessian (burlap), scrim or the top cover in place.

Steel pins hold fabric in place while you work. The most practical are 40mm (1½in.) long adamantine pins.

A table for working on. Upholsterers use a trestle table but a table top alone is satisfactory for most jobs.

Other tools which may be useful include a sharp craft knife; pliers; tailor's chalk; a soft tape measure and a straight length of wood for cutting piping, etc.

Materials used in traditional upholstery

Hessian (burlap) is made from jute and is available in three weights:

340g (12oz.) is used over webbing and/or springs as the base on which all the upholstery is constructed;

280g (10oz.) is used in much the same way as 340g (12oz.);

210g (7½oz.) is sometimes used instead of scrim to enclose the first stuffing.

Scrim is used to enclose the first stuffing. Like hessian, it is usually made from jute but the yarn used is finer spun. Linen scrim may be used on high-grade work.

The weight of both hessian and scrim relates to a piece of material 115cm × 90cm (45in. × 36in.).

Calico (muslin) is used under the top cover to enclose all the fillings. Either medium- or lightweight is the most suitable for upholstery.

Cambric is closely woven and waxed cotton used to make the inner feather-filled cases of cushions.

Bottoming, which is also sometimes called upholsterer's linen (though now usually made from cotton), is used for the base of chairs and catches any dust which falls from the filling.

Webbing is used as a support for all the other fillings. It can be either plain woven jute or twill woven cotton and flax (which is often termed English webbing). Both types are usually about 5cm (2in.) wide, jute webbing comes in rolls of 33m (36yds) and English webbing in rolls of 16.5m (18yds).

Linter felt, which is also known as cotton felt, is made from fine cotton fibres, and produced as a thick padding in rolls about 66cm (26in.) wide. It is used over the second stuffing but under the top cover.

Skin wadding (batting) is a very thin layer of wadding made of cotton with a 'skin' sprayed on to hold the fibres together. It is used in the same way as linter felt but on small chairs.

Left to right: *hessian, used as a base; scrim, to encase stuffing; calico, an undercovering; cambric, for cushion cases; bottoming, for catching dust; linter felt and skin wadding, for padding under the top cover; and herringbone webbing.*

Coir fibre.   *Curled hair.*

Curled hair, although referred to as horse hair, is today mostly a mixture of horse and hog hair. The best grade is still pure horse and should be long, stranded and very curly. Hair found in chairs can often be washed and reused. It is generally used as a second stuffing only today because of its high cost.

Fibre is a substitute for hair. Coir fibre (made from the husk of the coconut) is the most common today although hay, reeds and seaweed have all been used in the past. Coir is available either as a ginger fibre or dyed black; the latter is easier to work with but it does tend to stain the hands. Fibre should not be reused.

Upholstery tacks, also termed 'blued' cut tacks, have fine sharp points. There are two types: improved and fine. Improved have rather large heads and thick

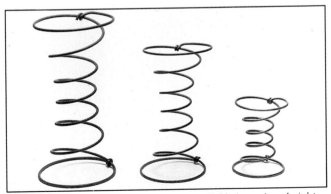

Double-cone or hourglass springs are available in various heights and wire thicknesses.

shanks, fine, as their name implies, have small heads and thin shanks. Tacks are available in various lengths but three are usual in upholstery:

15mm (⅝in.) are used for fixing webbing. The thickness of the timber dictates whether to use improved or fine, since a fine tack is less likely to split hard timber than the thicker improved tack;

12mm (½in.) are used for fixing webbing on light frames, such as you would find with a drop-in seat or delicate pin-stuffed work. Fine are used for temporary tacking hessian and scrim and fixing base hessian;

10mm (⅜in.) improved are used for fixing hessian and scrim, fine are used for fixing calico and top covers.

Gimp pins are mainly used for fixing gimp but are also useful for fixing the top cover on a fragile chair or in places where a tack would look unsightly. They are available in many colours.

Twine for use in upholstery is usually made of hemp and either jute or flax. There are three thicknesses: stout for sewing in springs and similar heavy work; medium for stitching edges; and fine for buttoning and for bridle ties. Nylon twine is now often used for buttoning work. Twine is available in 250g (8oz.) balls.

Laid cord is usually made of hemp, and its strands are laid together so that they do not stretch. Used for lashing (cording) springs, it is sold in 500g (17oz.) balls.

Piping cord (welting) is made of three-stranded soft cotton and sold by number (00,1,2,3, etc.). The lower the number the finer the cord, although thicknesses tend to vary from manufacturer to manufacturer. Pile fabrics may need finer cord than non-pile fabrics.

Slipping (buttoning) thread is used to hand-stitch top covers. Any good carpet thread is suitable if you cannot get upholsterer's linen thread. The thread is available in various colours, but natural is the most useful.

Springs used in traditional upholstery are termed double-cone or hourglass springs because of their shape. They are available in varying heights from 75mm (3in.) to 35cm (14in.) and wire thicknesses (SWG – standard wire gauge/metal diameter) from 8 to 15. Gauges 9 and 10 are used for seats (10 is the most useful); 11, 12 and 13 for backs and 14 and 15 for arms. Other types of springing are not covered in the projects in this section.

Basic construction

Traditional upholstery consists of layers of varying thickness of woven and loose materials. The number of layers varies, but they are always built up in the same way. Webbing tacked to the frame takes most of the strain and supports the springs, if there are any. Some chairs are unsprung, others can have them in the seat, back and arms. Both the height and the thickness (swg/metal diameter) of springs vary, but they are always attached to the webbing in the same way. The springs are then lashed (corded) together so that they move together to some extent.

A covering of strong hessian (burlap) is placed over the webbing or springs and the springs are attached to this in the same way as they were to the webbing. This forms a base for the first stuffing. This first stuffing is a loose material, either hair or (more usually, these days) fibre, and is anchored to the hessian by means of twine ties. Scrim encloses the first stuffing.

If the outer edge of the part being upholstered is of any height, a hard edge (edge roll) is constructed so that it holds its shape. A hard edge can be made on a straight or curved edge and on a seat, back, arm or wing, though not necessarily every edge on the same piece of furniture will have a hard edge. There are many ways of making an edge firm and able to retain its shape, but the one most often used is produced by forming rows of stitching with twine along the edge to hold the filling in place in the edge. One or more rows of blind (sink) stitches pull fibre into the base of the seat, and one or more rows of top stitches hold the edge firm. Other methods of constructing edges have been used over the centuries, but this is the most common among traditional upholstery craftsmen.

A second layer of stuffing, this time thin and unstitched, covers the scrim; this stuffing should be hair, and is held in place by calico (muslin). The calico also helps to create the final shape of the piece. A layer of wadding (batting) over the calico helps stop the hair filling working its way through the calico and sticking through the top cover.

Many different fabrics can be used for the top cover, but try to choose a fabric suitable for the piece – avoid large patterns for small pieces.

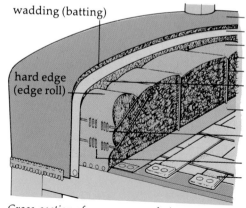

wadding (batting) · top cover · calico · scrim · first stuffing · stuffing ties · second stuffing · base hessian (burlap) · hard edge (edge roll) · top stitching · blind (sink) · stitching · webbing

Cross-section of an unsprung chair.

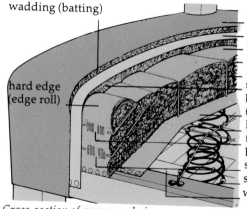

wadding (batting) · top cover · calico · scrim · first stuffing · stuffing ties · second stuffing · base hessian (burlap) · hard edge (edge roll) · lashing cord · top stitching · blind (sink) · stitching · springs · webbing

Cross-section of a sprung chair.

Although springs make a chair more comfortable, there is little difference in the basic construction techniques.

Chair frames

Most traditional frames are made of wood, usually beech or birch, and there are two basic frame types: stuffover, which are completely upholstered (excluding the legs) and show-wood, in which the wood, sometimes with decorative carving, is left exposed. The visible part of the frame can be made from any wood.

The joints used on the chair will depend on the quality and date of the piece. It will usually have dowelled or mortise and tenon joints or a combination of both. Although each part of the frame has a (usually obvious) name, all stuffover frames have one set of rails which are vital to the upholsterer; these are the stay or stuffing rails. These rails form a space at about seat height through which the covers pass.

Many modern frames (even of traditional style) are termed 'knock down' because the arms, back and seat are upholstered as separate units, which are then bolted together before the outside cover is attached. These frames, and iron-frame chairs, are not dealt with here.

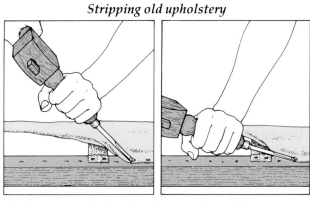

Stripping old upholstery

Use the ripping chisel and a mallet to strip the old upholstery off the frame. Work along the grain of the wood.

Stripping frames

If your chair is of some value or of a genuinely early date, consult a professional or your local museum before you do anything, even before you strip the upholstery off. Before you remove anything from the frame, make sketches or take photographs from all sides of the chair. Note things like the height of the seat at the edge, where the piping is and the size and shape at the front of the arms. You may think you will remember, but once the chair is stripped it will be too late to find out that you cannot. Begin by stripping the bottoming off the chair with the ripping chisel and the mallet. Work along the grain of the wood away from the corners, being careful not to split the wood. Next, remove the outside back and outside arms, making more notes and sketches as you go. You will need to know, for example, if the inside arm goes out through the back of the chair, or through the side of the arm close to the back. As you take the chair apart, look at the illustrations in this section which look similar; it may help you later.

When you have removed all the upholstery and tacks, look at the joints. If they are loose, reglue them. If the tacking area looks as though you may have difficulty anchoring the tacks in place, mix sawdust with a little wood glue and fill the holes. Glue strips of either hessian or calico over these areas to help hold the sawdust filling in place. If the polished show-wood needs repairing, get advice from a professional restorer.

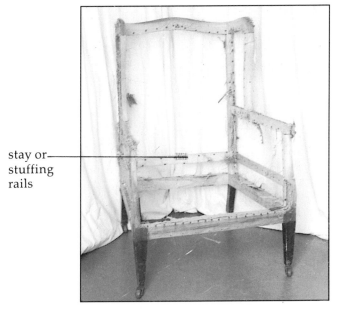

stay or stuffing rails

Most chair frames are simple and often look too fragile to hold the upholstery; the stay or stuffing rails are vital in re-upholstery.

Project 1: Drop-in seat

Simple seats

The upholstery in drop-in seats is simple and dates from about the seventeenth century, when the backs of chairs were sometimes constructed in the same way.

The frame to which the upholstery is fixed is usually made up of four battens of wood (usually beech) jointed at the corners. Some are serpentine-shaped along the front edge, but this makes very little difference to the way the upholstery is built up. The subframe sits in the main chair frame with a space between them – this is the space into which the covering fabrics fit.

Although, as a general rule, the edges of drop-in seats are not visible, sometimes the front and back edges are and the front edge is rounded off instead of flat. In this case, you must take care that both of these edges are very neat and that the undercovering does not show below the edge of the seat.

In spite of their simple construction, drop-in seats are not very easy to work on, simply because they move about easily. When you are fixing the webbing, either clamp the frame to the bench or tack a strip of old webbing to the bench across one corner of the frame – this will stop the frame from lifting up when you tension the webbing. When you strip the frame, note how many webbs there are in each direction. In almost all cases the old upholstery of a drop-in seat should be removed and discarded. The padding tends to flatten and the webbing stretch, and the result is a hollow seat.

Basic techniques

A drop-in seat is a good project to begin with because it involves many of the basic techniques of upholstery. Although there are variations from one piece to another, the application of these techniques and the method of working are the same whether you are dealing with a seat, back, arm or wing.

If you have more than one drop-in seat to re-upholster, work on two at a time so that they will look about the same when you have finished.

Left: *Re-upholstering a drop-in seat is a good project to start with because it is quite simple and relatively quick, but also involves many of the basic techniques of upholstery: the fixing of webbing and hessian; making bridle ties to anchor the filling; and fitting calico, skin wadding and top and bottom covers.*

Webbing

Webbing is usually fixed to the top of the frame in unsprung chairs and the bottom of the frame in sprung chairs. The top outer edge of a drop-in seat should be chamfered (beveled), so if your seat does not have a chamfered edge, you should put one on first. The webbing must be spaced evenly over the area formed by the seat rails, so start by marking the centre of all four rails on both the top and bottom surfaces.

Always work from a roll of webbing; you will have problems if you start cutting lengths off the roll to work with. Fold 2.5cm (1in.) of the cut end of the webbing over on itself. Line up the webbing at the centre back of the frame, with the fold about halfway across the width of the frame and hammer in five tacks in a W shape. Unless the wood is hard and liable to split (in which case you should use 12mm (½in.) fine), use 12mm (½in.) improved tacks. The cut end of the webbing should be on top (thus forming a 'washer' under the tack head). Thread the webb strainer and tension the webbing towards the front of the frame. Overstraining will warp a light frame but the webbing should still be drum-like, not saggy. Line up the webbing at the centre front and, again halfway across the rail, drive three tacks fully home into the single thickness of webbing while you are straining it. Cut the webbing about 2.5cm (1in.) from the tacks and fold this back on itself, then hammer in two more tacks. If you could see all five tacks at this end, they would make the same W shape. The number of rows of webbing you removed when you were stripping the chair is the best guide to how many rows you will need. Work outwards from the centre back and do all the back to front rows, then do the side to side rows, interweaving them.

Base hessian (burlap)

The base hessian covers the webbing and supports the filling, so if it sags, the filling will too. Measure across the widest part of the frame (side to side and front to back) and add about 5cm (2in.) on each edge for handling and turning over, then cut a piece of hessian to these measurements. Fold it in half, front to back and mark the centre then place it over the webbing, keeping the weave square to the seat. The hessian can then be temporary tacked. This involves driving the tacks only part way into the wood, so that they can be removed easily if adjustments have to be made. Use 10mm (⅜in.) improved tacks and start at the centre of the back rail. Strain the hessian to the centre front and temporary tack it there, then repeat at each side. Continue temporary tacking on the back rail, spacing the tacks about 4cm (1½in.) apart, then do the front edge, tensioning the hessian as you work, and then do the sides. When the whole frame is temporary tacked, hammer the tacks on the front rail home. As you do the back rail, tension the hessian slightly and when you hammer home on the side rails, keep checking that the weave is square.

Finish the edges as illustrated on the left.

Tacking the webbing and hessian

1 Tension the webbing, then hammer in three tacks.

2 Interweave the rows of webbing for strength.

3 Leave 2cm (¾in.) beyond the tacks and cut off excess.

4 Hold the hessian down with more widely spaced tacks.

Filling the seat

Bridle ties are made with a spring needle and thin twine. Start about 6.5cm (2½in.) from the edge of the frame, knot the twine, then make a looped running stitch around the seat, only knotting the twine again at the end of the run. The centre section will need some ties, though how many depends on size – for a small seat, one single loop down the centre is enough. The height of the loops varies according to how much filling you need; for a drop-in seat they need only be high enough to allow your hand to slide under them.

The best filling for a small area like a drop-in seat is hair. This is easy to handle and, unlike other fillings which go flat after only a short time, is resilient. To avoid lumps, tease the hair before you use it. To do this, take a handful and pull the fibres apart, letting them drop into a plastic bag. When you have a reasonable amount teased, take a handful and, starting at the back left-hand corner, tuck it under the bridle ties. As you tuck in each successive handful, tease it into the rest of the hair. Do all the sides of the seat first, then fill in the centre section. You should put slightly more here.

Covering with calico (muslin)

Measure over the filling at its widest point and round to the bottom of the frame and add about 5cm (2in.) on all sides for handling, before you cut the calico. The weave must be kept square at all times, so fold the material and mark its centre. If the space between the seat and the chair frame is not large enough to take the thickness of the tack head, calico and top cover, tack the calico to the underside of the seat. Normally, it should be tacked to the outer face of the frame. Using 10mm (⅜in.) fine tacks, temporary tack at the centres of the back, front and sides, keeping the calico square and quite taut. Place more tacks about 4cm (1½in.) apart along the back rail, then tension the calico towards the front rail and tack it there. Finally, temporary tack the sides. Take care that the filling does not slip on to the face edge of the frame at any point.

If, when you have finished, the shape is not quite right, take out a few tacks at a time and tension and shape again smoothing it over the edges and towards the corners. Finish the corners as shown on the right. Finally, tack home all around the sides.

Filling a drop-in seat

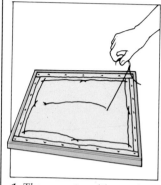

1 The correct position and height of bridle ties.

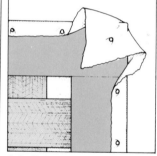

2 Teased hair will give a lump- and hollow-free filling.

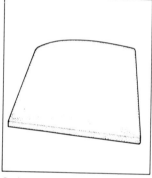

3 As you work, tension the calico to make the right shape.

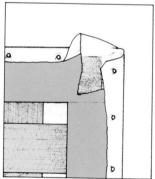

4 Pull the calico to the corner; tack with a gimp pin.

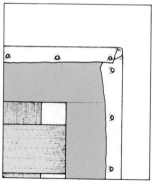

5 Pleat the first side, tack home and cut away excess.

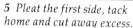

6 Pleat the second side over the first and tack home.

Skin wadding (batting)

Skin wadding is essential with a hair filling and is used on top of the calico to prevent the filling working through the top cover. It also adds softness to the surface covering. Cut a piece of wadding to cover the seat easily, then, holding it in place over the calico, pinch away any excess as far down as the top of the seat rail. This will prevent a hard edge showing on the top cover, which would happen if the wadding were cut. Take care that the wadding does not cover the face edges of the frame; if it does, you will find it difficult to fit the seat back into the frame.

Top and bottom covers

If the fabric you have chosen for the top cover has a pattern, remember when you are cutting out that you must centre the pattern. Tack the cover to the underside of the frame with 10mm (⅜in.) fine tacks. Space them as you did for the calico, about 10mm (⅜in.) in from outer edge, and, as with the calico, temporary tack first so that you can check the fit as you go. At the corners, fold the material to make pleats on the front and back edges.

Although the frame of this seat was not in perfect condition (left), the finished upholstery (right) should last for many years.

Fitting the cover

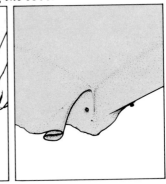

1 Pinch away excess wadding to prevent a hard edge.

2 Ease fabric to the back edge and fix with a gimp pin.

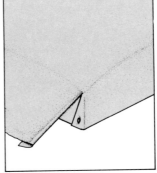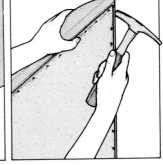

3 Pleat the fabric, cut away excess and tack home.

4 Tack one edge of the bottoming under the other.

Use gimp pins at the corners since they reduce bulk, and then cut off any excess.

The final stage is to fix the bottom cover, which catches any dust falling from the seat and also covers all the raw edges of the top cover. Although bottoming is usually black, you can use any close-weave fabric like curtain lining. Cut a rectangle of bottoming the same size as the base of the frame and temporary tack using 10mm (⅜in.) fine tacks, folding it under as you go. The fold should be about 10mm (⅜in.) from the edge of the frame, and the bottoming pulled just tight enough not to sag. Tack close to the fold so that the edge lies flat and space the tacks about 2.5cm (1in.) apart. This time, fold the corners one under the other.

Project 2: Stuffed and stitched dining-chair seat

Basic construction

There are several differences between a drop-in seat and this type of dining-chair seat. The first is that the upholstery is attached directly to the chair frame instead of to a subframe. Secondly, the filling here is much thicker than in a drop-in seat and therefore some way of keeping the shape of the stuffing has to be found. The stuffing in the drop-in seat was covered with calico (muslin) to create the seat shape; in the dining-chair, the shape is created by encasing the filling in scrim which is tacked to the edge of the seat frame – the top of the outer edge of the seat rail should be chamfered (beveled) for this purpose. Rows of stitching formed with twine are then inserted through the scrim and the filling to form a firm edge so that the seat keeps its shape even after many years' use. The stuffing, tacking and stitching described here constitute the basic and most often used method of creating an edge in traditional upholstery.

A further difference is that the drop-in seat had only one filling, while this seat has two. The filling over the hessian is called the first stuffing, the next (much thinner) filling is called the second stuffing. This is covered with calico, as in the drop-in seat.

Most chairs of this type are finished off on the lower edge by gimp or braid. Choose a gimp which is a suitable width in proportion to the depth of the upholstery – wide gimp or braid will tend to dominate a shallow seat. Always follow the line of the show-wood when you are fixing gimp.

Preparation

When you strip the chair, note how the corners are finished. Are there two pleats or one, for example? Note how high the seat is and where it comes to on the back posts, this will be a guide later when you build the seat. Measure the height of the front too.

If you have two or more chairs which are meant to be identical then work on them both at the same time; it will be easier to make them look the same this way.

Finally, before you start, remember to reglue the frame, if necessary (see p. 44).

Left: *From worn and collapsed* (top) *to firm and comfortable. The seat of this dining chair is stitched so that it holds its shape.*

49

First stages

Attach the webbing as described on p. 46. Use 340g (12oz.) hessian (burlap) as a base over the webbing. Fix it as described on p. 46, but at the corners, tack it on top of the front legs, and cut it to fit around the back posts. Insert bridle ties as described on p. 47 but here allow about three fingers' height. Although hair is preferred as a stuffing where only a thin padding is needed, fibre is acceptable as a first stuffing for most other work, so use that here. Tease and insert it in the same way as described for hair on p. 47.

Allow enough scrim to cover the filling and come down to the bottom of the seat rails. Fold the scrim to find the centre, and, keeping the weave straight, temporary tack it at the back, then smooth it to the front and temporary tack it there. Tack both sides. Be careful not to put the tacks into any show-wood.

Stuffing ties

Use a regulator or chalk to mark the position of the ties, which should run round the seat about 10cm (4in.) from the edge of the seat rail. Thread the stitching needle with no. 2 twine and, in the back left-hand corner (A), stab down through the scrim, stuffing and base hessian. Insert the needle in the hessian 12mm (½in.) along and push up and out through the scrim on top – the needle should come out 12mm (½in.) from where you stabbed down originally – and form a slip knot. Stab down again at B and come back up again. Continue doing this until you have a running stitch around the seat. Pull each stitch firm but not tight and then loosely tie off the twine at A. Then put a couple of ties down the centre of the seat to secure the filling there.

Once the stuffing ties are in position, the scrim can be turned under and tacked on to the chamfered edge. Remove the temporary tacks at the centre front. You will need to add more fibre to make the edge firm, so tease out a handful, lift the scrim and push the new fibre *under* the existing fibre mass. Work round the seat in this way, removing tacks from a section at a time, then fold the scrim under the filling (the regulator will help considerably here), and tack it on the chamfered edge using 12mm (½in.) fine tacks, about 10mm (⅜in.) apart. When you have tacked about 40mm (1½in.) either side of the centre, measure the height of the seat

Enclosing the first stuffing

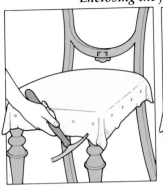
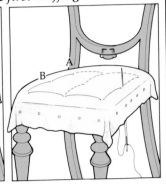

1 Temporary tack scrim with 12mm (½in.) improved tacks.

2 Put stuffing ties around the seat and down the centre.

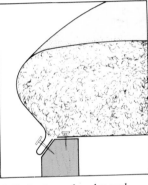
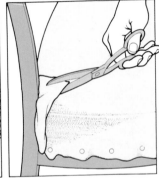

3 Scrim turned under and tacked on the chamfered edge.

4 Cut towards the corner post, but stop 15mm (⅝in.) short.

from the floor. Keep measuring from the floor as you work round and if your edge is too high at any point, remove the tacks and fold more scrim under the filling (if there is a lot of scrim to turn under, cut some away); this will lower the edge, but it must still protrude beyond the edge of the seat rail. Follow the shape of the seat rails and tack along the front, then the back, then each side, to within 50mm (2in.) of each corner.

At the back corners, fold the scrim back on itself, and make a cut. Tuck the scrim down between the back post and the stuffing, make a fold inwards, cut any excess off the bottom of the scrim and tack it. At the front corners, pleat the scrim, cut off any excess at the bottom, then turn it under and tack. Hammer all the tacks home.

Making a hard edge (edge roll)

The most common way of making a hard edge is by stitching: a blind (sink) stitch pulls fibre into the base of the seat, while a top stitch holds the edge firm. It is usual for this type of seat to have one blind row and two top rows of stitching. To make the blind stitch, thread the stitching needle with stitching (buttoning) twine, and starting in the back left-hand corner, insert the needle through the side of the scrim, close to the post and the tacks. The point should come out through the top of the seat about 70mm (2¾in.) from the edge. Do not pull the needle free (the eye should come to the top surface of the scrim). Make a circular motion with the

The stitched edge forms the shape of the finished seat.

eye end and push the needle down so that it comes out of the scrim near where you first inserted it. Take the needle out and make a slip knot. Tighten the twine gently but firmly. Insert the needle about 20mm (¾in.) along from the slip knot and make another stitch as before, but do not withdraw the needle this time. Loop the twine round the needle twice, withdraw the needle and pull the twine downwards. Work around the seat in this way, then work the back in exactly the same way.

Regulate the fibre into the edge of the seat, and keep regulating as you work around the seat. The rows of stitching must be evenly spaced up the height of the seat and about 12mm (½in.) apart. Insert the needle (eye end last) and stab upwards, coming out on the top surface a little way in from the edge. Pull the needle clear of the scrim, then push it down near to the back post. Pull it clear of the seat and form a slip knot. Insert the needle again about 20mm (¾in.) from the first stitch, come out on the top surface as before, stab down alongside the first stitch, then loop the twine twice around the needle, withdraw the needle, and pull the stitch tight. Work round the seat in this way, then work the back edge. Thread all the loose ends of twine up into the seat and tighten and tie off the stuffing ties.

The second stuffing should be a fairly thin layer of hair, inserted as described on p. 47. When you have finished, the surface of the chair should feel springy and the centre of the seat should dome slightly.

Blind (sink) stitching

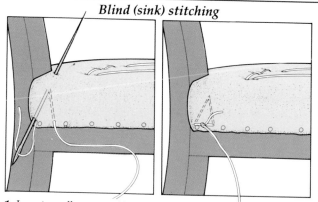

1 Insert needle, eye end last, through the scrim. Make a circular motion with the end, push needle back down, make a slip knot.

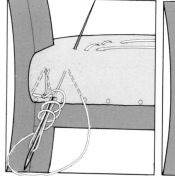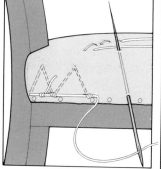

2 After the next stitch, loop left-hand twine round needle twice, withdraw the needle and pull the twine downwards.

Calico and wadding (batting)

Cut a piece of skin wadding to fit over the seat and cover the tacks, and trim away any excess by pinching as described on p. 48. Cut it to fit around the corner posts, easing down between the post and the seat.

Temporary tack the back using 10mm (⅜in.) fine tacks, then smooth and strain the calico to the front. Repeat at each side. The calico must be quite tight and tacked halfway down the seat rail, to within 50mm (2in.) of each corner. Finish the back corners as illustrated below. Use the flat end of the regulator to ease the calico between the stuffing and the post. If it puckers near the post, you will have to lift it and lengthen the cut a little.

Securing the back corners

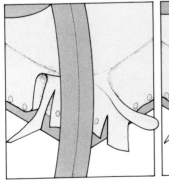

1 Slash the calico to within 6mm (¼in.) of the post.

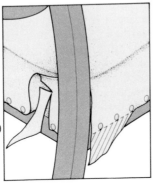

2 Ease it down between the post and the filling.

3 Tack almost on chamfered edge and cut near the tack.

4 Fold it to come to the post, and cut off any excess.

Find the centre of the front corners, strain the calico to that point, and fix it with a gimp pin. Tack that home. Put a pin each side of the corner, smooth the calico down and pleat it inwards. Use the flat end of the regulator to get a good fold line. Ease the calico into place, drive all the tacks home and trim off any excess.

Cut a piece of skin wadding to fit over the seat and cover the tacks, and trim away any excess by pinching as described on p. 48. Cut it to fit around the corner posts, easing down between the post and the seat.

Top and bottom covers

Measure for the top cover as you did for the calico, but remember that any pattern must be centred. The top cover must finish at the show-wood, so make sure that any gimp or braid you use will cover the tacks as you place them. Use 10mm (⅜in.) fine tacks and temporary tack first at the back, then smooth and strain to the front. Repeat at the sides, constantly checking that the cover remains straight and quite tight. Fix the corners as you did the calico, but remember that the tacks must not be visible when the gimp is applied. When you are satisfied that all is square and neat, hammer the tacks home, being careful not to damage the show-wood. Trim away excess fabric using a sharp knife or scissors.

Although gimp should be attached with matching gimp pins, gluing with a clear adhesive is easier. Do not use too much glue, which could bleed through the gimp and discolour it. Follow the show-wood line, and try not to stretch the gimp. The corners should be mitred.

Fit a bottom cover as described on p. 48.

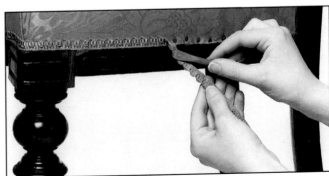

As long as you are careful, gluing gimp is quite acceptable and easier than attaching it with gimp pins.

Project 3: Wing armchair, with sprung seat and back, and scroll arms

Basic construction

The major difference between this project and the previous ones is that here the parts of the chair have to be upholstered so that they meet each other without gaps. Gaps look dreadful and adding bits of wadding (batting) when the top cover is partly fitted makes matters worse. The stay or stuffing rails are vital here – their position indicates the height of the seat.

The seat is usually the first part of a chair to fail. The webbing decays naturally and pulls away from the tacks and the base hessian (burlap) also sometimes rots with the result that the filling is pushed down into the spring area. The tops of the arms tend to lose their resilience and become dented where the elbows are rested. The back is usually the last to go. For this reason, it is not always necessary to strip all the upholstery off a chair but even if you can salvage the back and wings, the seat and arms should be stripped to the frame.

If you are in any doubt about how long the old upholstery will last if you leave it, remember that the covering material is the most expensive part of the job, except for your time, and that it will be better in the long run to start from scratch than to risk the chair collapsing after only perhaps a year or two.

Preparation

When you are stripping the chair, make drawings and notes of what sort of finish it has. Is there any piping (welting), if so where and how is it fixed? Where do the facings fit and what shape are they? It is not essential that you reproduce the original exactly, but it will be useful as a guide.

It is usually easier to webb, spring and base hessian the seat and back first, while the frame is free from upholstery, then begin stuffing the chair. Do the first stuffing of the whole chair, then the second stuffing and calico (muslin) of the whole chair, and finally the wadding and top cover. When a piece of furniture has identical sections such as arms and, as here, wings, work each stage of these sections at the same time; this will help you to make them match.

Left: *The seat of this chair had fallen out* (far left) *and extensive work had to be done on the frame; nothing could be reused. Most chairs look completely different when they are finished* (top).

Sprung seat

In unsprung work, the webbing is tacked on the top of the seat frame. In most sprung seats, however, it is fixed to the underside. With this exception, you should attach the webbing as described on p. 46. Use 15mm (⅝in.) improved tacks and be particularly careful that you tack the webbing halfway across the rail; if it is too close to the outside edge of the frame, it will show as ugly bumps under the top cover.

Check the notes you made when you were stripping the chair to see how deep the back and arms were. It is pointless to put springs too close to the back rail if they are going to be covered by the stuffing (filling) in the chair back, and, similarly, springs too near the side of the seat will be covered by the stuffing in the arms.

As a guide for the height of the springs you will need, first measure the height of the ones you removed, then measure from the webbing up to the stuffing rail. These measurements should be about the same, if they are not, compromise. Springs of 10 SWG (metal diameter) will usually be about right, but if the springs are very high, you should use 9 SWG. Your chair will probably have three or four springs along the front edge, and across the centre, but it may have fewer in the back row. Space them evenly and face them so that the knot at the top of the spring is inwards. (If the knot faces outwards it will cut through the base hessian.) Mark around the springs with chalk then remove all but the one in the back left-hand corner. Thread the spring needle with heavy twine and, starting with a slip knot, sew the spring to the webbing in three places. As you replace each spring in position, face the knot inwards.

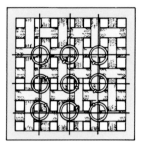
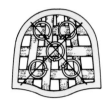

Spring patterns vary from chair to chair but the aim is always to distribute the springs evenly over the sitting area. Remember that most people move about on a chair – they don't sit in one spot the whole time.

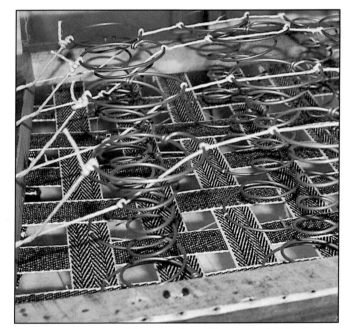

Here a space has been left at the sides of the seat and at the back because the arms and back would otherwise protrude over the springs. After the springs have been sewn in position, they must be lashed to hold them in place.

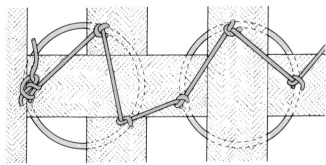

Attach each spring to the webbing in three places, beginning with a slip knot.

Lashing (cording) springs

When you have attached all the springs to the webbing, they must be lashed together with laid cord. Start by placing pairs of 15mm (⅝in.) improved tacks on the top of the seat frame at opposite ends of each row of springs, leaving enough space between the frame and the tack head to take the laid cord. Bear in mind that, after they are lashed, the springs should be vertical but reduced in height by 2-2.5cm (¾-1in.). Leave about 30cm (12in.) at the end of the cord, then loop it round the tacks at one end and drive the tacks home. You need to put two half-hitches (one each side) of every spring. When you reach the other side of the frame, pull the

The bridle ties are inserted around the edge and to form a squared S shape over the centre of the seat.

cord tight around the tacks and drive the tacks home. Cut the cord about 30cm (12in.) from the tacks, then tie both loose ends back up to the outside springs. You have to repeat this process across each row of springs from side to side and back to front. When you have finished, the springs should all be straight but reduced in height by about 2cm (¾in.). If any of them look crooked, you will have to relash them.

First stuffing

Cover the springs with 340g (12oz.) base hessian, as described on p. 46. Measure over the springs at the widest point and allow enough for handling. The hessian must be taut but make sure that it does not pull the springs down with it. Cut the hessian to fit around the back posts as described on p. 50. At the front corners, fold it back on itself from front to back and make a Y cut (see p. 56), level with the top outside edge of the front rail. Once you are satisfied that the hessian is in place, stitch the springs to it in the same way as you stitched them to the webbing.

Insert bridle ties around the outer edge of the seat as described on p. 47 but in the centre work the ties in an S shape. They should all be about three fingers high. Use fibre for the stuffing and tease it out and tuck it under the bridle ties as described on p. 47. Put more around the outer edge and enough to form a thin cushion over the springs in the centre. Press down on the filling and if you can feel the springs, add more teased fibre, but keep in mind the finished height of the seat and do not make this first stuffing too high.

Lashing (cording) springs

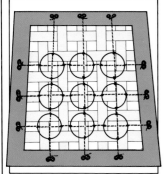

1 *Place pairs of tacks at both ends of each row of springs.*

2 Loop the cord round the tacks at one end.

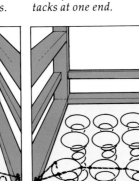

3 Place a half-hitch on both sides of every spring.

4 Tie the loose ends up to the first and last springs.

Stitching the seat

Cover the fibre with scrim and insert stuffing ties as described on p. 50. Be careful here that you only put the point of the needle through the base hessian (the twine must not go through the webbing). If you pull the twine too far down into the spring area it will get caught up around the springs and laid cord. The scrim should be tacked down as described on p. 50. When you get to the front corners, fold the scrim as you did the base hessian and make a Y cut. The scrim should now fit around the front post. At the back and sides, tack the scrim on the top of the rail. The seat itself should fit snugly up to the stuffing rails.

You will need to make a hard edge (edge roll) at the front of the seat; the number of rows of stitching required will depend on the height of the seat at the front edge, but usually in this type of seat, you will need two rows of blind (sink) stitching and two top rows (roll stitch). The top roll should be quite plump unless you want a sharp edge to the chair. Work the stitching as described on p. 51. When you have finished, tighten the stuffing ties slightly and knot off.

Second stuffing

Insert bridle ties around the edge of the seat and in the centre as you did for the first stuffing. This second stuffing should be hair, teased out and tucked under the bridle ties as described on p. 47. If your seat was domed slightly, add more hair in the centre and graduate it to the outside edge of the seat. Measure over the widest parts of the seat and halfway down the face edge of the seat rails and cut the calico to these measurements. Fit the calico as described on p. 52. Tack both the back and the front before you make a Y cut at the front corners, since once you have cut the calico, you cannot move it again. The cuts to fit the calico around the back posts are the same as described on p. 52. At the back and the sides (under the arms), tack the calico on top of the rails, as you did the scrim.

On armchairs linter felt makes a better wadding than skin wadding because it gives a softer feel to the surface of the top cover. Cut the felt to cover the seat and the calico at the front and go under the bottom edge of the arms and back. Be careful handling this felt as it tends to pull apart easily. Place it over the calico, press the seat down to leave a space, and tuck it under the back and arms. If it goes lumpy, it is best to take it off and start again.

Top cover

Cut a rectangle of top cover, remembering to centre the pattern. At the back and sides, the top cover will be tacked on top of the rails as the calico was, so measure to here and add about 5cm (2in.) for handling. If there is no show-wood along the front edge of the seat rail, the cover will go under the front rail and be tacked on the underside of the chair, so allow about 5cm (2in.) at this edge to go under the chair. Attach the top cover as described on p. 52. At the front legs, place a pin at the corner of the leg and rail, then cut the cover upwards to the pin. Cut off the excess fabric and turn it under, then fold and tack it under the bottom of the chair and across the top of the leg. Drive the tacks home along the sides then fold the top cover inwards on top of itself and tack it home using 12mm (½in.) fine tacks. Finally, trim off any excess fabric.

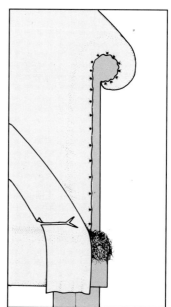 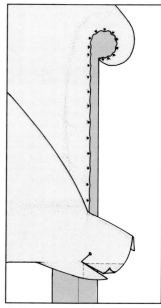

1 Make Y cuts in both scrim and calico to fit around the rails.

2 Place a pin at the corner of the leg and rail; cut the cover to the pin.

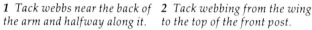

Scroll arms

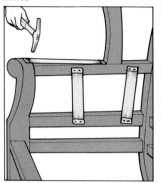

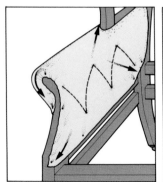

1 Tack webbs near the back of the arm and halfway along it.

2 Tack webbing from the wing to the top of the front post.

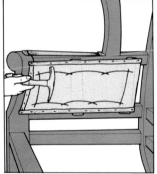

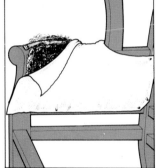

3 Fold the hessian round the webbing and insert bridle ties.

4 Tuck fibre under the webbing and fit the scrim.

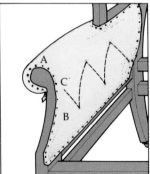

5 Tension the scrim to create a cigar shape.

6 Tack and smooth the scrim around the scroll.

Scroll arms

Fold a strip of webbing in half across its width and tack it as described on p. 46 on the inside of the arm, about 5cm (2in.) in from the back post. Tack a full-width webb about halfway along the arm. Both need only be hand tight. Tack a rectangle of 340g (12oz.) base hessian as described on p. 46 over the top of the arm rail to the stuffing rail, and from the front post to the back post. At the back, nick it top and bottom so that it folds around the back strip of webbing.

Insert bridle ties round the hessian, about 7.5cm (3in.) from the edge. Tack a piece of webbing on top of the arm rail close to the wing. Hand strain it over the top of the front post and tack it on top of the post. Prepare the first stuffing as described on p. 50. Tuck plenty of fibre under the webbing on top of the arm rail, then fill the bridle ties. Cut a rectangle of scrim to fit from the outside of the stuffing rail, under the rail, over the filling and around to the outside of the arm, and from the back post, over the filling to the front of the front post (the facing), and add 5cm (2in.) on all sides for handling. Temporary tack it on the outside of the stuffing rail, the underside of the arm rail and at the centre of the facing. Remove the original temporary tacks if necessary, and tension. Re-temporary tack along the outside of the stuffing rail and under the arm rail, and put two or three tacks down the front of the facing.

Put stuffing ties in a zigzag pattern along the arm. Tuck the scrim under the fibre as described on p. 50, and tack on the chamfered (bevelled) edge. Work the top of the scroll (the scroll is the curve at the top of the facing) first (A), then do about halfway down the front edge (B), and go back and fill in the space between (C). Do not make pleats down the facing, the scrim should be smooth but protrude beyond the facing. To finish the underarm, add more filling and tuck the scrim under the fibre. Tack the scrim low on the outside of the arm rail up to the wing rail. To finish the point of the scroll, cut off the excess scrim, tuck it under and tack. Complete the rest of the scroll, then drive all the tacks home right around the front facing.

To fit the scrim around the wing rail, fold it back on itself and make a long Y cut in to the wing rail. Fold it to fit around the rail, adding more fibre if you need to. Make Y cuts so that the scrim passes through and under the arm, and tuck this 'tongue' around the webbing.

Stitching the scroll

The next stage is to regulate and stitch the scroll. Use the regulator to help you work the fibre into the edge of the scroll so that it will be firm once you have stitched it. Work the blind stitch as described on p. 51 all around the front of the arm. The blind row does not need to go right to the point of the scroll since there is very little fibre there. Work a row of top stitches around the scroll, tapering the row so that it begins (or ends) at the point. Regulate the fibre into the edge as you make the stitches and remember that the roll should protrude beyond the facing when you have finished.

Remove the temporary tacks on the stuffing rail and add more filling so that the bottom of the arm sits neatly on top of the seat. Tuck the scrim under the fibre in the usual way and tack it on the outside of the stuffing rail. Make any necessary adjustments to the wing area of the arm and drive all the tacks home. The only part of the scrim not now tacked should be the tongue which you tucked around the webbing at the back of the arm.

To keep the shape of the arm, you should work a row of 5cm (2in.) top stitches (see p. 51) along the outside edge of the arm.

Make fairly tight bridle ties (as described on p. 47) to hold the thin hair second stuffing. Remember when you are doing the second stuffing to fill any hollows made by the stuffing ties and the rows of stitching; you should not be able to detect them when the calico is fitted. The hair must not come over the roll at the front of the arm, nevertheless you should put a reasonable amount on this edge.

Cut a rectangle of calico large enough to cover the whole of the stuffed part of the arm with about 5cm (2in.) for handling and temporary tack as described on p. 52. Pull it tight around the front of the scroll, and temporary tack on the outside of the stuffing rail and under the arm rail. Skewer (pin) the calico at the top of the scroll, smooth it over the front of the facing and temporary tack it in about three places. Make a cut in the calico, leave about 15mm (⅝in.) around the top of the scroll and trim off any excess.

Start at the top of the scroll, turn the calico under the hair and pin it. Work around the scroll, pinning as you go. Remember that the calico should be smooth and taut, so if it feels a bit loose, remove the temporary tacks and tension down the front of the facing again.

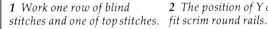
Shaping the arm

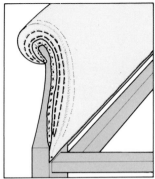
1 Work one row of blind stitches and one of top stitches.

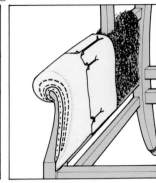
2 The position of Y cuts to fit scrim round rails.

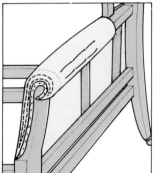
3 Make a row of top stitches on the outside edge.

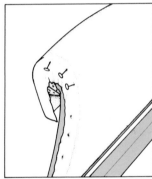
4 Skewer the calico at the top of the scroll.

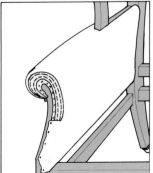
5 Turn the calico under the hair, then pin it.

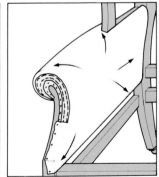
6 Tension the calico to keep the scroll shape as you go.

Finishing the scroll

At the back, remove the temporary tacks and fold the calico back, cutting it to fit around the wing rail, the arm rail and the stuffing rail, as you did the scrim, and re-temporary tack. Make a Y cut in the calico to fit around the front post and complete the tacking at the back, on the stuffing rail and under the arm rail. The calico should be quite tight – if it is loose it will make ugly wrinkles under the top cover – so when you are satisfied that it is taut in all directions, cut off all the excess. The calico pinned round the scroll must now be stitched in place. This is done with a knotted blanket stitch (sometimes called a joining stitch) and it is best to use slipping (buttoning) thread since this is less likely to show through the top cover. Work from where the calico was cut, round the top of the scroll to the point.

Use linter felt over the calico, ensuring that it covers all the stuffed part of the arm, but not the arm facing. Remember that it is far easier to pinch away excess than

The first stuffing is enclosed with scrim to create the required shape and the second stuffing is covered with calico, tacked and stitched into place. A layer of wadding is placed over the calico and the top cover encases them all.

it is to add more without it looking lumpy. Cut a rectangle of top cover as you did for the calico. It must run down the inside of the arm and both arms must match as far as possible. The tacks should not go through the wadding so pinch the wadding away as necessary. Temporary tack the top cover as you did the calico; it must be quite tight. Smooth the cover over the front facing, temporary tack at the top of the scroll first and then divide the fabric into pleats all around the scroll. Face the pleats downwards towards the seat – they should appear to radiate from a point in the centre of the scroll. The top of the pleats should not go over the top of the arm. Tension and tack down the rest of the facing as you did the calico.

At the back of the arm, fold the cover as you did the calico and make Y cuts to fit around the wing rail, the arm rail and the stuffing rail. At the front, make a Y cut to fit around the front post. Tack off, adjust the tension as necessary, then trim off any excess fabric.

Knotted blanket stitch

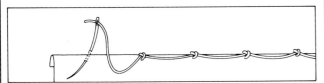

1 Make knotted blanket stitches with slipping (buttoning) thread, since this is less likely to show through the top cover.

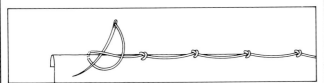

2 Place the stitches about 10mm (3/8in.) apart, round the scroll to the point.

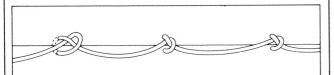

3 Use the same stitch on a button-back chair (see p. 66) to anchor the calico round the edge of the back.

Sprung back

Springing a back is in many ways similar to springing a seat, so follow the basic instructions given on pp. 54-6.

Attach the horizontal webbs first, then fix the vertical webbs to the stuffing rail and tension them up to the top rail. If the springs that you removed from the back are in a reasonable condition, sort them into heights and place them on the webbing, with the taller ones nearest the seat. Face the knot part of the spring inwards. The springs should sit over the area where the webbs cross. Position, stitch them to the webbing and lash them in place as described on pp. 54-5, but make sure you do not strain them down, since this would make the back hard and unyielding. Fix 340g (12oz.) base hessian over the springs (see p. 55), cutting to fit around the arm rails. Do not overstrain the hessian. Sew the springs to the hessian as described on p. 55. Work around the outer edge of the back inserting the bridle ties, as described on p. 47, then work some over the remainder of the back. They should all be about three fingers high. Insert the first stuffing as described on p. 55, but put more at the bottom of the back to give some support to the sitter's lower back.

The scrim should be turned under and tacked on the front (top) surface of the back posts, on the outside of the stuffing rail at the bottom, and on the chamfered edge on the top rail. Temporary tack each side of the scrim first, then do the top rail, then the bottom. At the bottom, tuck it down between the seat and the fibre in the back.

Insert stuffing ties as described on p. 50. The lower ones should be just below the top of the arms, so that the lumber support is free from ties. Avoid the springs and cords when you are inserting the ties. Remove the temporary tacks from the top rail, add more fibre, tuck the scrim under the filling and tack it on to the chamfered edge, as described on p. 50. Work to within 5cm (2in.) of the sides, then fold the scrim back down the sides and make Y cuts to fit it around the top rail, the arm rail and stuffing rail. Complete the tacking on the top rail right up to the wings. Do the sides in the same way, then do the stuffing rail.

Make a row of blind stitches (see p. 51) along the top edge of the back from post to post. Regulate the filling into the edge, then form a row of top stitching (see p. 51). Tighten the stuffing ties slightly, and drive all the tacks

Springs in the back of a chair are placed where the webbs cross (left); in the back, they do not add shape (right), merely comfort.

fully home. The second stuffing of the back is put on as the seat was done, so follow the directions on p. 56. Cut a rectangle of calico long enough to be tacked from the outside of the stuffing rail to the outside of the top rail, and wide enough to be tacked near the edge of the back posts. Tuck it down between the seat and the stuffing of the back and temporary tack it on the stuffing rail. Tension it up and over the hair, and temporary tack it on the outside of the back rail. If the calico is tight enough, it will not have to be retacked so fold it back down each side and make Y cuts to fit around the top, arm and stuffing rails. Smooth it back into place before tacking it in its final position. Tension it up and out towards the corners, folding it under and angling it out as you go, them form a mitre in the calico across the top of the back post at each corner.

When the tension is correct, hammer all the tacks home and trim off the excess calico.

Cover the whole of the back with linter felt, pinching away the excess around the arm and wing rails. At the top edge, the felt should not go over on to the outside back of the chair. Cut the top cover as you did the calico, but remember to centre any pattern. Place the cover on the wadding and temporary tack. Fold it down the sides as you did the calico and make Y cuts to fit around all the rails. Smooth it back into place and tack. Test for tension in both directions, and, when you are satisfied, drive the tacks home and trim off any excess fabric.

Wings

Tack a strip of webbing to the top of the arm at the back of the wing parallel to the back post, strain it up to the top of the wing rail, and tack it off on the inside. Tack a rectangle of 340g (12oz.) hessian on the inside of the wing; allow enough to enable you to tack it off on the inside of the back post. Tack it on the top of the arm, strain it upwards and tack it to the inside of the wing. Fold it back on itself, tack it again, then cut off any excess. Insert bridle ties as described on p. 47.

Fill the inside wing with hair, putting more where it meets the inside back. Cut a rectangle of calico large enough to be tacked on the back posts, to come over the hair and be tacked on the outside of the wing rails. At the bottom, it should fold under the hair and sit neatly on top of the arm; the hair must not come over the edge of the rails here. At the back, fold the calico back parallel to the back post and make a Y cut (see p. 56) so that it fits around the top rail. Temporary tack the calico to the back post from the outside, then strain it to the front and temporary tack on the outsides of the wing rail and the top rail. There will be quite a lot of fullness around the curve of the wing but you can get rid of this by straining the calico out between the two sections you have already tacked. Drive all the tacks, except those down the back post, fully home.

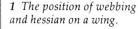

Wings

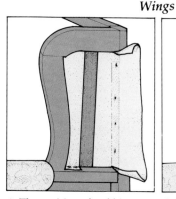

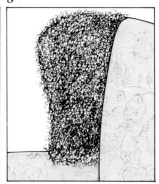

1 *The position of webbing and hessian on a wing.*

2 *Fill the inside wing with hair.*

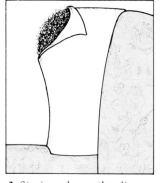

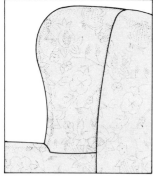

3 *Strain and smooth calico to create the shape.*

4 *Press all the fillings inwards down the back post.*

Most wings are simple in construction; webbing and hessian support the filling, and the shape is created by the calico – rather like the drop-in seat.

Use skin wadding over the calico, pinching away the excess as necessary, and tuck it under the wing where it sits on the arm. Cut a rectangle of top cover the same size as you cut the calico, and place it over the wadding. Tuck it under the wing to sit on the arm, and temporary tack it on the back post. Strain it over the wing and temporary tack on the outside of the rail as you did the calico. Make Y cuts to fit it around the top rail. Fold it to form a mitre across the top of the back post and to join up to the inside back cover. Press all the layers and filling inwards down the back post so that the back of the wing sits neatly up to the inside back and tack through all the thicknesses. Fold all the thicknesses inwards and add two or three more tacks.

Outside covers

Cut a rectangle of base hessian to cover from under the arm down to the bottom of the chair (it does not need to go under the chair), and from the back post to the front post of the arm. Cut the top cover as for the hessian but allow enough to go under the chair and around the back and front posts by about 5cm (2in.).

With the chair on its side, place the top cover on the outside of the arm, fold the top edge under the arm, and pin it at the back and the front along the fold line. Gently lift the cover and hang it over the arm. Fix it in place with two or three tacks under the arm rail. Position the hessian over the top cover and fix that

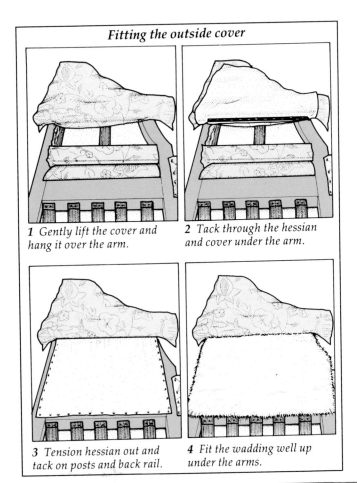

Fitting the outside cover

1 *Gently lift the cover and hang it over the arm.*

2 *Tack through the hessian and cover under the arm.*

3 *Tension hessian out and tack on posts and back rail.*

4 *Fit the wadding well up under the arms.*

under the arm with two or three tacks. Use a length of back tacking strip and tack through the hessian and top cover underneath the arm. Make sure that the tacking strip is in line with the outside of the chair.

Fold the hessian down flat on the side of the chair, tension it out and tack on the posts and bottom rail. Leave it raw at the edges, but cut off any excess. Place a sheet of skin wadding over the hessian, making sure it fits well up under the arms. Fold the cover carefully over the wadding so as not to disturb it. Make sure the cover is square, then temporary tack it underneath the chair, on the back of the back post and on the front facing. Cut it to fit around the legs of the chair as described on p. 52.

Cut a rectangle of top cover large enough to cover the facing easily, and ensure that it is square. Use some linter felt to pad out the facing, then lay the cover over it. Trim off any excess, but leave enough to tuck under the wadding – about 12mm (½in.) should be sufficient. Starting at the top of the scroll, tuck the cover under the wadding and pin it up to the edge. Work all round the facing, including the bottom, in this way. You will have to snip the cover at the point of the scroll, but be careful not to snip too much. When this is all pinned in place, slip-stitch the facing to the cover, using slipping thread and a curved needle. Work all around the facing, making two or three stitches, then pulling them gently to close up the seam. Remove the pins as you work.

Tack a piece of hessian over the wing area. Leave the edges raw and trim off any excess. Cut a rectangle of top cover large enough to cover the outside wing and to turn under at the edge and along the bottom. Pin the cover to the edge and slip-stitch it in place all around the wing. Tack it off on the outside of the back post.

Cut a rectangle of hessian to cover the chair back and tack in place, then place skin wadding over it. Cut a rectangle of top cover large enough to cover the outside back, allowing enough to turn under the wadding along the top and down the sides, and to be tacked under the bottom of the chair. Place the cover over the wadding and, starting at the top rail, turn the edge under the wadding, pinning it in place as you work. Pin down each side and cut to fit around the legs at the bottom as described on p. 52. Tack under the bottom of the chair and then slip-stitch it in place.

Finally, put on a bottom covering to keep in the dust; follow the directions given on p. 48.

Project 4: Nineteenth-century button-back nursing chair

Basic construction

The major difference between this and the previous projects is in the construction of the back. Here, a roll of stuffing around the edge of the inside back is created, leaving a space in the centre. Calico (muslin) is anchored at the points where you will put the buttons and is stuffed to give it shape. The calico is then covered with wadding (batting), and the top cover is fixed in place by the buttons in the centre section and by tacking around the outer edge to just inside the show-wood line. The area for tacking is usually very narrow and close to the show-wood in this type of chair and you must take care not to split the wood at this point. Use smaller tacks, and, if possible, fewer of them than usual. Slip-stitching the outer covers in place is not possible here. The outside back has to be fixed to the wood with tacks which are covered with gimp or braid. Glue this in place in the usual way, but be careful on the inside back as there is very little space and it is easy to get the adhesive on the top cover.

Preparation

It is vital to make notes when you are stripping down a buttoned chair, and it will help if you keep the top cover for the pattern of the buttoning, and to enable you to make a rough calculation of the top covering. Before you remove the base hessian (burlap) from the back of the chair, measure the distance between the twines used to hold the buttons in place. Make a diagram of the pattern and the distances between the buttons from the centre of the chair. With this type of chair, you will have to work the back first; it is far more difficult to do both the back and the small sections each side of the back, rather like very low arms, when the seat is in position.

Choose your top cover fabric carefully. Buttoning will send stripes crooked, and a very large pattern is lost in the buttoning. An all-over pattern of small or medium size is usually acceptable, but avoid glazed cottons – they are rather stiff and are not easy to work into pleats. Unglazed cottons work very well.

Left: *This chair is a good choice for a first buttoning project because the buttoning is fairly simple. The construction of the back is different from the pieces discussed so far, but all the other techniques involved are familiar from previous projects.*

Back

Place two strips of webbing (see p. 46) on the inside of the back of the chair. Tack them to the stuffing rail at the bottom, then hand tension them to the top of the chair. Leave as much space as possible between the show-wood and the edge of the webbing.

Cut a rectangle of 340g (12oz.) hessian large enough to cover the inside back area. Leaving as much space as possible between the tacks and the show-wood, temporary tack it on to the stuffing rail, then tension it to the top. Keep the tension vertical to retain the curve of the chair. If the horizontal tension is too great, the back will be very flat when you have finished. Tack all around the back, cut off the excess, fold the hessian over and tack it back on itself (see p. 46). Mark a line down the centre of the back.

Cut a rectangle of scrim about 18cm (7in.) larger all round than the base hessian, fold it in half and mark a vertical centre line. Skewer (pin) the scrim to the base hessian, matching the centre lines, then secure it with a running stitch 9cm (3½in.) inside the show-wood. Stitch it along the bottom of the chair about 16cm (6in.) up from the stuffing rail. Use a curved needle and fine twine and make small stitches.

Place the chair on its back and support it with pieces of padded wood to prevent damage to the show-wood. Start in the centre top, and stuff teased fibre under the scrim; turn the scrim under the fibre (see p. 50) and temporary tack it in place. This roll needs to be firm and to follow the line of the frame. Work the top centre section first, then do the middle of the sides and then fill in the gaps between. Trim the excess scrim away as you work, so that you reduce the amount that has eventually to be turned under.

At the bottom, fill the lumber region well to give support to the sitter. This part should also sit neatly on the seat when the chair is completed so keep this in mind as you work. When you are satisfied with the shape, drive all the tacks home.

Stitch around the edge roll so that it holds its shape. Use a fairly large curved needle in place of the usual bayonet needle, and if you can get a double-ended one, the stitching will be quite easy. (Filing a point on the eye end of a large curved needle will help if you can't.) Form a row of blind (sink) stitches (see p. 51) very close to the tacks all around the edge but not along the bottom, then form a row of top stitches (see p. 51) above the blind row, remembering to regulate the fibre into the edge as you work. The edge roll should now be wedge-shaped.

When the wedge-shaped edge roll is complete, you have the basic shape of the back. The stuffing under the calico and the final buttoning are all within this edge, although the outer pleats are tacked to the frame.

Making a buttoning plan

Marking out the button pattern can be confusing, so plan it out on a sheet of paper, using the measurements you took between the twines on the base hessian when you were stripping down. Remember that the diamonds should be equally spaced and taller than they are wide.

Place a tack on the centre line where the bottom row of buttons will be. From this point measure half the width of the diamond each side of the line and place tacks at these points (A). Now measure up from these tacks the full height of the diamonds (B). From the original tack measure up half the height of a diamond (C). Make sure that the distance from the centre line at B is the same as at A. Continue measuring the button points and placing tacks in the scrim, ensuring that both the horizontal and vertical lines run parallel. None of the tacks on the outside should be closer to the show-wood than half the size of the diamond. If the pattern of diamonds formed by the tacks looks too close to the edge at some points, adjust the diamonds until they look acceptable. Check that you have the number of rows and lines correct by referring to the original top cover. The distances between the buttons marked on the top cover will be up to 4cm (1½in.) longer than on the base hessian, to allow for the filling. When you are satisfied that the tacks are in the right position, remove each one in turn and mark its position carefully with a permanent marker.

Mark out the calico (the top cover will have the same markings so note the button distances). To calculate how much calico you need, measure over the edge roll at the widest point and add 3.5cm (1⅜in.) for each button; if, for example, the width is 60cm (23½in.) and there are three buttons at the widest point, the calico should measure 60cm + 10.5cm = 70.5cm (23½in. + 4⅛in. = 27⅝in.) total width. Calculate the length in the same way, measuring from the outside of the stuffing rail.

Fold the calico in half vertically to find the centre and mark it with tailor's chalk. Mark the position of the bottom row of buttons (A). To find this line, measure from the stuffing rail up to the bottom buttons. Strike two lines (B and C), each the full height of the diamond, plus the 3.5cm (1⅜in.) allowance, for example 13cm + 3.5cm = 16.5cm (5in. + 1⅜in. = 6⅜in.) On line A measure out from the centre line half the width of the

diamond – including the 3.5cm (1⅜in.) allowance, for example 10cm + 3.5cm halved = 6.75cm (4in. + 1⅜in. = 5⅜in. halved = 2¹¹⁄₁₆in.) – on both sides and mark these points (D). Repeat at lines B and C (the height of one and two diamonds) and mark points E and F. From points D, E and F, measure and mark the full width of the diamond, i.e. 13.5cm (5⅜in.); this will give you points G, H and J. Join these points up diagonally; the points where the lines cross give you the other button points. Mark only the points that will have buttons with coloured chalk.

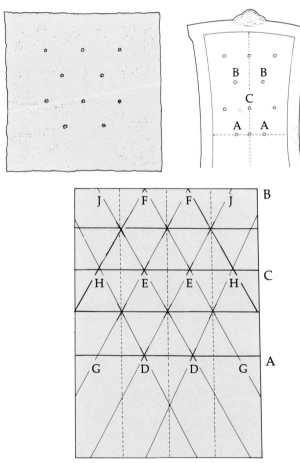

Make a rough buttoning plan from the original base hessian (top left), then mark out the button pattern on the chair with tacks (top right). The points that will actually be buttoned should be marked on both the calico and the top cover with coloured tailor's chalk.

Attaching buttons

Cut lengths of twine about 30cm (12in.) long, thread a buttoning needle and stab through the calico, scrim and base hessian, slightly to one side of the first button point. Pull this end of the twine through, rethread the needle with the other end of the twine and stab through on the other side of the button point. Form a slip knot with these two ends to hold the calico firmly in place. Place a small 'butterfly' of calico or wadding under the twine loop to stop it tearing the calico. Repeat this at all the button position(s) on the bottom row, then do the next row up.

Tease some hair and tuck it under the calico to pad out between the button points. Add more hair *underneath* the first handful. The calico should form diagonal pleats between the button points. Ease these into place as you put in more filling, making sure there are no hollows under them. When you have filled the gaps between the first two rows of buttons, do the third row and fill that, and so on until you have worked the centre of the chair. Then work round the outside, so that the whole of the back is full and level with the top of the edge roll.

Skewer the calico all round the edge. Cut off the excess, tuck it under the hair and pin it slightly over the edge of the roll. Fold the pleats in place on the edge, then work a knotted blanket stitch as on the scroll arm to hold the calico in position (see p. 59). At the bottom, add more hair over the scrim and tack the calico on the outside of the stuffing rail. Fold the pleats straight down from the bottom buttons.

Cut a rectangle of top cover a little larger than you cut the calico and mark out the button pattern with tailor's chalk on the *back* of the cover.

Cut a piece of linter felt to cover the whole of the chair back and place it over the calico. Carefully make holes in the felt by gently easing it apart at the button points on the bottom row. Position the top cover. Insert the twine through the top cover but this time thread a button on to the twine before you stab back through. Ease the button down into the hole in the felt and pull the twine taut. Make a slip knot on the back and insert a butterfly of fabric or webbing between the hessian and the knot. Use the regulator to ease the pleats, which should face down towards the seat, into place. When all the buttons are in place, tighten the twines and tie them

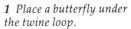

Attaching buttons

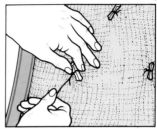

1 Place a butterfly under the twine loop.

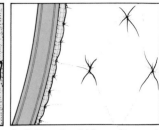

2 Calico should form diagonal pleats between button points.

3 Thread buttons on twine; knot twine at the back.

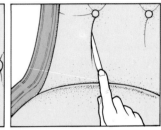

4 Use the regulator to ease pleats into place.

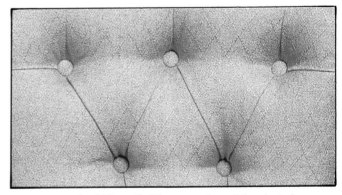

The buttons should be pulled down evenly and the pleats form as near perfect diamond shapes as possible.

off. Fold the pleats at the top and sides into place and tack off. The side pleats should all face down but the top and bottom ones can face either in or out. Temporary tack the bottom on to the outside of the stuffing rail, and leave it like this until the seat is complete. Cut off the excess fabric.

Side sections

The small section each side of the seat, where the back curves around it, should be completed before you start the seat. Tack a small piece of top cover quite close to the show-wood. Pad it with linter felt and ensure that it lines up with the bottom part of the back. Tack it off below the line of the seat.

Seat

Fix the webbing, springs and base hessian as described on pp. 54-5. Apply the fibre filling, tack down the scrim and work the stitching as described on p. 51, and follow the directions given on p. 52 for the front corners. Attach the second stuffing, calico, linter felt and top cover as described on pp. 51-2, but take the top cover under the seat rails and tack it on the bottom of the chair. At the back, tack off the top cover on the top of the seat rails.

Outside covers

Work this step with the chair facing down. Draw a line in chalk around the back of the chair where the cover will finish – this may already be marked out but they are frequently lopsided. Tack a piece of 340g (12oz.) hessian in place over the whole of the back using 10mm (⅜in.) fine tacks. Cut off the excess up to the tacks.

Place a piece of skin wadding over the hessian. Lay the top cover in place and, making sure it is straight, temporary tack it at the top, bottom and the sides. Start in the centre of the top and turn the cover under so that the fold is level with the chalk line. Trim off the excess and tack home. Work all around the back curve in this way. At the bottom, cut the cover to fit around the legs and tack off under the seat rail.

If the side sections are short, take the cover around the back in one piece. If they are rather long, you will have to cover them separately. Treat them as small versions of the back but where they meet the back make a neat fold; alternatively, machine stitch them. Lay the top cover fabric on the back of the chair, pin, then machine, the extra pieces in place, and then tack permanently, as described above. Finish all the edges with gimp (see p. 52).

Fix the bottoming as described on p. 48.

Once the techniques of buttoning have been mastered, there is no reason why you should not attempt more complicated buttoning projects.

3

WOOD FINISHING

There is possibly more mystique in finishing than in any of the woodworking skills, and with (arguably) less good reason. Anyone with time and patience can master the encyclopedia of wood finishes and finishing techniques, because manual skill is less important than a painstaking, methodical approach, and an understanding of your materials.

Much of wood finishing is common sense. Always read the instructions on containers; always ask suppliers for help if there is something you are not sure of; *never* put a liquid or paste on your precious work if you are unsure what the effect will be. If there is one golden rule of wood finishing, it is *always experiment before applying*.

Finally, the essential ingredient of this, as of all the forms of working wood, is love. Wood responds to your touch and state of mind, becoming implacable if you are impatient, and 'coming up' beautifully if you put care and enjoyment in your fingertips. This is why, however many machine processes you use to get a smooth surface, at the end there is no substitute for using your hands.

Finishes and stains

Right from the start, be assured there is no perfect wood treatment. All are compromises between durability, appearance, and ease of application, so you must know what final effect you want before you start.

Staining is not always essential. Many craftsmen abhor the use of wood colouring, maintaining that if something is not the right colour, a different wood should have been used in the first place. For re-finishing, however, you are bound to be 'matching up'. Dyes and stains have traditionally been used to make cheap wood look better, or to give a uniform appear-ance to a hodge-podge of timbers in one construction. Different woods behave differently with the same application, so test your colour on inconspicuous parts.

Some stains darken if you put more on; some do not. Some are difficult to apply evenly, but do not fade; some are easy to apply, but are not so light-fast. The actual colouring agent can be a pigment, which does not soak into the wood, or a dye, which does. Finishes also penetrate, or lie on the surface. They dry by evaporation, or by reaction with the air. Waxes and oils are absorbed into the wood, allowing it to breathe and move, and give a warmth unequalled by harder finishes. Oils do not alter the texture of the wood, and waxes, like the scented carnauba and bees' waxes, add their own aroma to a wood's distinctive smell; neither oils nor waxes, however, protect the surface from dents, although some oils are very good for heat and water-resistance. Waxes need a lot of maintenance; oils give a flat, dull sheen which you do not get with any other finish. Teak and Danish oils contain synthetic resins, which add to their durability and ease of application.

French polish, the shellac finish of tradition, is prized for its clarity, brilliance and depth. It is soft enough to allow the wood to move a little, but it does need protection from liquids and sunlight. While not as difficult to apply as you might think, it requires more processes and a special 'knack'.

There is quite a range of hardness and methods of application even among the varnishes. The traditional types are based on natural resins and gums, the modern ones on synthetic resins – alkyds, phenolics, or polyurethanes. Phenolic-based spar or marine varnish is softer to allow wood movement; polyurethanes are household-hard but difficult to apply well.

Lacquers are either cellulose or synthetic, and be-cause of their speed of drying, most used in furniture production. If you can master spraying – which is not difficult – there is no real reason why they cannot be considered as alternatives to french polish, but it is difficult to apply them with a brush. The vapours they give off are highly noxious, which is perhaps why they do not find their way on to the domestic market. For the purposes of this book, the word 'lacquer' refers to all these finishes.

Left to right: *The high gleam of the french polish on this dressing table may be dulled; light chairs can be given elegance with dark stains; work upwards when staining, keeping one 'live' edge; stripped-pine stain gives new furniture an antique patina.*

Tools and brushes

A lot of edge tools will not be necessary, but for good-quality work they must be sharp. You will need a block plane, preferably with an adjustable mouth, and, perhaps most important in finishing, a cabinet scraper.

Sanding

Sanding blocks made from cork or rubber can be bought, or you can stick a piece of felt or rubber to a block of wood. The block should be big enough to wrap a quarter-sheet of standard-sized abrasive paper around. Apply pumice and rottenstone with a felt-based block.

Sticks and dowels are useful. Wrap the abrasive round ordinary round-section pieces for mouldings, or profile your own for unusual shapes.

Machines can do some of the hard work. Disc sanders for electric drills leave nasty circular scratches. Do not touch them. Belt sanders are heavy, powerful, expensive machines for removing the really rough stuff. A moment's inattention and you will find you have gone right through a veneer or dug a trench in the wood. Rub the (expensive) belts with a wire brush to unclog them. Orbital and finishing sanders are the best bet.

Stripping

Wire (steel) wool is the standard stripping material, and you will also need putty and decorators' filling- and scraping-knives (a hook scraper is efficient but easily scars the surface).

A wire brush will remove every bit of waste from the grain; a small brass shoe-cleaning brush, a nailbrush, and a toothbrush will all be needed at times.

Pointed dowels and toothpicks will all come in useful for carvings and mouldings.

Hot-air strippers make more sense than blowtorches for furniture, but be very gentle. They are best for paint on flat surfaces, and useless for synthetic lacquers. Never use heat to strip veneers.

Brushes

For varnish (which here includes polyurethanes) buy a best-quality 35-50mm (1½-2in.) brush and never use it for anything else. Real bristle is always better than nylon for a good finish. You need full bristles, slightly tapered, with some flagged tips to control the flow. In cheap brushes, the two rows of bristles are set too wide apart to hold the liquid and let it flow well.

Fine artist's brushes will be necessary for touching in colours; bear-, sable-, or squirrel-hair 'mops' for shellac in awkward corners and a 'grass' or nylon scrubbing brush for bleaches. The finest is a 'dulling' brush (furniture rubbing brush), for laying pumice powder on to a bright finish.

Brushes should always be finest quality. You will need artist's brushes, and a first-class varnish brush; the wire brush is indispensable for stripping.

Orbital sanders move in 3mm (⅛in.) circles, which can leave scratches that you do not see until the finish is on; finishing tools move straight back and forth.

Repairs

Minor repairs demand a tenon or dovetail saw, sharp chisels, block plane, and a selection of the invaluable G-cramps (clamps).

For veneer work, add a scalpel or other sharp, thin-bladed knife, a veneer saw and an electric iron.

The cabinet scraper

A favourite finisher's tool, the cabinet scraper is merely a rectangular piece of tool steel which can take four sharp edges. It will produce a smooth cut, however wild the grain is, which is why it is indispensable for work on veneers with decorative, curly grain.

To use the scraper, hold it in both hands, with your thumbs in the middle, flexing it and pushing away from you at a 45° angle to the surface. It should produce a shaving and leave a very smooth surface. If you get dust, it is blunt; if the grain cuts up rough, push it the other way. It can heat up very quickly and burn your thumbs, so take a slight warmth as a warning.

To sharpen the scraper, the thin edge must be dead square to the flat face, and dead straight. Hold it in a vice (vise) and draw a flat file along the edge to get the right angle. You have to produce a burr and wipe (curl) it back – it is the burr itself that cuts. Draw the edge back and forth on an oilstone, keeping it absolutely square to the stone, or trap it between the two halves of the box and rub on the stone's edge, if you have one in a box. When you feel a burr on both sides of the edge, lay it flat on the bench and strop it with a round piece of spring steel or the back of a gouge (the ticketter/burnisher). This brings the burr over in line with the flat face, so the ticketter must be flat to that face.

Now hold the scraper on end on the bench and pad your hand with a cloth. Run the ticketter up the narrow edge, angling it back towards the flat face very slightly. Do this three or four times on all the corners, angling the ticketter back slightly more each time till it is at about 70°-80° to the flat. Try the cut; if you get dust not shavings, take it back to the stone.

Old finishes are hard, and will blunt this burr quite quickly. The last two ticketter stages will 'dress' the cutting edge again, but after three or four times, you will need to take it back to the stone.

The cabinet scraper

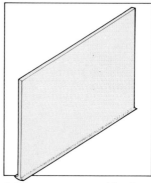

1 *The scraper cuts with a burr on the narrow edges.*

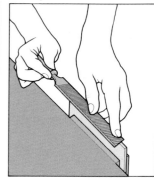

2 *To sharpen, draw a flat file along the edge.*

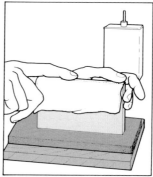

3 *Draw the edge back and forth on an oilstone.*

4 *Lay it flat and strop it with the ticketter.*

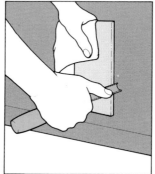

5 *Run the ticketter up the narrow edge.*

6 *A sharpened scraper produces shavings, not dust.*

Abrasives and adhesives

A clear finish may sometimes disguise or obscure the grain, but it will *never* cover imperfections in the surface of the wood. Rather, it will emphasize them. The more work you put into sanding, the better your chances of a first-class finish.

Abrasives

Abrasive papers are made from glass (flint), flour, garnet, aluminium oxide or silicon carbide. Glasspaper is the cheapest, but it also wears out quickest. It has no real advantages over garnet, which gives a more 'sympathetic' cut, and hardwoods seem to like it better. Aluminium oxide papers are expensive, long-lasting, and are usually used with machines. Silicon carbides (wet and dry), though available in coarse grades, tend to be used for cutting back between coats, especially of hard synthetic lacquers. Lubricate them with water, white spirit (paint thinner) or mineral oil. Avoid using liquid paraffin or mineral oil, which are insoluble in meths (wood alcohol), on raw wood. Raw linseed oil is usually better.

There are at least three marking systems, of which the easiest one is the 'ordinary' numbers, starting at 30 or 40 for the coarsest grades. A 30/40 grit size is the same as S2 for the glass and 1½ for the garnet; 100 grit is F2, 2/0 garnet; and 150 is 1 glass, 4/0 garnet.

Black silicon carbide is best for smoothing an already finished surface; red garnet papers suit hardwoods very well.

Steel wool is used for stripping in nooks and crannies where no tool blade will go, for surface repairs and reviving, for cutting back between coats, and for final burnishing, usually with wax or oil. The coarsest grade available is 3, the very finest is 0000 or 4/0.

Pumice and rottenstone are fine powders – pumice is the coarser – usually mixed with oil to make an abrasive burnishing paste. The friction they create is also an effective remover of blemishes in shellac finishes.

Car polishes, including T-Cut, can be used. Any really fine abrasive paste, even toothpaste, is good in the last burnishing stages.

Adhesives

Animal (scotch) glue was about the only furniture adhesive there was until the 1950s, and you are bound to come across it in repairs. It is used hot, and can be melted – with care – with hot water or an iron to make it stick again.

PVA (yellow) is the most commonly used adhesive nowadays. While not waterproof, it is extremely strong. Time and pressure are needed for it to set effectively.

Formaldehydes are usually bought in powder form and mixed with water for application. They are harder to use than PVA, but are waterproof.

Impacts (contacts) are good for sheet materials but unforgiving because they stick immediately, unless you use a 'thixotropic', which allows some re-positioning.

Two-pack epoxies set rock-hard. They are useful for filling and building up in woodwork.

Safety, comfort and conditions

Most of the materials you will be using are highly flammable, highly corrosive, or both. Do not smoke; do not leave saturated rags lying about; always put the caps back on containers, and store them where they will not be knocked over. Label the jars in which you keep your own concoctions, noting the exact proportions of the mix so you can reproduce them. You will *want* a face mask when you use acid-catalysed lacquers, never mind need one, but it is easier to be lazy about eye protection when you are stripping. Splashes go a lot further than you think and it is not worth risking damage. Rubber gloves are a must for these liquids too, although if you wear them for french polishing you will lose the feel of the rubber. Shellac, although not harmful to the skin, is no cosmetic, and you just might discover some interesting allergies.

Dust is your major enemy. Any sticky surface is like fly-paper, and once dust sticks, you will only do more damage to the finish trying to get it off. You can only really guarantee a dust-free atmosphere if you work in an operating theatre, or have got an extraction system, but there are ways of minimizing it; aim not to disturb it, rather than to be completely rid of it. You need good ventilation for your lungs' sake and for drying, but try to arrange it so the air does not cause draughts near the work, or bring dust in from outside the room. Damp the floor and sweep it thoroughly, then lay your cloths or newspapers – polythene (plastic) sheeting is melted by strippers and many of the finishes – and do not sweep again until the finish is completely dry.

For your own comfort and the sake of the finish, the workspace must be neither hot nor cold, and certainly not damp. Moisture creates 'bloom' (a white haze) in french polish, which also will not harden below about 18°C (65°F). Varnishes and lacquers, on the other hand, dry too quickly if they are too hot; a skin forms which prevents the reaction with the air, and they do not harden underneath.

Light is also important. Work near a window if possible so you can see exactly what you are doing, and do not fool yourself about imperfections in the surface.

Be methodical, be patient, and do not hurry. Allow time to get started and to clear up. Always add one-third to your estimate of how long something will take, and you will not be far off. Impatience is a guarantee of eventual dissatisfaction, and more than likely a lot of time wasted redoing a finish. Your standards are up to you, but you are unlikely to be reading this if you do not think something worth doing is worth doing well.

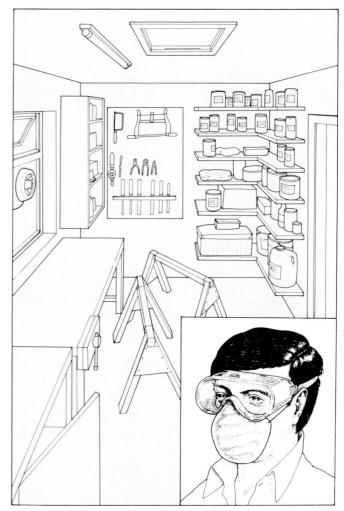

You can never, of course, have enough space in a workshop. This small area is neatly arranged and well-lit: note the trestles (saw-horses), padded for protection, and the clearly labelled jars.

Preparation

Recognizing the finish and deciding to strip

The first refinishing decision you will have to make is whether you need to strip the entire piece. A scruffy, dirty finish does not automatically need stripping; basically, as long as there are not too many scratches and they are not too deep, there are quite a few ways to avoid going back to the bare wood.

Clean your piece thoroughly with detergent and warm water, and, perhaps, use a mild abrasive like steel wool. Try not to get the surface too wet, particularly veneer, which will lift if water gets under it. Shellac and lacquer cloud if water is left lying on them. White spirit (paint thinner) or methylated spirits (wood alcohol) will shift stubborn grime, but be careful – if the rag is really soaked, it could start dissolving the finish.

To establish what the finish is, test an inconspicuous part with solvents. Meths will dissolve french polish, which will set again, but varnish will merely crinkle and lift. Cellulose and the acid lacquers will soften and set again when treated with their own solvents (thinners), but meths alone will not affect them. Scraping with a chisel is another way of distinguishing varnish from cellulose; varnish comes off in a yellow shaving, the lacquers make white dust. A certain amount of common sense helps you narrow the options, in that a battered antique is obviously not going to have a thoroughly modern finish. Once you know what you have, use a cleaner that will not dissolve it.

If the finish is basically intact, sand it with fine paper or steel wool and prepare it for a new coat of the same thing. If, however, it is worn right through, chipped, and peeling, you will need to remove it all. Sometimes the top of a table or sideboard is badly damaged, and the rest is sound, in which case it is possible to strip and recoat just the top, although matching colours could be a problem. Crazing and cracks in french polish and lacquered surfaces can be healed, if they are not too deep, by reamalgamation (see p. 80). If you are going to be repairing the wood in any way, clean the finish off around where the repair will be, but wait till the gluing and clamping are over before stripping completely.

Left: From flat and dull to a rich colour and a deep sheen . . . be meticulous in removing every trace of old finish. This table has been stained and varnished; the curved front is veneered.

Stripping

There are basically three stripping methods open to you – sanding, heat and chemicals – and you will probably find yourself using at least two, whatever the piece. Regardless of the method(s) you intend to use, you will find it easier to take the piece apart as far as possible: remove drawers, fittings, shelves and so on and treat them all separately.

Because it is mechanical, sanding is a more controlled way of stripping, but it is unlikely that you will be able to remove everything, especially from the nooks and crannies, without chemical help. The belt sander's power and weight is ideal when you have a lot of layers to get through, especially paint, but it really is not the right tool for valued pieces of furniture.

You can use heat, although a blowlamp (blowtorch) is far too violent for furniture. The hot-air strippers popular nowadays are more gentle, but it is still all too easy to burn the wood if you look away for so much as a second. Bubble up the paint and lift it off with a decorator's knife, layer by layer. Heat does not really work on french polishes and lacquers, except for the highly risky business of flashing, a trade practice that involves wiping a meths-soaked rag over french polish and setting it alight. It *is* very effective, but the risks are obvious!

Chemicals are most efficient, and do the least damage to the wood, but bear in mind that they and their waste are highly flammable; that they are very harmful to skin and eyes, so you must wear goggles and rubber gloves; and that you *must* neutralize them.

Proprietary strippers are usually methylene chloride based; pastes are generally a better idea than liquids, because they stick to vertical surfaces. Dab the stripper on with a grass or nylon brush, or a dispensable paint brush and dollop it, rather than brushing. The idea is to leave a thickness that will soak in and lift up the old finish; putting it on too thick or leaving a thick coat over-long does not increase the product's efficiency. Work layer by layer, scraping with a knife, or wire wool for awkward bits.

Ready-made strippers are usually neutralized by water or white spirit, which dissolves the wax that some of them use to prevent quick drying. Remember that if you get old furniture and veneers too wet, you will melt the glue. Some strippers are promoted as 'no-wash', which is useful, but (apart from veneers) there can be no harm in wiping over with water or white spirit.

Caustic soda is still popular, if not so easy to use as proprietary strippers. It needs to be thickened into a paste with whiting, starch or even wallpaper paste, and used as strong as you dare to avoid the water wetting the wood too deeply. A kilo (2-3lb) of crystals to a bucket of water should give the right consistency. Do not use it on veneered pieces, and remember to mix the crystals into the water, not the other way round. It also darkens the fibres, which will need to be bleached out again (see p. 86). Neutralize it with vinegar.

There are commercial stripping firms, who use large tanks of caustic solution in which the whole piece is submerged; this 'dipping' is an easy alternative to taking the work on yourself. It is good for, say, a staircaseful of balusters, but the trisodium phosphate darkens the wood, damages the fibres, and attacks the glue in joints. It is also unlikely that your furniture will be given the careful treatment you would give it yourself, and naturally everything you give an operator is given at your own risk.

You will often find a white deposit in the grain of mahogany furniture that will not come out when you have stripped the piece. This is plaster of paris, used as a grain filler, that has hardened; scrub it out with a wire brush and linseed oil, and resign yourself to a lot of sanding and smoothing afterwards.

Stripping

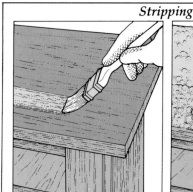 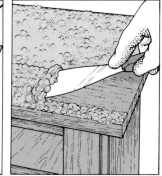

1 *Dab on stripper with an old paint brush.*

2 *Lift paint off layer by layer with a decorator's knife.*

Repairs to existing veneers

Although a discussion of the numerous repairs you are likely to come across in revitalizing old furniture is beyond the scope of this book, it is useful to know how to treat and patch veneers and surfaces.

There is much more veneer around than you might think. Before the days of manufactured boards, pine was often overlaid with mahogany as an inexpensive way of making expensive-looking furniture. If it is chipped or blistered, it will be easy to identify as veneer, but if it is still in good condition, you can tell by looking for the telltale thin edge at the back of, say, a chest of drawers, or checking inside a cabinet or underneath a table to see whether the grain and colour of the wood are different.

Older items will be glued with animal (scotch) glue, which can be softened and made to stick again with heat. If the veneer has lifted at an edge, try to see if the glue is crumbly and crystalline by poking it gently with a thin blade. If it is granular, scrape it out as far back as you can without splitting the loose piece and scrape the 'ground' – the base wood – to uncover a raw surface, then slide a blade or piece of card with some white (yellow) glue on it to coat both surfaces, and clamp it with a G-clamp. If the glue has not broken up completely, heat it gently with an iron through several thicknesses of brown paper (*not* newspaper). Keep testing as it softens and once it has become sticky, clamp the loose piece down.

Repairing superficial damage to veneer

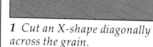

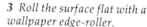

1 At an edge, slide in glue with a palette knife.

2 Make one cut along or diagonally across the grain.

Treating bubbles in veneer

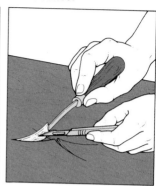

1 Cut an X-shape diagonally across the grain.

2 Lift the veneer and carefully scrape out the old glue.

3 Roll the surface flat with a wallpaper edge-roller.

4 Put a heavy weight over it until the new glue is dry.

Blistering or bubbling in the middle of a surface is another common phenomenon. If the veneer is not chipped, cut it with a razor-sharp blade like a scalpel, from edge to edge of the lifted part. Try the iron and brown paper first; roll the veneer flat and weight it down to set with a heavy weight on some greaseproof paper. (This will stop the weight sticking to the veneer and pulling it up again when you take it off.) If the old glue does not work, you will have to scrape it out and reglue. Be as delicate as you can – veneer is brittle at the best of times, and it is going to be messier if you break a piece and have to glue that as well. Slide the new glue in with an artist's palette knife or something similar. When the glue has set, sand it smooth and refinish.

Veneer, marquetry and solid wood patching and replacement

Often in a veneered surface there are pieces missing, which need to be replaced. Inlay lines and marquetry pieces tend to shrink and become loose so although specialist suppliers keep a wide range of ready-made inlays, be careful ordering the size. It is safer to order oversize, and reduce the insert by rubbing the edge on 120 grit sandpaper laid on the bench. Replacements for marquetry panels may need specialist identification; keep the piece you remove to use as a pattern.

When you have a good piece of matching veneer, plan a patch so that the grain and figure blend in as closely as possible. Cut a piece slightly larger than the damaged area. A veneer saw is the most reliable tool for cutting brittle veneers; even the sharpest of knife-blades can drag along an edge and pull a chip of grain out. The diamond should be lengthwise on the grain, to avoid obvious repair lines going across. Clean out the waste with a chisel, bevel downwards, back to the lines. Fit the patch tightly, using a file or garnet paper to reduce it, working *with* the grain. The points of the diamond are extremely fragile. When the piece is a perfect fit, coat both the surface and the veneer with white glue, position the patch and weight it to set.

Solid patches are cut in much the same way. You will need to chisel out a depression to hold the patch, but the fit along the edges is much more important than the flatness of the gluing surface. Anything less than razor-sharp tools will pull the edges of the repair down rather than cut them, and make the patch very noticeable. As with veneers, the repair should be slightly proud of the surface when you set it in, so you can sand it back flush when the glue has dried. Letting pieces into an edge also demands that you fit an oversize piece and plane and shape it back to blend after the glue has set.

A dent in raw wood can often be steamed out. A hot iron on a damp cloth can swell the fibres enough to bring the surface level. Try once and repeat if it does not work; if the dent is too deep, you might have to wax fill it (see p. 79). If you have to prick the surface, fill the holes later with wax or shellac stick.

Patching veneer

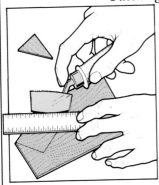

1 *Cut a diamond-shaped patch with a veneer saw.*

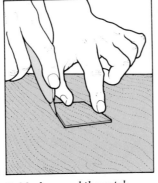

2 *Mark around the patch, bevelling the edges inwards.*

3 *Cut away the veneer inside the marks.*

4 *When the glue has dried, sand the patch flush.*

Treating surface damage to raw wood

1 *A hot iron on a damp cloth can steam out a dent.*

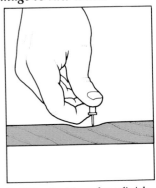

2 *If the dent is under a finish, prick the finish, then steam it.*

Treating superficial damage to a finish

If the wood itself is not damaged beyond the scope of a filler or stopper, but the finish has generally deteriorated, there are numerous remedies.

For localized problems like shallow scratches, try furniture polish, shoe polish, or even the kernel of a nut to wet, darken and blend the lighter area. Often it is only a matter of colour, and ordinary wax crayons work very well in small amounts. You can get different colours by mixing and melting shavings. The more specialized wax and shellac sticks are good for deep blemishes, even those that have gone right through to the wood. They have to be heated on a hot knife-blade – preferably curved – and dripped into the scar, then smoothed over while they are still warm, but left proud of the surface and sanded back when hard. Paint in grain lines before the finish coat. Do not hold these sticks in the flame – they are highly flammable.

White rings or spots, an overall 'bloom', or a smoky blue haze are common results of damp in or on french polish and cellulose. If a general bloom does not disappear when wiped (hard) with white spirit, camphor oil and tobacco ash, or meths, then it is likely that the damp is under the finish, which will have to be stripped. Be careful with meths – if your rag is too damp you will dissolve shellac. The smoky blue effect is usually the result of wax or oil being rejected by a silicone polish beneath; upper and lower layers are usually easily dealt with by white spirit.

This pine table has been re-varnished, but the scratches and marks of age have been left under the finish.

The way to deal with the white rings or blushes that have been caused by cups and glasses, or other damp from on top, is friction. Start with the finest abrasive, even 'extra bright' toothpaste, and get progressively stronger if you get no result. Abrasive car polish, rottenstone or pumice powder mixed with mineral oil and rubbed on with a felt pad, salt with oil, salt with vinegar and fine steel wool and oil all abrade, and some have a chemical action as well. If you rub patiently, after a while the finish will be re-fused by the friction.

Buff the area, which will now be much duller, with a soft cloth, and apply wax or oil, unless you intend to renew the whole finish.

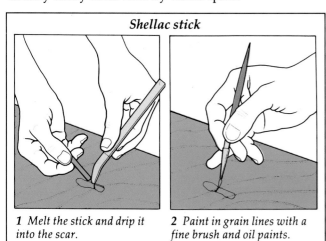

Shellac stick

1 Melt the stick and drip it into the scar.

2 Paint in grain lines with a fine brush and oil paints.

In apparently severe cases, check that the wood itself is also damaged.

Repairing more severe damage to a finish

Chips and holes in a varnished or french polished surface can be built up by applying a 'touch-in' of the same finish in the depression, letting it dry, and adding more until you bring it level. For huge gashes, make cellulose 'jam' by pouring a capful of cellulose lacquer into a tin lid, letting it evaporate to become sticky, adding a bit more and letting that dry out, and so on. This is an ideal thick filler for damage to cellulose surfaces. Use a fine artist's brush, and make sure your previous coat is hard before you apply the next one.

A scuffed, dull surface with multiple light scratches can be brought back into condition with fine steel wool (000 or 0000) and mineral oil, rubbed in the direction of the grain. Wipe the oil off, then wax or furniture polish the surface. You can buy french polish 'revivers', which should be applied in the same way and buffed, first with steel wool and wax and then a soft cloth.

For even more severe deterioration of french polish and cellulose, reamalgamate the finishes with their respective solvents. Varnish will not respond to this treatment because it hardens by reaction rather than evaporation, as do the acid lacquers. For french polish, soak fine steel wool in meths and rub it along the grain so that both the liquid and the action fuse the surface. This needs a delicate touch; you have to dissolve the finish enough to move it around, but not so much as to create ridges or inadvertently strip it. Wipe the meths off with a rag before the finish starts to go. The same method works for cellulose using thinners. If cellulose is badly cracked, paint the thinners along the lines with a fine brush and fuse it by pushing gently with the heel of your hand before you wipe the solvent over.

Reamalgamation

1 For cellulose, paint thinners along the cracks.

2 Fuse it by pushing with the heel of your hand.

3 For french polish, use steel wool and meths.

4 Wipe the meths off with a rag.

A professional's trick for reamalgamating is flashing, in the same way as described for stripping french polish on p. 76, but with the important addition of a wiped layer of mineral oil before you apply the meths. The finish softens and moves, but is not burned off because of the protective oil. Have the surface vertical so the flame travels upward, work quickly, and take every fire precaution.

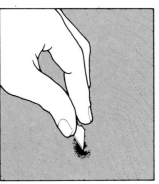

Left: Remove burns and charring by scraping the area from side to side with a sharp blade held upright.

Right: Scratches and burns on this table have broken the finish and affected the wood. Use wire wool and stripper (far right) to remove as many marks as you can, then scrape, fill and touch in.

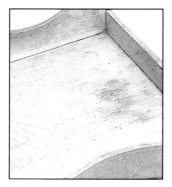

Chemicals; mixing, colouring and tinting

The chemical reactions of acids and alkalis with the wood's own constituents give a deep-laid colour which is comparatively inexpensive and (in most cases) lasts well. These are traditional stains, the only ones available before modern industrial chemistry, and are still used in antique restoration or where, say, new church furniture has to be matched to very old. White vinegar

(acetic acid), if left with a handful of iron nails in it overnight, will turn oak almost black a matter of seconds after you apply it. A stain made from potassium permanganate crystals dissolved in water will bring out a warm brown shade, and makes a good dye for floors because it is inexpensive, although it does fade. Potassium bichromate crystals, which are yellow and orange, dissolved in warm water, darken oak, ash, mahogany and other high tannic acid-content woods without affecting the basic colour. Burnt sienna – a pigment – dissolves in stale beer and makes a very effective mahogany-coloured stain; and there are many more.

If you want to mix your own stain, start with a decision about the colouring agent and the base, and then experiment. Pigments are really best for touching up over an already sealed surface; water as a medium will give you problems with raised grain; slow-drying oils are easiest to apply evenly, but might strike through a finish; spirit-based dyes dry very quickly. Keep a careful record of the proportions you are using, and *always test*.

Touching in, painting grain lines over stopping (wood filler) and so on, is best done with oil (white spirit) and pigments – artist's oil pigments are fine. For french polishing, you can tint the finish by adding pigment or spirit aniline dyes to the shellac itself. Use a fine artist's brush, so that you can control exactly what colour goes where. Cellulose and synthetic lacquers have their own tinters. These fine touches should always be sealed on top; the order is stain, sealer, touch-in, finishing coats.

Coloured varnishes are already pigmented, and can be used to carry more. Used on their own, they are popular because they are not difficult to mix or apply but they are a quick compromise solution, and show up as such. There is nothing to recommend them in terms of appearance, in that they combine uneven pigment spread with the thick 'plastic on top' look of polyurethane. These too should be given a top coat of clear varnish or polyurethane, whichever you are using.

Left: *Traditional stains: (from top) white vinegar and iron nails; vandyke brown, ammonia and water; potassium permanganate crystals and warm water, all on oak; mahogany crystals and water; potassium permanganate crystals and warm water; burnt sienna and stale beer; potassium bichromate crystals and warm water, all on beech.*

Grain filling and bleaching

Bleaching is done before staining, grain filling after. You might have deep marks to remove, such as those that water makes on oak (a particularly reactive timber), or you might want to lighten the whole surface generally, especially if you have used a caustic soda stripper.

Bleach works well on open-grained hardwoods like ash, beech or elm, but not on the close-grained ones like cherry, rosewood or padauk. Neutralizing bleaches, like strippers, is vital; they are corrosive and dangerous, so be careful – always add crystals or solutions to water, not the other way round. Sand with medium grit paper (100) to open the grain before you bleach – you'll be sanding with finer papers afterwards – and do not bleach veneers.

The weakest and easiest to use is household bleach. Start with a weak solution to see how it works, then strengthen it if you need to. Mop it on, leave it to dry, and rinse it thoroughly with clean water and vinegar. Oxalic acid is the next in strength, and is widely used in the trade. It is good for removing water-stains from oak. Use 50g (2oz.) of crystals per 500 ml (1 pint) of hot water, mop it on hot, leave it to dry, and neutralize it with a solution of 1 part ammonia to 10 parts water. Two-part 'A & B' solution (a mix of hydrogen peroxide and ammonia or caustic soda) is very strong and quite dangerous. Apply the first coat, leave it for about 10 or 20 minutes, then apply the second. Neutralize – stop the action if you want to – with full strength vinegar. Do not use this solution on oak.

Grain filling aids your smooth build up of finish – the glassy feel – and, if you put it on right, it will not obscure the grain pattern. It also surface-levels the pores, which would otherwise give your clear finish a pitted effect, however many coats you put on.

Proprietary fillers come in a wide range of colours, and should be used one shade darker than the wood, which itself will darken as if it was wet when the clear finish is applied. Thin them to a paste for the hardwoods and a thick liquid for soft, open-grained pine, using the correct solvent – white spirit or meths. Rub in the filler with a coarse cloth across the grain, let it 'go off' – begin to dry – and then rub off the surplus, also across the grain, packing it hard into the pores. Finish by wiping hard along the grain.

Colour-matching any additions in this old pine kitchen must start with bleach. Only when you have got a neutral ground will you be able to build up the characteristic washed-out grey tones.

The thinner fillers should be pushed in with a brush. Leave them to dry for a day, then fine paper the surface down, and rub in raw linseed oil to clear the muddy appearance. Wipe the surplus off thoroughly.

You can mix your own filler with superfine plaster, french chalk, or silex (china clay). Use pigments or oil stains to colour it, and a solvent compatible with the colour and the top finish. This is especially important for cellulose, which has its own nitro fillers, and will not take to oils. There are shellac-based liquid fillers available for french polishing close-grained woods.

Wax and oil finishes

For ease of application and softness of sheen, wax and oil are hard to beat, but offer comparatively little surface protection. Both need constant maintenance, although both are easy to maintain. Many coats of wax, however, built up over the years, will yellow and obscure grain and colour, and will also collect grime. That definite but intangible glowing warmth of an old finish – patina – is the product of waxing, buffing and normal wear over the life of the piece, so if you do strip and rewax a surface, expect to take time to regain the patina.

These finishes are more attractive on hardwoods. Silicon waxes should be treated with caution, since they are incompatible with any other sort, and give much more of a 'household sparkle' than a warm finish. There are many good-quality traditional furniture wax blends on the market, which use carnauba, beeswax and other additives; use these. A word of warning – once wax is applied to a raw surface, you must give up the idea of using any other finish at all over it. You can strip it with white spirit (paint thinner), but some wax will certainly remain in the pores of the wood.

Use wax on pieces that get no hard wear, like carvings, decoration, marquetry, hall furniture and so on. It is also commonly applied inside drawers and cabinets, where its fragrance mixes with the wood's natural aroma, and on drawer sides to facilitate running.

Oil finishes give durable, deep-wood protection against heat and moisture, have a distinctive flat, dull sheen, and are the only treatments through which you can feel the grain texture. Application is easy, but demands a lot of time and work. Linseed is traditionally used, either raw, which takes a long time to dry, or boiled, which sets more quickly but becomes gummy during application. It soaks deep into the grain and hardens by oxidation, allowing the wood to shrink or expand freely. Oil forms no barrier to surface knocks or bruises, but is untouched by heat and liquids and can be easily touched up, which is why it is a good choice for table-tops. Teak, tung and Danish oils (penetrating wood sealers) carry added resins which leave a harder surface film; they do, however, require much more careful application than linseed.

Left: *A penetrating oil finish would be very suitable for this dresser* (top), *whose rustic style would be spoiled by a high gloss; wax over french polish would give a beautiful patina to the writing table* (bottom).

Wax application

Grain filler is not necessary if you are applying wax; the wax itself does the job most efficiently. To avoid many applications and an unnecessary amount of absorption, you can seal the surface first with a thin coat or two of shellac; rub it down with wire wool or fine garnet between coats. You can also increase protection deep in the fibres against heat and water by applying a warmed, thinned mix first. Melt 50/50 wax and white spirit in a can in a pan of hot water, stirring it to a thick liquid, and brush it in hard with a shoebrush. You might have to reheat it to keep it runny. Wipe off the residue, and when it has set, cut it back with wire wool, then apply full-strength, normal temperature coats with a soft rag. They will buff up easily.

It is usual to apply wax with a rag; wipe it on, leave it for a few minutes to 'go off', and buff. The main point is not to get lumps in the rag or on the surface, which will smear, and which can be avoided by making sure the wax is soft enough and warm enough to spread easily. Put on as many coats as it takes to bring up a deep shine, and expect to rewax a surface regularly. Once or twice a year, depending on how often you wax, you should clean as much off as you can with white spirit and start the build-up process again.

For pieces that get harder use, wax can be used as a 'disposable protection' skin over a clear finish. It gives a softness to an otherwise hard brilliance, and when applied with wire wool has the added advantage of removing the final nibs and giving a sheen at the same time. It is also a quick way of finishing low-wear surfaces which have been sealed with the economic minimum of lacquer or varnish.

Oil application

The traditional oil-finishing work schedule is daunting, to say the least: 'Once a day for a week, once a week for a month, once a month for a year, once a year for the rest of your life.' The principle, if not perhaps demanding quite such a taxing regime, is that you soak the wood until it will absorb no more, wipe off the surplus, leave it to set for 24 hours, paper it down, and soak it again. When it will take no more, or after a week, whichever comes first, buff it long and hard with a cloth wrapped in a brick. 'Top it up' regularly.

Liquid waxes with pigments have deep penetration, but melting beeswax and carnauba gives control over consistency, and a lighter tone.

There are ways round this off-putting schedule, such as using the 'oil-resin' finish. This is an equal-parts mixture of varnish, white spirit and linseed or proprietary oil, soaked, wiped, papered and burnished in the same way, which offers a particularly effective combination of flexibility and durability. The 'buffing with a brick' part – the extra weight gives extra friction – could be eased by fitting a cloth pad to an orbital sander; as with any finish, the result is in direct proportion to the amount of work you put in.

If you use the proprietary teak, tung or Danish oils, a first-class brush is extremely important as poor or old brush will produce a poor finish. Brush the first coat on, brushing along the grain initially, to leave a film which you should cut right back to the wood the next day. Then do three or four more coats, wire wooling each one, but merely de-nibbing, not rubbing back so much. Burnish with wax and wire wool, pumice or rotten-stone. Extra penetration can be achieved by laying these oils over an initial soaking of 50/50 raw linseed oil and white spirit.

Both these and linseed oils can be tinted with pigments, oil stains, or oil-soluble aniline dyes. *Beware seepage* – an oil-finished piece should stand on plastic until you are sure no more will seep from the legs on to the carpet!

French polishing

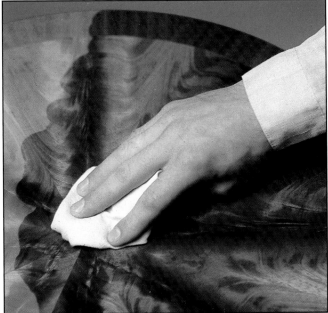

Introduction

Generally considered to be the most prestigious and desirable of all the clear finishes, french polish is the best looking, but in many ways the least practical. Its depth and brilliance are unequalled by varnishes or lacquers, because the surface it forms is actually wafer-thin, and gives grain pattern and colour a particular clarity, almost a transparency.

The French Martin brothers developed a polish based on shellac in the eighteenth century, a version of which was being used in England for pianos by 1815. By the late nineteenth century it had become the most popular treatment for high-quality furniture and joinery, especially mahogany. This timber still looks beautiful french polished, but other woods (though not wide-pored oak) can be treated equally successfully.

French polish is resistant to neither heat nor liquids, and is particularly susceptible to alcohol, so table tops are usually waxed to ease maintenance. This is not to say that the finish cannot be repaired at all (see pp. 79-80) but rewaxing is a great deal easier and quicker.

There is a certain mystique about polishing, probably because application with a rubber is an involved process, and recognizing the stage it has reached demands experience. Once you have developed a 'feel' for the rubber, however, you will find that it is a great deal easier than generations of craftsmen would have us believe. Doing it is really the only way to learn.

If you are finishing a new piece there is very little to be said for french polishing it, if it will be getting ordinary household use. But you will find it on antique, old or reproduction furniture and will need to know how to apply it when you are refinishing.

French polish is particularly reactive to damp; white blotches will appear in the finish if you apply it in a humid atmosphere, and it will not harden if the temperature in your workspace is less than 15°C (60°F). If conditions are bad and you still have to french polish, fix up a non-flammable heater over the surface, or warm it over with an iron on top of a blanket. This can also eliminate damp patches in the wood fibres.

Left: *This curl mahogany veneer is greatly enriched by staining before french polishing; without the colour, the surface would be dull and lifeless. A wax layer over the final coat gives easily maintained protection.*

Shellac

The basic ingredients of french polish are shellac and methylated spirits (wood alcohol). The secretions from the lac insect, found in India, Africa and the Far East, were originally used for red dye; while commercial chemistry has evolved better and cheaper colouring agents, there is still no synthetic equivalent of lac for french polish. The fluids secreted from the larvae encrust the twigs of infested trees; the 'stick lac' formed like this is harvested, pounded, melted, refined and filtered through 'seed' and 'lump' stages to make wafer-thin sheets. These sheets are then flaked and exported as shellac.

The decorative detail of these boxes would be best suited by the hardness and clarity of transparent white polish.

Types and mixes of french polish

The shellac/meths mix includes gums like arabic and copal, plus drying and hardening agents, to make the polish as it is sold. The off-the-shelf product is likely to be a '3lb cut' – in other words, 1.3kg (3lb) of shellac dissolved in 5l (1 gal.) of methylated spirits. The thicker '5lb cut', the other basic British mix, is for brushing, and is often sold as 'brush polish'. It is worth remembering these proportions when you are thinning or mixing different polishes for colouring or sealing.

French polishes come in a handful of basic varieties, according to the purity of the shellac; all can be intermixed, and both pigments and the clearer spirit aniline dyes can be used to tint them. Be careful, however, if a polish you buy is obviously a manufacturer's 'special'; it might have synthetic ingredients which demand special mixers. Always ask.

Button polish, so called because the shellac comes in little cakes or buttons, is brownish with a yellow tinge. Brown or 'orange' polish is a standard, made from orange shellac, and commonly known as just 'polish'. It is usually used for mahogany, as is garnet polish – a red- rather than a yellow-brown which gives clarity and warmth to mahogany that brown and button polish lack. White polish is milky in appearance and is made from acid-bleached shellac, which has a very limited shelf-life – two years at the absolute outside. It darkens the light woods on which it is used only slightly; there is no way of telling if it has deteriorated until you find it has not hardened after application, so buy only as much as you can predict you'll use. Transparent white is bleached twice, is clearer still than white polish, and is especially suitable for marquetry and inlays where no colour darkening at all is desirable.

You can buy ready-coloured polishes like red and black, and other proprietary makes may include acid or melamine hardeners for tables or bar-tops, or even exterior use. They are usually thicker, and formulated for application with a brush.

A '2lb cut' of white or transparent white polish is generally used as a sealing coat to protect stain from bleeding, or just to limit the absorbency of the wood before final finishing. Varnish can be put over shellac, but never for outside use; cellulose and the synthetic lacquers, which have their own 'sanding sealers', will not 'take' over shellac.

Making and using a rubber

Although you can use mops, brushes and spray guns for french polish, by far the most important method of application is with the rubber. This is no more than an absorbent pad, but making a good one and mastering its behaviour are essential to good french polishing.

Take a piece of cotton wadding, about 25cm (10in.) × 12.5cm (5in.), and fold it in half to make a square. Fold across three of the corners to make a pointed oblong, then place it on a fine, clean white rag. A well-washed linen handkerchief is ideal; it must be lint-free, colourless, and have no embroidery or stitching that might mar the surface.

Fold the rag over the pointed front of the wadding, then fold the sides in. The rest of the rag should be folded over the back of the wadding and screwed up so the lump rests in the palm of your hand. You should be able to squeeze the wadding by screwing the linen on top up more tightly, and it should also be easy to unfold the linen so you can charge the rubber.

Polish is dripped into the wadding from the top with the linen folded back. There must be no creases or folds, which will leave uneven marks and troughs in the surface, in the base of the rubber. Hold the rubber gently but firmly, with your fingers all round it to keep the shape and the flat base. When polishing a horizontal surface, drop your wrist so the weight of your arm works parallel rather than at an angle to the surface; this is especially important for circular motions, where there is a tendency to press harder on the outer sweep than the inner. Even pressure is vital.

Charging the rubber correctly is also important. Drip some polish into it a little at a time then dab the rubber on some (clean!) scrap wood to bring the polish through. It must not be so wet that too much polish flows, but if it is too dry the friction will cause the rubber to stick. An even flow is just as vital as even pressure, so as the charge is used up, press harder on the rubber to keep the same amount coming out. It is a common mistake at first to overcharge the rubber and not press hard enough: just wiping over the surface is no good, because the damp polish holds the rubber back and makes the action jerky. In the initial stages, you are forcing the polish into the grain, while in the latter, friction itself plays an important part in getting the brilliance of the finish.

The rubber

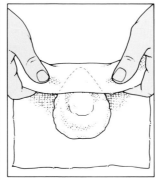

1 Fold the rag over the pointed front of the wadding.

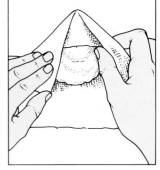

2 Fold in the sides so they leave a pear-shaped point.

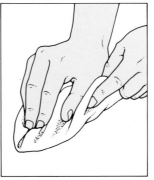

3 Screw up the remaining rag into your palm.

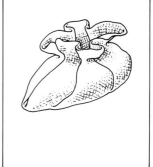

4 The pear-shaped point is for getting into corners.

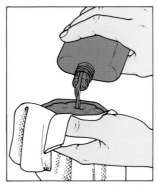

5 A v-groove cut in the cork helps to control the flow.

6 Keep the weight of your arm parallel to the surface.

Applying french polish

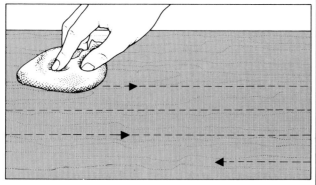

1 Bodying up: first apply the polish in overlapping circles, and glide on and off the surface at the sides and edges.

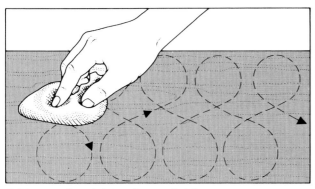

2 Next, apply polish in a figure-of-eight movement; even pressure and flow are vital.

3 Spiriting off removes the cloudiness of the oil; sweep the meths rubber along the grain.

Bodying up and spiriting off

The first operation, 'skinning in' or 'fadding', coats the grain with shellac. Charge the rubber and wipe it across the grain in straight, overlapping strokes, then do the same along the grain. Aim for even pressure and flow. A whistling sound from the rubber indicates there is a crease or fold, which you must deal with immediately.

The next stage is bodying up. First apply the polish in overlapping circles, going along, down, along and down again. Then lay more polish on in a figure-of-eight movement; if you see ridges building up as a result of uneven pressure, go back to moving straight along the grain to wipe them down. If you cannot wipe the ridges away, leave them to harden and paper them back. Try not to recharge the rubber in the middle of one going-over of the surface; as the polish is used up, press harder until you have finished one covering, then recharge.

Five or six applications, waiting only a minute or two between each, should be enough to build up an even coat, filling the grain and leaving a body of polish. In this part of the process you will find the rubber wanting to drag. Lubricate it by rubbing a fingertip's worth of raw linseed oil on the pad, using as little as possible because its cloudiness must be removed later.

After these bodying coats, leave the work to harden, preferably overnight. The polish will have sunk somewhat and you will be able to feel any imperfections. Wipe the surface carefully with fine, worn garnet paper, clean it meticulously, and do some more bodying until there is no hint of grain texture to the touch. You might need another five or six applications; in the last two, charge the rubber with 75/25 polish/meths, then 50/50. Depending on how much oil you have used, the surface will be smooth but smeary, and by now well-built-up.

Spiriting off removes the cloudiness of the oil. Make a new rubber, with three or four layers of rag this time, and charge it with meths so it is just damp enough to feel cold on your cheek. Sweep the meths rubber along the grain; it will lift the oil, which will form a tide-mark round the edges of the linen, out. If the surface clears then clouds over again, you are merely moving the oil around, not lifting it out, and you will have to take the dirty rag off and use the clean one underneath.

Go through these stages until you have a clear, brilliant, french polished surface.

Hints and problems

A finished french polished surface should be left at least a week to harden before you use it. Wax will protect it, but reduce the brilliance a little; if you want an eggshell or a flatter finish, apply pumice with a felt pad and oil or rottenstone powder dry with a dulling brush (furniture rubbing brush). Be extremely gentle; if you use oil, wipe it off and buff the surface with a clean soft cloth.

For awkward corners, mouldings and carvings, you can apply polish with a soft bear-, squirrel- or sable-hair mop, or use glaze, which is easy to apply and quick-drying. In fact a spirit varnish (gum benzoin in meths), glaze can be bought from trade suppliers. It is, however, less durable than polish itself. Lay a body of polish, then finish off with two or three coats of glaze, allowing them to harden properly between applications.

For the insides of cabinets and desks, where you want to seal and protect the surface but do not need a full french polished finish, use dry shining. This is basic polishing, without the grain filling or the use of oil. Fad and body enough just to fill the grain, using straight then circular strokes; after three or four applications, charge the rubber slightly more fully than usual and finish off with long, even strokes. Oil would have to be spirited off, defeating the whole object of speed and ease, so do not use any, but be extra careful to prevent the rubber sticking.

'Stiffing' is a technique for cabinet interiors and other areas where you cannot glide on and off the edges. Start at the edges and work towards the middle, lifting the rubber as you get there to overlap a stroke you have made from the other side. It takes a lot of practice to be able to do this without building up ridges; if you do get some, they can be smoothed very delicately with a spirit rubber after about half an hour's hardening time.

Lubricating a french polish rubber with oil can be less controlled than just lubricating one sticky area of the surface, which many professionals prefer to do. Always be sparing with oil, and do not use it unless you really have to. Do not keep worrying away at a problem area, it will only get worse. Leave it to harden a few minutes and then see whether a wipe with polish will smooth it out. If not, paper it back when it's hard.

Make sure there is no dampness in the surface. When repolishing an old piece, dismantle it as far as possible,

Though the polish of this low-boy is pitted and marked, the superb patina makes it unwise to strip and repolish the piece.

taking off removable mouldings and marking them so they go back in the same place. Mount them on a strip of hardboard and fix them to a board to work on them, so the edges are held away from the surface. If you have stained a repair to match in and it lightens under the polish, tint some polish and brush that over the area, let it harden and seal it with a thin coat, then continue over the whole surface. If you are making panelled doors, try to polish the panel before you glue up the frame – the glue will not adhere to the polish, and there will be no problem getting your rubber into the corners. Otherwise you must use the pear-shaped point of the rubber.

Make up felt- or blanket-covered battens to protect a polished surface when you have to do the other side; pad vice (vise) jaws like this too. Do not trail your shirt-buttons, jewellery or a loose edge of rag from the rubber over the work; keep your hands as free from flaky dried shellac as possible; pour polish and oil well away from the work; and, above all, start on small, unimportant surfaces and move on to more ambitious projects as you get the feel of the rubber and the polish.

4

OLD CHINA
and
CERAMICS

Due to the very nature of the material, much old china and pottery has suffered damage to some degree, and favourite ceramic items are easily chipped or broken. A missing hand on a figurine, or an ugly discoloured chip on a bowl, detracts greatly from the beauty and integrity of the piece. The effect of even quite a simple restoration can be extremely pleasing and worthwhile.

Although every damage is in some way different, all the types of repair you are likely to come across are described as separate projects. The techniques are those used by professional restorers, but they are explained in a way which anyone can follow.

As with any skilled activity, do not be too ambitious at first. Start with some simple repairs, learning the basic bonding skills on a piece with one or two breaks. Restore a few chips around the edge of a bowl or vase, before embarking on the more complicated tasks of replacing missing parts and more elaborate modelling.

Tools and materials

All the tools and materials you will need to complete the projects in this section should be available from either a hardware or DIY store; an art and/or craft shop; good toy shops, especially those which specialize in models, or specialist model shops; chemists (pharmacists); and, finally, car accessory shops. Department stores with good toy departments are worth investigating.

Art shops are often prepared to order goods in small quantities if they do not stock them, and you should look through their catalogues for various alternatives. Similarly, chemists will usually order goods which they may not have in stock.

As a general rule, buy the smallest quantities available.

The workspace

You need a table (or bench), a chair, a good light, and adequate ventilation. Many of the solvents you will be using are highly flammable – do not smoke and do not have any naked flames in your workroom. A laminate (formica) top is excellent, but if you are using your kitchen table, for instance, cover it with a board, or lay down some newspaper, and cover that with one or two layers of tissue paper taped down on to the table. Throw away the tissue when you have finished and want to use the table for something else.

General

This section includes those materials and tools which have a variety of uses.

An apron, besides keeping your clothes clean, will ensure that if you drop something, it will be caught in your lap.

An eye-dropper is used for transferring drops of acetone, glaze, paint thinners, and so on.

Small clear glass jars with lids are useful for decanting large amounts of filling powders, liquids and so on, for ease of access. Do not use plastic ones which may dissolve in acetone and paint thinners. The more you have the better. Ask for them in your local chemist.

A white tile, preferably several; these are used for mixing fillers and paints.

Petroleum jelly is used as a releasing agent.

A domestic oven or low temperature plate warmer is useful for a variety of jobs, but only vital if you decide to use stoving enamels (p. 119). An electric oven is best. Never heat china to more than 120°C (250°F).

Acetone is the best and most easily available all-round solvent and cleaner for china restoring. You can use it, for example, to clean adhesives before they dry. Paint thinners are alternative solvents.

Soft toilet paper and small cotton rags are used mainly for cleaning-up. Make sure rags are cotton, not man-made fibres, which can dissolve in acetone.

A scalpel (or similar sharp knife) is important and a no 15, with its curved blade, is the most useful. Buy a no 11 next. If, generally, you use more than one type of blade, use a separate handle for each.

Scissors and **tweezers** will also be necessary.

Dismantling

Stipple on water-soluble paint stripper with an old paintbrush to break down old glue.

Water-soluble paint stripper is the best product for breaking down glues, but treat it with caution. If you get any on your skin, wash immediately in cold, not hot, water. *Never* pour hot water on to ceramics covered with paint stripper – noxious fumes are given off.

An old stiff paintbrush is used to apply paint stripper.

Cleaning and stain removal

Washing-up (dishwashing) liquid is the standard cleaning material. With the possible exception of some soft-bodied ceramics (see pp. 122-3), all pieces, including (especially) the joins, should be washed thoroughly in washing-up liquid and warm water. Do this after dismantling (if dismantling is necessary) and before bonding. Be sure to rinse thoroughly after washing.

A toothbrush is especially useful for washing and cleaning joins and difficult, inaccessible places.

A plastic bowl or bucket is a safer container to wash and soak things in than an enamel or metal sink.

Water softener is sold in a powder form. This is *not* the same as fabric softener.

Biological detergent

Hydrogen peroxide 100 volume is used to remove stubborn stains (see p. 101). Make sure you get the full-strength 100 volume. Buy it from the chemist.

Cotton wool (absorbent cotton)

Bonding

Slow-setting epoxy-resin adhesive is the basic and best adhesive for china restoration. It is widely available under various different brand names, but they all consist of two tubes, a *hardener* and a *resin*, which have to be mixed together in equal quantities. Ensure that the two parts are thoroughly mixed together before use. The mixture remains usable for at least an hour, and sets hard after 24 hours, though full strength is achieved only after several days. Slow-setting epoxy resin is also used as the base for filler.

Some people are allergic to epoxy resins, so avoid getting them on your skin.

Fast-setting epoxy resin is not as strong as the slow-setting variety, but it can be useful (see p. 100).

PVA, or wood glue is used for bonding soft-bodied ceramics.

An orange stick or similar tool is used for mixing and applying adhesives and fillers. Orange sticks are available in packets from a chemist. Clean them in acetone before the adhesive dries.

A palette knife is more permanent and versatile, or any small modelling tool with a thin, flexible, metal end can be used. A no 15 scalpel can also be used for applying adhesive.

Thin white card or white cartridge paper is useful for mixing up adhesives on. This can be thrown away after use, which is much easier than cleaning off your white tile. Save the backs of old greeting cards for this purpose.

Razor blade

Filling in and modelling

Slow-setting epoxy resin is used as the base for making up filler (see pp. 97 and 107).

Ready bought epoxy-resin putties are more convenient to use than home mixed, especially for modelling. They tend to dry a little faster than made-up filler, which is often an advantage. Buy them in craft, modelling or DIY (hardware) shops. See p. 107 for more details.

Titanium dioxide is a strong white pigment, available from art shops.

Kaolin, or fine dental plaster is used to give the filler 'body'. Kaolin powder is probably easier to obtain (from a chemist) than fine dental plaster, although they are equally effective.

Cellulose filler is a more suitable filler for earthenware, terracotta and other soft-bodied ceramics. It is available from hardware or DIY shops, where it is sold as a filler for small holes in walls.

Fine surface filler is used for filling tiny holes. You can buy this in the same range as cellulose filler, or make your own from epoxy resin, titanium dioxide and talcum powder.

Talcum powder can be used with epoxy resins for making up a fine surface filler (see above).

Dividers or callipers are very useful for comparing sizes when you are modelling, as well as measuring distances between repeated painted patterns.

Modelling tools will be necessary. A spatula with a fine, flexible, metal end is probably the most useful all-round tool. A palette knife, small boxwood tools, orange sticks, wooden cocktail sticks, scalpels, dental probes and so on, can all be used.

Rubbing down and abrading

Needle files are available in a variety of shapes. The rounded ones tend to be more useful.

Abrasive papers are essential. The following grades should cover most needs.

Coarse or fairly coarse grade glasspaper is useful but be careful how you use these papers, as they can scratch the glaze on the original china if you are careless. Medium grade glasspaper is probably the most useful. Flour paper is a fine abrasive paper for finishing.

Silicon carbide wet and dry paper (grade 1200) is available from car-accessory shops, and used for very fine smoothing, especially between coats of paint and varnish.

Moulds

Liquid rubber latex is usually sold as fabric adhesive, and is a good, easily available material from which to make moulds (see pp. 114-15).

Fine sawdust is used for strengthening moulds.

Cotton-wool buds (Q-tip swabs) are useful for applying latex to a model.

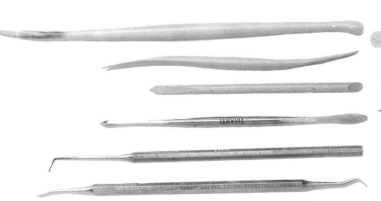

A palette knife or small metal spatula, orange sticks and a scalpel are the basic modelling tools you will need. They should be either metal or wooden – not plastic, which can dissolve in some solvents.

Painting and colouring

Artist's dry fine-ground pigments are very strong, so buy the smallest quantities you can. They are often sold in small glass tubes. A list of the colours you will need is given on p. 118. These are *not* the same as the school-type powder paints.

Ready-made paints are a convenient alternative to dry pigments, or you can invest in both. The most common available series are those sold for painting model aircraft, but you might find a specialist set for china restoring or glass painting in a good art or craft shop.

Glazes or varnish mediums are discussed on p. 119.

Thinning agents or thinners are used for thinning glazes, varnishes and paints, and may be used instead of acetone for cleaning.

Metal dippers from art and craft shops are useful for mixing paints in.

A black tile is good for practising white and background painting.

An old, fairly soft brush (about a size 6) can be used for mixing paints on your tile or in a metal dipper.

Best-quality sable brushes should be used for painting. Cheaper brushes do not last as long, and will soon start to leave hairs on your work. Look after them, they are both delicate and expensive. To begin with, a no 00, for fine decoration, and a no 2 are the most useful.

A hard lead pencil is useful for lightly pencilling in complicated patterns.

Talcum powder can be added to paints and glaze for a matt effect. Pumice, or abrasive powder will give a coarser, gritty effect.

Gilding and lustres

Ready-made gold paints, as well as silver and copper, are available from art shops.

Bronze powders are an alternative to ready-made. They tend to give a slightly better finish, and are more versatile. You can also buy silver and copper powders.

A soft cloth can be used for burnishing.

Ready-made gold paints and bronze powders are generally more appropriate on oriental gold; use transfer gold leaf for a brighter finish.

Gold- and silver-leafing materials

Transfer gold leaf is discussed on p. 101.

Imitation transfer gold leaf is much cheaper than real gold leaf, and on many jobs is just as good, if not better.

Silver leaf is applied in the same way as gold leaf, but tarnishes quite quickly, unless you cover it with a coat of varnish.

Agate burnisher

Advanced painting

Although hand painting gives a very good finish on many pieces, it is not the best method if you have a piece of china with large areas of light washes of colour. In this case, an airbrush is really the only effective way of invisibly restoring pieces. There are many books on the subject if you intend to try this technique.

Basic techniques

Supporting

Before you begin any bonding job, you must consider how the item is to be supported and strapped together. Clear adhesive tape and tourniquets can be used to strap tight and secure simple breaks together while the adhesive cures. But these are not appropriate when you are bonding small or awkward pieces on an ornamental figure, for instance.

Many amateurs attempt to overcome the problem by using fast-setting glues, the most extreme being the 'superglues' (cyanoacrylates) which set in under a minute. These are not suitable for use on china. For one thing, mistakes cannot be rectified without dismantling the join and starting again. With slow-setting epoxy resins, you have the time necessary to achieve the most perfect join. In addition, no available adhesive has the strength of a slow-setting epoxy resin.

Always position the piece you are working on in such a manner as to maximize the effect of gravity.

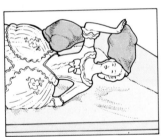 

Support an arm with modelling clay, and use a core of it in a spout as a support when filling.

Support bonded plates and cup handles in a sandbox at an angle to maximize the effect of gravity.

A tourniquet is the best way to hold the two sides of a simple crack or break firm while the glue dries. An old pair of tights makes an ideal tourniquet. Tie them round the vase or plate with a loose knot, then insert a stick in the knot and twist the stick until the tourniquet is tight.

Clear adhesive tape (Sellotape/scotch tape) is useful for holding both sides of a break together while slow-setting epoxy resin dries. If it leaves a sticky residue on the surface, clean it off with acetone. Do not use this tape on gilding – it can lift gilding off.

Stationery clips (bull-dog clips) are useful for holding the sides of a join in a plate or saucer in perfect alignment.

A sandbox or a tin full of sand or salt is a valuable aid for positioning pieces of ceramics at whatever angle is most appropriate. Use a cake tin or a box – a cat-litter tray is an ideal size.

Plastic modelling clay (plasticine) is almost indispensable for propping up and supporting in position. It becomes soft and pliable when warm, yet maintains its shape well, and can be removed easily. Do not allow it to come into contact with the join.

Fast-setting epoxy resin can be used if you can find no effective means of support. This is not as strong as slow-setting, but on many small pieces, great strength is not of crucial importance.

Mix up the fast-setting resin in the same way as you would the slow-setting type, and apply it thinly to one side of the join. Make sure you have practised joining the broken piece without adhesive to familiarize yourself with the join, and the best way of holding it together with your fingers.

Fast-setting epoxy resin takes 10-15 minutes to harden, so after mixing, leave it for five minutes, then press the broken piece on to the join and hold it there for between five and ten minutes more until the adhesive has hardened. Use a firm even pressure. Do remember, however, that holding something for five or ten minutes without moving is not easy.

Whatever method of support you choose, check its effectiveness after two hours. Make sure none of the pieces have moved, and if one (or more) has, then readjust it.

Gilding

Whatever the job, always apply gold decoration last, and make sure before you begin that any other painting is finished and completely dry. Highly mirrored gold is impossible to reproduce well. Fortunately, this is only found on modern pieces. Antique gold is duller, although even the finest quality gold leaf cannot perfectly match some finishes.

Many art shops sell **ready-made gold** and silver preparations. These are simple to use and it is worth buying as many different shades as possible, because gold decoration is so often found on china. After painting them on, burnish with a soft cloth.

Finely ground **bronze powders** give a gold with a slightly better finish than ready-mixed paints, and they are more versatile. Again, buy as many shades as you can. Mix them together dry, then, when the required shade has been reached, add a few drops of glaze medium (too much glaze tends to give a duller finish) to bind them together, plus a little thinner if necessary. Apply them with a paintbrush. Do not apply a coat of clear glaze over the top, as it will dull the shine, just burnish with a soft cloth. These preparations can, of course, be mixed together and pigments and paints added.

For large areas of bright gold, **gold leaf** can give the best results. Gold leaf is difficult to apply, and sometimes the results are disappointing. It is expensive as it

Applying gold leaf

1 With a very sharp scalpel, cut a square of gold leaf

2 Transfer the leaf and its tissue backing to the piece.

3 Gently rub the tissue backing with your fingers.

4 Peel off the tissue; burnish when the varnish is dry.

comes in books of 25 leaves. There are cheaper imitation gold leaves available, which on some pieces are just as good. There are various shades available, so if you want to try it, take the piece of china to your supplier (not all art shops sell it) and find the closest match. For china restoring purposes, *transfer gold leaf* is the most convenient form to use.

Gold leaf application is illustrated above. Apply a thin even coat of varnish with a little yellow pigment or paint to the area of china to be gilded. Wait until the varnish is tacky (15-30 mins) before applying the leaf.

When the varnish has dried, burnish with an agate gold leaf burnisher, or a very hard smooth rounded gemstone (for example in a ring). More than one coat of gold leaf may be needed.

Lustre finishes usually have a copper base. Pigments and paints can be added to them to achieve different lustrous shades and effects. Many lustre effects consist mainly of pigments with just a small amount of copper added. Unfortunately, however, it is impossible to match some of these effects well.

An effective way of using bronze powders for an area like the base of this jug is to sprinkle them on to a tacky coat of glaze. When the varnish is dry, wash the piece – the 'gold' will be left adhering to the glaze underneath. Burnish it when the piece is dry.

Project 1: Cracked oriental vase

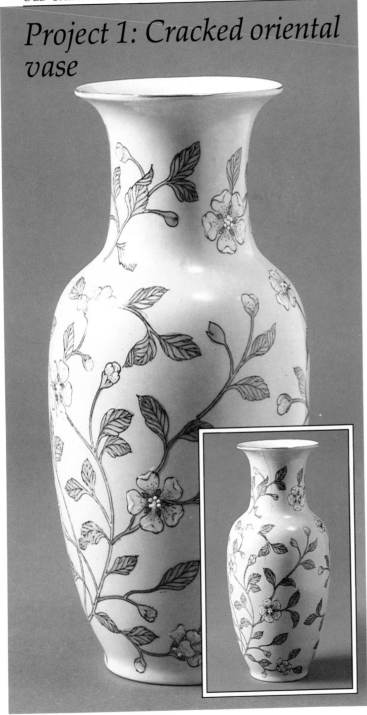

This vase, with its long vertical crack, is in danger of splitting in two, and the crack is so visible because of its accumulation of dirt and grease. The first step is to draw out all the dirt. For this you will need biological detergent and water softener, but if this method fails, you may need hydrogen peroxide 100 volume. Slow-setting epoxy-resin adhesive is used to bond the crack. When heated, this adhesive turns liquid, before setting rock hard. If you first warm the vase, the epoxy resin will seep right into the crack.

A tourniquet ensures a tight, neat join while the adhesive dries, by exerting a strong pressure in one direction. Sometimes this is not appropriate or possible, in which case use clear adhesive tape to strap the join as tightly as you can.

If you have a piece of china with an unsightly hairline crack, use the stain removing techniques alone. It is not necessary to fill in the crack, because the piece is unlikely to be in any danger of splitting.

A near invisible repair can be made using these techniques.

Left and above: *On a crack such as this, the secret of a really invisible repair is to ensure that all the dirt and grime are removed before the crack is secured with slow-setting epoxy-resin adhesive.*

To remove dirt and staining

Mix up in a plastic bucket a weak solution of equal quantities of water softener and biological detergent. Add warm water to a level which will enable you to submerge the vase completely. Do not use very hot water as this reduces the effectiveness of the cleaning solution. Leave the vase in the solution for several hours or overnight. If the crack is still dirty, scrub at it with an old toothbrush, then repeat the soaking in a new cleaning solution. Repeat as often as necessary.

If the soaking method does not completely remove every particle of dirt, try pouring a small quantity of hydrogen peroxide 100 volume on to a saucer. *Be careful* not to touch this with your fingers as it is corrosive. With some tweezers, soak a swab of cotton wool in the peroxide, and place the swab along the crack – you might need several swabs depending on the size of the crack. Leave these for several hours, then remove them. The hydrogen peroxide will cause the dirt to leach out into the cotton wool. Repeat the process if necessary.

Do not use peroxide on soft pottery or earthenware; it can cause the stain to spread.

Rinse the vase thoroughly in clean water, and leave it to dry in a warm place.

Securing the crack

Gently warm the vase in an oven at its lowest setting for about 10 minutes, or use a hair dryer to heat the crack. While the vase is warming, mix up some *slow-setting* epoxy resin on a square of white card. Use an orange stick or palette knife to mix the two parts together.

Remove the vase from the oven – use a tea towel (pot holder), it might be hotter than you think. Insert a razor blade in the crack, and carefully open the crack a fraction. Apply the adhesive liberally to the crack – because of the heat, the adhesive will immediately seep into it. Remove the razor blade. If there is a good deal of adhesive around the cracked area, carefully remove it with acetone or a similar solvent, but do not allow the solvent to touch the crack itself. Any remaining adhesive around the crack can be removed later.

Tighten the two sides of the crack together using a tourniquet and leave it for at least 12 hours. Remove the tourniquet and pare off any excess dried adhesive with a scalpel or a similar sharp knife.

Cleaning and repairing a crack

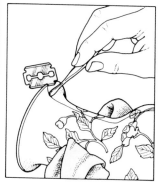

1 Soak vase in water softener and detergent.

2 Lay cotton wool swabs along the crack.

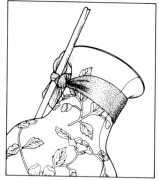

3 Open crack a fraction and apply the glue.

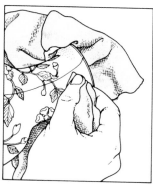

4 Clean off excess adhesive with acetone.

5 Use a tourniquet to ensure a clean join.

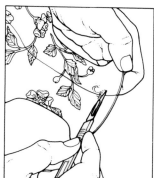

6 Pare off excess dried adhesive with a scalpel.

Project 2: Broken plate

Simple breaks

Technique, in an apparently simple job, can make the difference between an amateurish, weak join, and a near invisible professional repair.

The plate illustrated had been badly glued together. The old glue was applied too thickly, and had in time turned a lumpy, dirty brown. The first task was to dismantle the original repair, then clean off every trace of the old glue before rebonding the pieces.

For dismantling, you will need hot water and a plastic bowl. It may seem surprising, but with prolonged immersion in water alone, most glues will soften and break. If soaking alone does not work, you will need water-soluble paint stripper and, possibly, acetone. Water-soluble paint stripper will not damage the ceramic or glaze, but it will dissolve old restored materials and, occasionally, old gilding. If your plate has gilding, be a little wary and test a tiny part first.

Slow-setting epoxy resin is used for bonding. While the adhesive is drying, the two parts of the plate need to be held together as tightly as possible. Clear adhesive tape and a tourniquet are used for this, although you may also need metal stationery (bull-dog) clips to hold the two sides of the break in good alignment.

One of the interesting things about china restoration is that no two repairs are exactly the same. However, the same basic techniques apply whether the mend is simple or complex. They are not difficult, but forethought and planning are essential. Do not embark upon one step before you are sure of the next, and have all the appropriate materials to hand.

These projects are intended to show you how to repair ornamental china and ceramics. Domestic china, especially plates, can only rarely be satisfactorily repaired. All adhesives will eventually break down in water, especially in a dishwasher, and, of course, on a broken plate, dirt and grime will soon start to accumulate in the crack, however perfectly you have joined the two halves. It is worth repairing the broken handle on your favourite cup, or one of a set, if you bond and strap it properly. But be careful when you wash it, and use it as little as possible.

Left: *The combination of adhesive tape and a tourniquet, as well as the use of a minimum amount of adhesive, enables you to make a really tight, neat and secure join on a two-piece break.*

Dismantling the old join

Place the plate in a plastic bowl, pour in enough very hot water to cover it and leave it to soak for a few hours or overnight. Repeat every few hours as necessary.

If, after a few days, the join refuses to come apart, take it out of the water and dry it off. Stipple water-soluble paint stripper on to both sides of the join, leave it for about 20 minutes, then wipe off the stripper. If the join is really stubborn, stipple on the stripper, then enclose the plate in a plastic bag; this will stop the paint stripper drying out and give it more time to work.

It is not uncommon to find a broken plate or bowl which has been riveted together with metal staples, held in place with plaster. To remove these, soak the piece in warm water for a few hours. This should dissolve most of the plaster, making it fairly easy to lever out the staples with a scalpel. Start from the middle one and work outwards to the edges.

A certain amount of old glue will probably still adhere to each side of the now-broken join. Apply paint stripper to each edge, leave it for 20 minutes, then carefully remove the stripper and dissolved glue with a scalpel. Be careful not to damage the broken edges of the plate with your scalpel. Repeat this process if necessary. If the old glue has stained the joined edges, use the methods outlined on p. 103 to remove the staining before you proceed.

Clean the plate thoroughly with a toothbrush and washing-up (dishwashing) liquid. Rinse it in clean water and leave until it is bone dry.

Dry run

Before you start applying any adhesive, always work out how the pieces fit together. *This is a must for every bonding job.* If you find your join is not perfect, examine it carefully under a good light or a magnifying glass, to check for minute deposits of glue, or tiny shards of china. Carefully remove these with your scalpel, not your fingers. Position the broken pieces together several times, so you are familiar with their alignment.

Bonding and strapping

On some white card, thoroughly mix up a small quantity of slow-setting epoxy resin with an orange stick or similar tool. The adhesive will remain workable for at least an hour, so do not hurry these stages.

Cut up about a dozen strips of clear adhesive tape, and make sure they are easily to hand.

With your orange stick, carefully apply the epoxy resin to one side of the join only, making sure that you do not miss any area. Contrary to what you might think, the thinner the layer of adhesive, the stronger and closer the bond.

Press the two pieces of china together. Be firm but gentle, or you might chip off tiny pieces of ceramic in the join, which will cause it to misalign. Test the alignment by running a scalpel across it from side to side; it will catch where one side is higher than the other. Adjust as necessary. While maintaining the pressure, strap the join with pieces of clear adhesive tape on both sides of the plate.

Support the join as shown opposite. After 24 hours, remove the clips, tourniquet and adhesive tape and pare off any excess adhesive with a scalpel. If the tape has left a sticky residue, clean it off with acetone.

Repairing a simple break

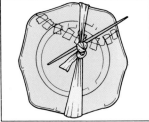

1 Apply adhesive to one side of the join.

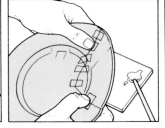

2 Strap the join with adhesive tape on both sides.

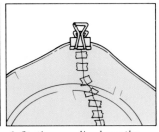

3 Use a tourniquet to maintain firm pressure.

4 Stationery clips keep the rim well aligned.

Project 3: Chipped vase

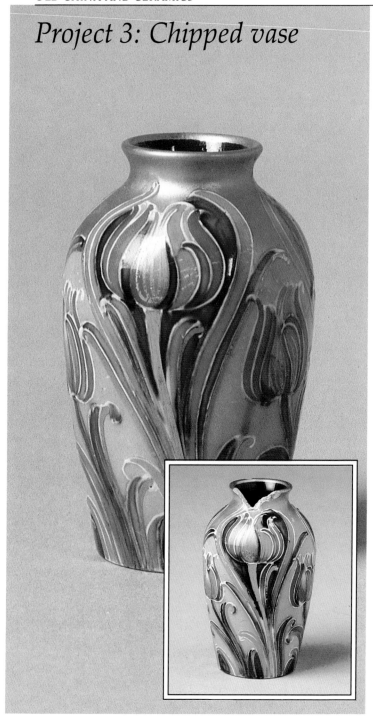

The use of coloured filler

This project demonstrates how to fill in chips and make up simple missing parts. There are two ways of colouring a filled-in piece: you can either use coloured filler, or paint. Painting is a more complicated procedure and is dealt with in full on pp. 116-21. Here, we will use coloured filler, which is simpler, but more approximate in matching colours than painting. It can give good results, however, especially when the piece to be filled is a uniform colour.

If your piece has an intricate design, you can use coloured filler for the background colour, and paint the decoration on top, or use plain white filler and paint it all (see p. 120).

Even if you decide eventually to paint, follow the instructions for making filler and filling in chips and breaks which are outlined here.

Materials

To make the filler you will need some slow-setting epoxy resin, a selection of dry artist's pigments (the colours you may need are discussed in more detail on p. 118), some kaolin or fine dental plaster, and, possibly, a fine surface filler. Mix up your filler and colours on a plain white tile. Have several to hand if possible – they are very useful – and keep a small bowl of water and some acetone handy.

An alternative to making up your own filler is to use one of the ready-made epoxy-resin putties on the market. If you buy an opaque type, you will also need some titanium dioxide to whiten it. These putties can also be coloured with artist's pigments.

Any small modelling tools you can find are helpful, in particular a small metal spatula. For rubbing down, small metal files are useful, but the various grades of glasspaper are a must. If you want a glass-like finish, use one of the glazes discussed on p. 119. You may also need clear adhesive tape and plastic modelling clay for support as you work.

Left: *The edges of plates, cups and as here, vases, are the parts most prone to chipping. There are two basic types of chips – glaze chips and V-shaped chips. Repairs to a V chip like this one are more time-consuming because you have to model on both the inside and the outside of the piece.*

Making epoxy-resin filler

Make up some slow-setting epoxy resin on a piece of white card as described on p. 103. When it is thoroughly mixed, transfer some to a clean white tile.

Look at the vase and study its colour. Select the dry fine-ground artist's pigments that you think are the nearest to the ones you need. Carefully decant tiny piles of each pigment on to another tile, but keep them well away from each other. Many pieces of china have a predominantly near white background colour, so you will probably need some titanium dioxide which is a strong white powder pigment. If this is the case, mix it in first.

Carefully add grains of the appropriate pigment(s) to the mixed epoxy resin (a scalpel is useful for transferring pigments), and mix it up with your orange stick until you have a uniform colour. These pigments vary in strength, but many are very strong indeed, so be cautious and introduce just a few grains at a time (for hints on colour matching, see pp. 120–1).

Have some acetone and a cotton rag handy to clean epoxy resin off your tools and so on, but remember that it will not work on dried epoxy resin.

When the colour is to your satisfaction, you will need to add 'body' to the epoxy resin so it will maintain its shape while it is setting. There are several filling powders you can use, but the two most readily available are kaolin and fine dental plaster. The more filling powder you add, the thicker your putty will become. If you want to fill in small holes or cracks, then the mixture can be kept quite thin, with only a small addition of filling powder, and spread on to the crack or small hole with a fine modelling tool or orange stick. If the chip is more substantial, keep adding filler until you can pick it up in your fingers ('flouring' your fingers with the filler powder helps). Keep adding filler until it is really stiff, so that when you incorporate it on to the missing area, it will keep its shape.

Keep a little filler on a piece of white card, so that if you do need more, you can match up the next batch to the first. If the match is not good, the slightly different shades will give a 'blotchy' look.

Ready-made putties

There are a number of ready-made epoxy-resin putties on the market. These are convenient and save time; they are also easy to work with and hold their shape well. In addition, many do not dry as hard as the made-up filler; this makes them easier to rub down. The only disadvantage is that when they are mixed, some of them have a green, blue or grey colour. There are some which are white or opaque, so buy these for preference.

Tools for filling

The method of filling and the tools you will need depend on the type of chip or missing parts to be filled in. Fingers, scalpels, small metal spatulas and fine modelling tools can all be used, but don't feel you have to invest in a vast range of them. Your fingers, an orange stick and perhaps a small metal spatula or even the blade of a scalpel will do for most jobs. Other tools are useful, but you can buy (or make) them as you see the need, and experience has shown you what might be useful.

Preparing a coloured filler

1 Make up some slow-setting epoxy resin.

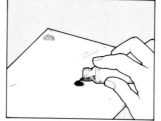

2 Decant piles of powder pigments to a clean tile.

3 Transfer pigments to resin with a scalpel.

4 Add filling powder until the filler is stiff.

Filling

As carefully as possible put a layer of filler in the chip. If the area to be filled is large, do not try to fill all of it at once, as it is bound to sag as it dries. Instead, build up the filling in layers, leaving each layer to dry, or at least partially dry, before adding the next. Try not to overfill the chip more than a fraction. If you do, when the filler dries, you will have to spend many tiresome hours rubbing it down with files and abrasive papers until it is flush with the unbroken edge. If you are in doubt, underfill it, and add more later.

Remember that you are always working in three dimensions, and that you must take into account the curve of the lip of the vase. Water is useful to smooth the filling into shape, as is acetone, but be careful: too much acetone on your modelling tool will temporarily turn your filler into a liquid 'sludge' until the acetone evaporates. Use filling powder on your fingers to 'pat' the filler into shape without it sticking to them.

On a small missing piece, you can save a lot of time by using clear adhesive tape as a backing to press the epoxy-resin putty against. This can be easily removed when the filler has dried. On larger areas, use plastic modelling clay in the same way, but be careful not to allow it to touch the broken edges of the china.

Drying

The filler is ready to be sanded down when it is hard enough to be rubbed by abrasive papers without it peeling off in lumps – usually between six and ten hours, depending on room temperature. However, this 'curing' process can be speeded up by placing the piece in a warm environment such as an airing cupboard (linen closet). If you put the object in an oven at the lowest possible temperature, the filling will harden in about 20 minutes. But beware: if you do cure it in an oven, although you can proceed more quickly, the filler will be very hard indeed and, consequently, much tougher to rub down.

A further word of warning if you are using an oven to speed-cure your filler – leave it to part dry naturally for about two hours before you put it in the oven. If you put it in immediately, the epoxy resin in the filler liquefies with heat and then hardens, so your filler will lose its shape. (See also stoving enamels, p. 119.)

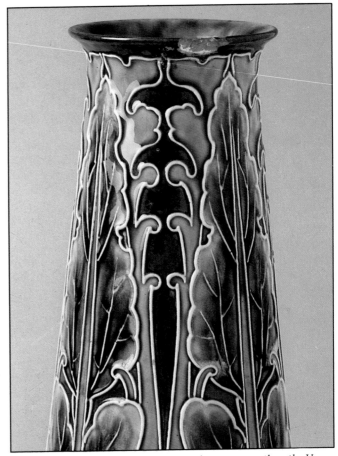

While this glaze chip is obviously simpler to restore than the V-type chip on the gilded vase, it involves filling in and rubbing down on a curved area, which is always more difficult than on a flat surface.

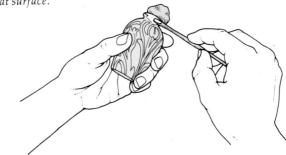

Use a wodge of plastic modelling clay as a backing to build up your filler against.

Rubbing down

When the filler is dry, it will probably need rubbing down with abrasive papers. You can buy small metal files of various shapes to rub away excess filler and you should start with these if you have grossly overfilled. Be very careful not to touch the original glaze on the vase (this is easy to do), which will scratch and damage.

Next, use glasspaper, cut up into 25mm (1in.) squares to finish the rubbing down. Start with a fairly coarse grade, then a medium (the most useful) and finish off with the finest grade you can buy (often called flour paper). This will give you a smooth finish, which can be further improved by rubbing in a fine abrasive metal

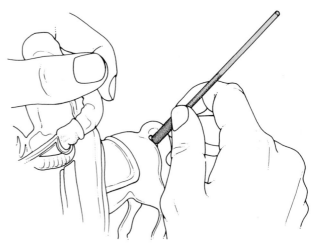

For rubbing down awkward areas, wrap a square of glasspaper around a thin stick or round needle file.

polish paste. As you rub down, be constantly aware of the contours of the shape you are trying to achieve.

As a rule, rub down from the china side to the filler in separate strokes, not the other way round. If you rub down the other way, or you rub along the join with the china rather than across it, you will inevitably rub too much off and will have to fill in around the edge again with new filler. For rubbing down awkward areas, wrap a square of abrasive paper around the end of a small round stick or round needle file.

Filling in

You may need to make up more filler several times, rubbing down between each layer, until your final rubbing down is satisfactory. Tiny holes in your filler can, at this stage, be carefully filled with epoxy resin, or a fine surface filler (see p. 98), both coloured to match.

Finishing

When you have finished all your filling in and rubbing down, examine the surrounding china and clean off any filler that has stuck to it with a scalpel.

If you require a glaze-like finish, paint on a thin coat of varnish (see p. 119).

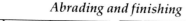
Abrading and finishing

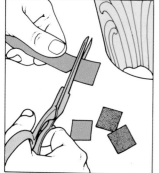
1 Cut up small squares of glasspaper.

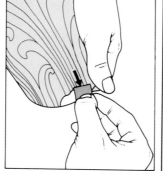
2 Rub down from the china side to the filler.

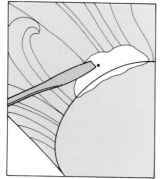
3 Fill in tiny holes with a fine surface filler.

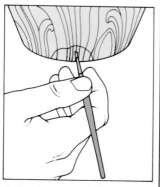
4 Apply a coat of glaze medium.

Project 4: Advanced modelling

Do not be put off by the thought of modelling – you do not have to be the world's greatest modeller to achieve excellent results. What you need are good observation, an eye for fine detail, and patience.

Apart from chips (see pp. 106-9), hands, handles and flowers are probably the commonest parts which need to be replaced on ceramic ornaments and figures. The techniques outlined here can be adapted for just about any other kind of piece you are likely to encounter.

You have one great advantage when you are modelling. If you need to make a hand, you can copy the style, size and colour from the other hand on the figure. On a decorated ornament, an intact flower will be your model for a new one. A missing cup handle has a twin somewhere. If you don't have it, do some research. There are plenty of books illustrating different styles of cup handles (and, for that matter, figurines). Use your library, investigate museums. If you intend to repair more than one or two pieces of china, paste pictures from old antiques magazines into a scrapbook for future reference.

Materials and tools

Epoxy-resin putty (either home-made or ready-bought, which can be easier to model with, see p. 107) can be used for all kinds of intricate modelling. To model fine details, make sure the epoxy build-up is really thick by adding plenty of filling powder. If you intend to paint, add a little titanium dioxide to give you a white base colour. If you wish to use the coloured filler method (see pp. 106-9), add the appropriate pigments.

Do not begin modelling immediately, because the material is initially too soft to support its shape when you are making something as delicate as fingers or a complicated flower. Leave the filler for about two hours, depending on room temperature, by which time it will have started to harden; you will still have at least an hour before it becomes too hard to manipulate.

Orange sticks, wooden cocktail sticks, scalpels, tweezers, probes and any other small modelling tools, dipped in water or acetone, are all useful for modelling – the more you have on hand the better.

Left: On a figurine, the parts most prone to damage – some may even be missing – are the extremities. This harlequin is a valuable Meissen piece.

Cup handle

Research the missing cup handle as discussed on p. 110 then draw it out on a piece of card. Make your drawing lifesize so that you can use it as a template. Hold your drawing against the cup and check that it looks right.

Make up some stiff epoxy-resin filler (see p. 107) and leave it for about an hour, then roll it thin. If it does not roll out well, leave it for another half an hour or hour and repeat. Place the roll on your template, bend it to the correct shape and cut it to size. Make sure that your core of putty is thinner than the finished handle, then leave it until it is nearly dry.

Take this cup handle core and bond it on to the cup with some fresh epoxy-resin adhesive, with a little filling powder added. Stand the cup in a sand or salt box, and support the cup handle core with plastic modelling clay.

Once the core is firmly set, build up the handle with more putty and add any necessary embellishments.

Abrade and finish as described on p. 109.

If you have to replace a cup handle, make sure that the style is in keeping with the rest of the cup – this may require research.

Modelling a cup handle

1 Draw out the handle on a piece of card.

2 Check that the shape looks right against the cup.

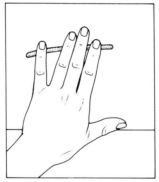

3 Roll out a thin core of epoxy-resin putty.

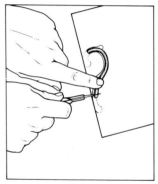

4 Bend it around the template; cut off the excess.

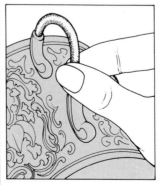

5 Bond the core to the cup with epoxy resin.

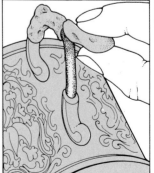

6 When the glue is dry, continue modelling on the cup.

Flowers

Use partly hardened epoxy-resin putty to make flowers, petals, leaves and so on, and put a little filling powder on your workboard or tile to prevent the putty from sticking.

Petals and leaves

For missing petals and leaves, roll or press a pellet of putty to the required thickness and cut it to shape using a scalpel dipped in acetone. Scrape a little adhesive on to the broken china and carefully transfer your petal or leaf. Support it with plastic modelling clay. If necessary, carry on modelling once it is attached to the piece, then leave it to dry. Finish as described on p. 109.

Whole flowers

There will probably be unbroken flowers on your ornament and you can copy from these as you model. Examine them carefully to see how they were made. The more closely you copy the methods of the original modeller, the better match your own flowers will be.

Simple flowers on china were often made in one piece, and consist of four or five petals, sometimes with a slightly raised centre.

With your fingers, make a small ball of putty and shape it into a cone – the pointed end will be the stem of your flower. Hold the stem in one hand, and, with a round stick, make a hole down the centre of the wide end of the cone. With a sharp stick or scalpel dipped in acetone, indent or cut away the edges to make the required number of petals. If you need a raised centre, add a small 'dome' of putty. Leave it to dry and finish as described on p. 109.

Roses are easier to make than they look. Flatten an oval of putty into an elongated shape, and curl it round a tiny ball for the centre. Flatten petals into fan shapes and place them alternately round the folded centre, so that they stand slightly higher than it. Tease the petals outwards into naturalistic shapes with your fingers or modelling tool, then gently roll and squeeze the base of the flower into the shape of the stem. Leave it to dry and finish as described on p. 109.

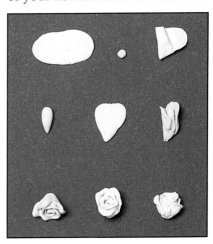

Leave the modelling material until it is firm enough to be pressed out very thin and will hold its shape without drooping.

Modelling replacements for missing flowers is very satisfying and not as difficult as it looks.

Hands

China figures with missing hands or fingers present the restorer with the most difficult job he is likely to undertake. Nevertheless, with a little perseverance, and practice, excellent results can be achieved. The best way to practise is to make hands in plastic modelling clay.

Look carefully at the figurine. Can you visualize a natural position for the hand? It is dependent on the posture of the whole figure, especially the arm. It may help to try out different hand positions *in situ* using plastic modelling clay. Perhaps the hand is holding something? If you cannot find an exact copy in a book, study as many similar figurines as possible; china figures are usually very stylized and themes and postures are repeated endlessly.

When you have decided on the positioning of the hand and fingers, study the style. It would be quite out of keeping to model a beautiful hand showing every knuckle and fingernail on a rough Staffordshire figure, for example. The intact hand is the most valuable guide for this. Next, consider the size. As you model, keep checking the other hand, making sure the one you are working on is the same size, not only in length and width, but in thickness. A pair of dividers or callipers can be a great help here. Note that a hand is just a little smaller than a face.

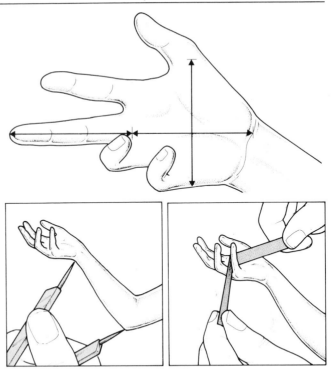

Note the proportions of your own hand, and use callipers to check the length of a modelled arm, for example. Use a thin strip of glasspaper to rub down between fingers.

Refer constantly to your own hand. If it is awkward to put your hand in the position of your modelled hand, then adjust your modelling. Study your own hand, each finger has three sections, and the tip of each is turned up (this is often exaggerated on china figures). See how the thumb is placed in relation to the fingers. The length of the longest finger is about the length of the palm, which is also the width of the palm, including the thumb (see above).

Always dip your tools, probes, scalpels and so on in water or acetone as you model. This will stop them sticking to the putty and pulling it out of shape.

When the hand is roughly correct but still pliable, bond it on to the arm with slow-setting epoxy resin, then make any minor adjustments. Support as described on p. 100. When the hand is dry, carefully abrade it with files and abrasive papers, then add more putty, modelling as necessary. Make sure that the join is smooth with no filler overlapping.

When you model replacement hands, make sure that they fit the style of the piece; they may be naturalistic or stylized.

Project 5: Art deco clowns

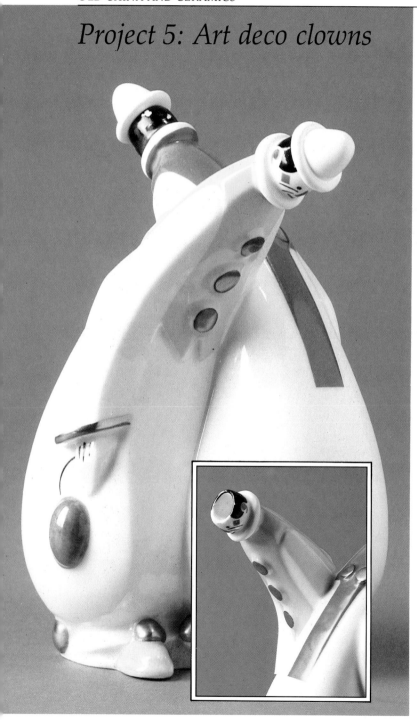

Making moulds

Although, as we have seen (pp. 110-13), modelling missing parts is not as difficult as first impressions might suggest, if you have an exact replica of a missing part, you will save a lot of time by making a mould. This is quite a common occurrence. You might, for example, have a double-handled vase, with one handle missing. In this case, make a mould of the handle you have and use it to produce an exact copy. Even if both handles are missing, you will still save time by modelling only the first and making a mould for the second.

The photograph illustrates this problem. These amusing art deco clowns were probably made to hold oil and vinegar. A photograph showed that their original tops were conical hats with corks embedded in them. Both tops are missing, but it will only be necessary to model one, and then construct a mould to make a copy.

For the mould, you will need some liquid latex rubber, which can be obtained from art or hardware shops where it is often sold as carpet or fabric adhesive. Briefly, the outside of the modelled hat is covered in latex which forms the mould. This is then removed and a liquid filler poured in. The most suitable liquid filler to use is liquid epoxy resin, but this is not always easy to obtain. You can, however, use ordinary epoxy resin if you heat it carefully first. This, when it has solidified, will give you a replica of the first hat.

You will also need a handful of sawdust, cotton-wool buds (Q-tip swabs), and, finally, an ordinary domestic oven.

A word of warning about latex: it can sometimes lift gilding off, so if you want to use this method on a gilded piece, test a tiny area first.

Modelling the first hat

Find two suitably sized corks. Model a hollow hat using an epoxy-resin putty (see pp. 107 and 110) and check that half the cork will fit inside.

When the first hat is modelled to your satisfaction, wash it to remove any dirt, grease and loose filling powder, and leave it to dry.

Left: *The most efficient method of replacing these clowns' hats is to model the first, make a rubber latex mould of it, then use this to make an exact replica.*

Moulding the second hat

Pour some liquid latex on to a saucer and dab it on the outside of the hat to the edge of the rim with a cotton-wool bud. This first coat of latex is the most important. Latex is very delicate, so do not touch or disturb it in any way. You will need three coats of latex, and should leave each to dry before applying the next.

Finally, to ensure that the mould is strong and fairly rigid, mix some sawdust with more latex and 'pat' it on with your fingers. Leave that until it is dry, then carefully remove the mould.

To make a liquid filler, mix some slow-setting epoxy resin and transfer it to a small, preferably disposable, container. Mix in some titanium dioxide to give it colour, then stir it thoroughly. Leave it for about 15 minutes to give the mixture time to settle, then place the container in the oven at a low temperature (about 120°C, 250°F). Check it every few minutes, because the resin only remains liquid for a few minutes, after which it hardens, so it is easy to leave it too long. If you do, discard the resin and begin again.

After about 10 minutes, the resin will have liquefied. Take it out of the oven (do not forget that the container will be hot, so use a tea towel/pot holder), invert the mould – a sandbox is ideal for holding it steady – and slowly pour the filler into the mould. So that you can embed the cork in the clown's hat, only half-fill the mould with resin and leave it for 24 hours to dry. Then make up some more liquid filler, place the cork in the centre, and fill around it to the brim. Leave this to dry for 24 hours, then remove the mould. The new hat will not be perfect, so abrade and fill it as described on p. 109. Finally the hats can be painted (see pp. 116-21).

Leave the liquid epoxy resin to harden for at least 24 hours before you remove it from the mould.

Making a latex mould

1 Dab latex on to model with a cotton-wool bud.

2 Speed drying under the heat of an angle-poise lamp.

3 Use three layers of latex; mix sawdust with the third.

4 Fill the mould with liquid epoxy resin.

Two-part moulds

If you need a mould of something like a whole head, or a complete handle, you might find it impossible to remove the mould without distorting or breaking it. In this case, you can make a two-part mould. With a head, for example, make one mould for the face, and one for the back of the head.

Before making the face-side mould, press some plastic modelling clay over the surface of the back of the head, to act as a barrier against the first mould and to define its edge. Make one or two indentations on the clay, where it meets the first mould, to help you align the two half-moulds. Make the first half-mould as if it were a one-piece mould and leave it to set. When it has set, remove the modelling clay. Smear some washing-up (dishwashing) liquid or petroleum jelly around the edge of the set latex – this acts as a releasing agent when you need to separate the half-moulds. Now make the second mould, and when this has set, remove both. Join them together with a thin coat of latex, and proceed as for one-piece moulds.

Project 6: Eagle figure

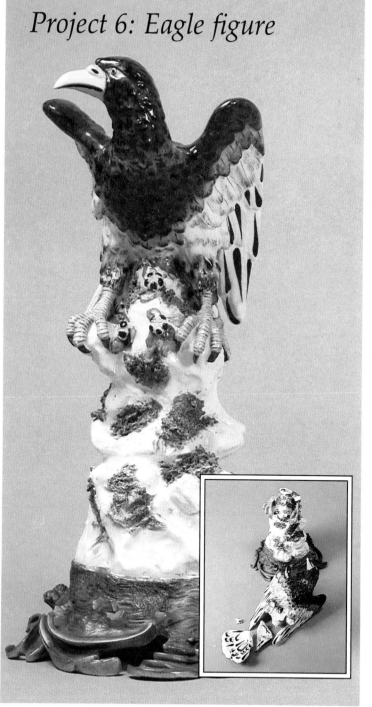

Painting techniques

Earlier (pp. 106-9), coloured filler was used to fill in a chip in a vase. Coloured filler is an easy and effective way of making breaks and chips more acceptable to the eye; but they are never invisible. If you want to achieve an invisible or near invisible repair, it is necessary to paint.

Painting well on ceramics can be difficult and time-consuming although the results can be spectacular on many pieces of decorated and ornamental china. Such results are well within the capabilities of the amateur, given practice and the right methods and materials, though of course some pieces are by their nature more difficult to repair invisibly than others.

At first sight, this broken figure of an eagle may look like a daunting repair for an amateur to undertake. All the techniques involved in the reconstruction of the figure, however, have been discussed already in relation to earlier projects; here, they are all brought together and can be adapted to any other figure.

Whatever paints, pigments or glaze mediums you use, the painting technique is the same. The background colour (often, as here, white or nearly white) is applied first, followed by the decorative shades. Look closely at the eagle to determine the order in which the colours were originally applied; if you are able to copy this process, your repair and restoration will be more authentic.

Left: *Do not be tempted to save time by filling in and retouching a previous repair. As with this eagle, first dismantle and thoroughly clean each piece, then reconstruct the figure.*

116

Reconstructing the eagle

Remove every particle of glue, old filling material and paint, and clean each piece of the eagle carefully (as described on p. 103), then wash, rinse, and leave them to dry.

Reconstruct the eagle one piece at a time with slow-setting epoxy resin. Each added piece must be left to dry, strapped and supported in a way which is appropriate to it, before the next is joined on (see p. 100). As a general rule, on ornamental figures, do not be tempted to try bonding more than one piece at any one time.

Filling and modelling

Use made-up or ready-made white epoxy-resin putty to fill in chips, and to model the missing flowers and legs (see pp. 107 and 110-13). All the filled surfaces, but especially the joins, must be perfectly smooth to the touch before you begin to paint; if they are not, the base coats of paint will always highlight, rather than mask, the discrepancies (see p. 109).

Filling in joins

However well you have bonded together two pieces of china, there will be, at least, a hairline crack. For an

To achieve an invisible restoration, all the joins and cracks must be filled in and rubbed down level with the surface.

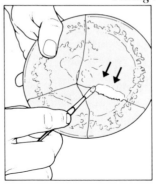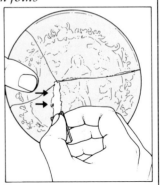

Filling in joins

1 *Fill joins from the lower side to the higher.*   **2** *Rub down from the higher side to the lower.*

invisible repair even these cracks must be filled and smoothed before you start painting. One side of the join will probably be a fraction higher than the other, so run a scalpel across the join to detect which. Sometimes, the alignment will change along the crack, from one side to the other.

Make up some thin putty as described on p. 107, using less filling powder than for modelling or filling in chips, and fill the join from the *lower* side to the *higher*. Be as neat as you can and try not to overlap far on to the 'higher' side. When it has dried, rub down from the *higher* side to the *lower* in separate strokes. The filler should feather off on the lower side and leave a join that you cannot feel with your fingers. Repeat the process as many times as necessary.

Finish with a fine surface filler, or if you have difficulty obtaining that, make up your own (see p. 10) and apply this to the required area. Rub down the final thin filler with flour paper, once again working from the higher side to the lower.

Keep some of your used pieces of flour paper. They are useful to give an extra fine polish on your work; alternatively, buy the finest grade (1200) of silicon carbide wet and dry paper.

When the filling in and rubbing down have been completed, take your scalpel and scrape off any superfluous bits of filler on the piece. Wash the eagle thoroughly to remove any loose filling powder, dirt and grease, and leave it until it is bone dry.

It is now ready to be painted.

Pigments and paints

In project 3 (pp. 106-9), we saw how dry ground artist's pigments can be used to colour filler. These pigments can also be used as a base for your paints. Buy them in the smallest quantities you can, as a little tends to go a long way.

Pigments have to be mixed into a glaze or varnish medium (see p. 119), so that they can be applied by brush. Some pigments disperse better than others. As a convenient alternative, small pots of ready-mixed enamel paints are widely available in model shops, toy shops and department stores. Initially, they are cheaper than buying a full range of powder pigments, but more expensive in the long run and less versatile.

In some art or craft shops, you may find ranges of enamel-type paints specially designed for painting on china or glass. If you buy ready-made paints, make sure you purchase the clear varnish or glaze, and plenty of the thinners which are sold with them.

Colours

The names of the same colours can vary according to the manufacturer, so if you are in any doubt, take this colour chart to the shop and check them.

Metallic colours see pp. 99 and 101.

White
You will already have titanium dioxide, which is essential for whitening filler. Buy this pigment in larger quantities, unless you are using ready-made paints.

Black
The densest is the best; this is usually called *lamp black*.

Blues
Ultramarine: a warm blue with a slight red hue.

Monastral, or astral blue: a cool blue tending towards green.

Indigo: a dark blue with a violet tone.

Greens
Monastral, or astral green: a rich green, tending towards blue.

Oxide of chrome: a lighter, more yellow green.

Browns
Burnt umber: a rich, chocolate brown, tending towards red.

Raw umber: an earthy, yellow-brown.

Yellows
Yellow ochre: an earthy, slightly brown yellow.

Lemon yellow: tending towards green.

Cadmium: a sunshine yellow.

Reds
Cadmium red: a bright red, tending towards orange.

Crimson alizarin: a red tending towards maroon.

Venetian red: an earthy red-brown.

Varnishes and glaze mediums

If you use powder pigments, you must also buy a clear glaze or varnish medium and the appropriate thinning agent. Art and craft shops sell various types of varnishes, some of which are suitable for china restoration, so check the labels or instruction leaflets. Also, the clear varnish sold with the ready-made enamel-type paints can be bought separately and mixed with artist's powder pigments.

Most professional restorers use one, or both, of two types of glazes, which are not generally available. However, some art or craft shops do sell (or may order) them. If you can buy these, do so, as they are superior in various ways to most other varnishes.

The first type of glaze (a urea formaldehyde resin) sets with the addition of a catalyst, and is then workable for 24 hours if you keep it in an airtight bottle, or for two days or more if kept in a refrigerator.

The second type is stoving enamel glaze. For this you need a (preferably electric) oven or plate warmer. After each application the piece is placed in the oven for an hour at a very low temperature (90-120°C, 200-250°F). Once removed from the oven and left to cool, the glaze is very tough and the next stage of painting can be overlaid immediately, unlike all the other varnishes which often need up to 24 hours to harden. Stoving enamel glaze is probably the hardest and most yellow-resistant varnish available. Most pieces can be treated with stoving enamel but exercise discretion and do not put very delicate or old pieces in an oven. Always remove any metal rims, bases and so on before stoving any piece.

The setting time of all varnishes (except the stoving type) can be speeded up if you place the piece in a warm environment, such as the top of a radiator, or under an angle-poise lamp. Do not be tempted to add more coats of paint until the one underneath has set to its maximum hardness.

When you buy them, varnishes are usually thicker than you will need for china restoration. It is a good idea to decant some into a small jar and add thinning agent; the amount will depend on the varnish (experience will teach you the correct proportion), and work with this thinned varnish.

Always keep a separate small glass jar of thinners for cleaning brushes, tiles and so on.

Painting techniques

1 Mix paints and pigments in a metal dipper.

2 Transfer thinners and varnishes with a dropper.

3 Use finest quality sable brushes for painting.

4 Cure stoving enamels in an oven.

Painting

Your paintbrushes should be finest quality sable, and numbers 00 and 2 are probably the most useful to begin with. Look after your brushes, clean them in whatever thinning agent you are using before the paint on the brush dries out. Do not use your sable brushes to mix pigments – they will quickly be ruined. Instead, use an old, larger, *clean* brush (about size 6).

The more tiny glass jars with lids you have the better. These are useful for keeping and decanting solvents, made-up paints, thinners and so on. Use an eye-dropper for transferring thinners and varnishes – never a brush, however clean you may think it is.

Small metal dippers for mixing up pigments or paints can be purchased from art shops. Clean them in thinners immediately after use. Metal bottle tops, small egg cups and so on can be used instead, in fact, any small clean receptacle, as long as it is not plastic. Use soft toilet paper or cotton rags dipped in thinners for cleaning up.

Base coats and background colours

Almost all pieces of china have a white background. If you look more closely, however, the white background is actually never pure white; observe this yourself by comparing a pure white tile with any piece of china. You must aim to match the background perfectly; this is sometimes the most difficult part of colour matching.

Applying base coats

Before you apply the background colour, paint a coat of pure white colour along the lines of the cracks, joins, and modelled parts to cover all the filler. Try not to overlap on to the original china by more than a fraction. A number 2 brush is usually appropriate. Apply the paint, which should be the consistency of thin cream, in one smooth stroke over each area, so there are no brushstrokes visible.

There will be a hard line at the edges of the paint where it meets the original china. You can feather this out by cleaning your brush and applying short angled strokes of pure glaze along the edge. Do this immediately before the paint starts to dry, which it will after only a minute or two, for all paints other than stoving enamels. Practise this feathering out technique on a black tile. Feathering out hard lines is important – the join will never become invisible if you don't do it.

After about 10 minutes, depending on the medium, apply a coat of clear glaze or varnish over the painted

After you have finished filling in and modelling, apply the first base coat; this should be pure white, followed by a tinted background colour.

area. Paint it as lightly and swiftly as possible, or the thinners in the glaze may disturb the painting underneath. If it does, try applying a slightly thicker glaze (that is, with less thinners).

When this first coat has thoroughly dried (or stoved if you are using a stoving glaze), examine the restoration so far. The paint will highlight any discrepancies, holes, ridges and imperfectly filled cracks and joins. Small blemishes may disappear with subsequent coats of paint, but you may well have to return to the filling in stage, using a fine surface filler, then rub that down and paint on another coat of white paint and glaze. To obliterate the joins completely, you may need several coats of white paint, each covered with a coat of glaze. To avoid a lumpy look and feel, carefully abrade with the finest flour paper or wet and dry you have, after each coat of glaze or varnish. Rub down from the centre of the paint to the outside. If you work from the outside inwards, you may lift off the paint.

Colour matching the background

When all the joins are invisible, you are ready to paint on the background colour. This is white, with minute quantities of colour. Take a number of pieces of china, both ornamental and domestic, and study their background colours. Almost invariably you will find they are either a 'cool' tone, tending towards blue, or a 'warm' tone tending towards yellow. Most oriental and hard-paste chinas are cool, while softer paste ceramics tend to be warm. For cool tones, with your white, mix in tiny amounts of both ultramarine and yellow ochre. For warm tones, mix in a few grains of burnt umber and lemon yellow. Occasionally, you may need to add traces of other colours; the exact amounts, of course, vary from piece to piece.

In a dipper, put some white, plus a little glaze and thinners to make the consistency of thin cream, and adjust it to the correct background colour. Add drops of thinners occasionally with an eye-dropper, so that the paint does not dry out. Test your colour matching by dabbing a little on an original part of the china. Clean it off with thinners immediately afterwards.

Apply the background colour in the same way as you did the white base coats, finishing with a coat of glaze. If the match is not perfect, leave it to dry, rub it down lightly and try again.

Decoration: transparent and semi-transparent colours

A transparent colour is pure colour, semi-transparent colours contain some white. Look closely at your piece. On the eagle, there are a number of bright colours; a yellow beak, green foliage, purple flowers, and black, grey and brown feathers. There are also light washes of colour underneath some of the bright colours. In fact, there are fewer colours than appearance suggests. The grey, for example, is a watery black and the light yellow is the same as the yellow on the beak but less dense.

For light washes, put some glaze medium into your dipper or, if you need only a small amount of paint, on your tile. Then add pigments or paints, until you achieve the correct tint. Add thinners as necessary. These washes are often semi-transparent colours and need some white in their composition.

Apply the paint by flowing it on to the china rather than in neat brushstrokes. Test on a nearby, but unrestored, part for colour match. Once painted, protect the coat with a layer of clear varnish.

The denser, bright colours, are mostly pure colour with little glaze added, or, if you are using ready-made paints, no glaze at all. Adding a tiny bit of raw umber is often the best way to darken a colour.

Remember that you are working over a delicate background colour. If you make a mistake in decorat-

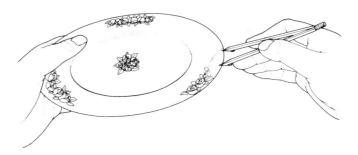

If you have a repeated pattern, round the edge of a plate, for example, use callipers to measure distances.

ing, cleaning it off with thinners can disturb the base coats. If this happens, leave it to dry, rub down and apply more base coats. However, if you have painted a thin line too thickly, you can take a clean brush, barely dampened in thinners, and run it along the edge of the line. This will thin and neaten the line without disturbing the paint underneath. Do this as soon as possible, before the paint dries too much.

To finish, cover all your work in a final coat of clear varnish or glaze medium.

If the decoration stands too proud of the surface, after applying the final coat of varnish and letting it dry, lightly rub down the surface with your finest abrasive paper, then finish off with more clear varnish. This process can be repeated again if necessary.

Hints on painting

Difficult decoration can be pencilled in lightly on the area to be painted with a hard pencil.

For a **matt finish**, add some talcum powder to the glaze medium. The more you add, the less glossy will be the finish.

Some **crazing** on china can be effectively imitated by very thin lines of paint (often raw umber and a touch of white, in a suitably thinned medium).

On **blue and white ceramics**, use ultramarine and indigo, *never* astral blue for the blue.

Flesh colour is semi-transparent, that is composed of glaze medium, white and thinners, plus some yellow ochre and cadmium red. If there is a 'flush' of transparent colour over this semi-transparent one, use the same formula, but without the white.

Typical crazing on a Staffordshire figure. With practice, it is possible to paint lines thinly enough to simulate crazing.

Project 7: Ceramic tiles

In this section, we will examine the techniques involved in restoring old ceramic tiles. They also apply to other soft-bodied ceramics, such as pottery, earthenware and plaster figures.

Cleaning and bonding

Be more careful than usual when you clean soft-bodied ceramics. Unglazed ceramic crumbles and flakes quite easily when subjected to a scalpel or even medium-grade abrasive papers. Also, the material can be so porous that it soaks up water like a sponge. Although it will dry out again, if the edge of the break is very grimy, the water may carry the dirt underneath the glaze and leave a stain. For this reason, never use the hydrogen-peroxide method of stain removal (p. 103). Similarly, prolonged soaking in water softener and biological detergent is not recommended. Soapy water can be used to clean many types of soft ceramics, but if you are in any doubt, just de-grease and try to remove stains by using the various solvents like acetone. Test them on a small piece first.

Soft pottery is so porous that bonding with epoxy resins is not very effective, because much of the adhesive soaks into the pottery. Use PVA (yellow) adhesive, which is usually sold as wood glue, instead.

It is unlikely that you will be able to achieve the sort of hairline join on soft pottery possible on china because it crumbles so easily, and flakes and chips of pottery will probably have broken off when it was originally damaged. Once you have bonded a piece, you should fill the imperfect joins.

Filling in soft-bodied ceramics

The smooth, hard, china-like finish of epoxy-resin filler is not appropriate to unglazed soft-bodied ceramics, which are more easily damaged when you come to sanding down. Also the texture is quite different. You should use a filler which is softer when set, and gives a matt, coarser finish – the types sold for filling in small cracks and holes in walls and plaster are ideal. You can also add dry artist's pigments to them if you want coloured filler; this often looks very effective on pottery.

Left: *These typical Victorian tiles are made of a soft, porous ceramic with a glaze on the top surface.*

Filling in tiles

Tiles, though composed of soft pottery, have a tough glaze on the surface, so filling in with epoxy-resin filler is quite suitable. Fill in and rub down as described on pp. 107-9. To fill a missing corner make a wall of small toy interlocking bricks or use plastic modelling clay or other straight-sided objects to support the filler.

Put the tile and wall on a disposable piece of card in case the filler runs underneath. Smear petroleum jelly on and under the wall and tile; this acts as a releasing agent when the liquid filler has dried. To reduce run-off, either place weights on the wall, or attempt to seal around it with plastic modelling clay. Underfill slightly, rather than overfill. When it has dried, this filler is very hard, and it is very time-consuming to rub it down even if you have only slightly overfilled.

When the filler is dry, remove the wall, then fill in and rub down as described on p. 109.

Painting

Paint the tile as described on pp. 120-1. Use several white base coats, and then apply the background colour. Use a coat of glaze medium over each, and lightly rub down all the coats except the last one.

Hand paint the decoration, using either ground pigments in a glaze medium or ready-bought paints, and finish with a coat of glaze.

Simple breaks

Bond a simple break, such as in the tile illustrated here, which is broken in half, with PVA adhesive (wood glue). First, make a thin solution of PVA by adding water, and then paint it on to both sides of the break with an old clean paintbrush. It will be soaked up immediately, but it will form a barrier so that when you apply neat PVA (to *both* sides of the join), it will work effectively.

Clear adhesive tape does not stick well to unglazed surfaces, so to support the tile while the glue dries (about 24 hours), bring the two halves together on as

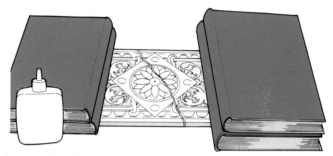

Use woodworking glue to bond tiles and support the join between two heavy books until the adhesive is dry.

level a surface as possible. If one side of the join is slightly higher than the other, place pieces of plastic modelling clay underneath the lower half of the tile to raise it up slightly. Adjust it in this way until the join is level. You should now put some weight on either side of the tile – heavy books are ideal. Do not use a tourniquet on broken tiles, or other flat objects – since it is not usually very rigid, it often tends to make the joins misalign.

As we have seen, often the most difficult and time-consuming aspect of painting a piece is to match the background colour satisfactorily. In many cases, however, this is not necessary and, if you wish, quite acceptable and fast results can be achieved by omitting this stage and simply painting on the decoration once the piece has been bonded and filled. This is particularly suitable for tiles with large areas or flat colour.

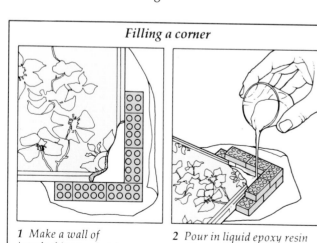

1 Make a wall of interlocking toy bricks.	*2 Pour in liquid epoxy resin and leave until set.*

Filling a corner

5

RUGS
and
CARPETS

The hand-woven oriental carpet can be one of the most beautifully made objects in the world. This is in part due to their status, for to their makers oriental carpets are not just functional coverings. Rug-making occupies the greater part of the weavers' daily life, and with their delicacy of design and artistic interpretation carpets are a vital element in their history and culture.

As all oriental rugs are made from perishable, natural fibres it is inevitable that over the years even the best-cared-for rug will suffer some kind of deterioration, either in the loss of pile, damage to the side cords or fraying of the fringes. Although rugs often have complex patterns, the basic techniques of rug repair are not difficult to learn; what they call for is a painstaking approach, common sense and the correct guidance, but with all these the amateur can achieve excellent results.

This section has been organized into chapters covering the kind of damage commonly found in old rugs, with simple and easy explanations of how to restore them. Before looking at them, however, you need to learn something of how oriental carpets are made.

Basic rug techniques

Oriental rugs fall into two types, depending on the way they are made: knotted-pile rugs, and flat-woven or tapestry-type rugs. Flat weaving is by far the older technique and pre-dates pile knotting considerably. Pile knotting, which seems to have begun some time after 1000BC, produces rugs of a soft rich texture particularly suitable as floor coverings.

The pile of an oriental rug is usually made of spun sheep's wool, although goat or camel hair is occasionally used by nomadic tribes. Cotton and jute are used principally for the warp and weft foundations of rugs, though not for the pile. An exception to this is to be found in Turkish Kayseri rugs, which are woven completely of cotton; it has first undergone a chemical process known as mercerizing, which gives the surface of the fibre a very high, shiny finish and is thus sometimes called artificial silk.

Many fine pile rugs are made of natural silk, either in the foundation warps or in the entire rug. Such rugs are the most prestigious and sought-after of all oriental rugs. Flat-weave kelims and soumaks are nearly always made of wool, although sometimes of silk, cotton or of part-cotton.

The loom

Handmade rugs are still woven on a loom that has remained basically unchanged for centuries, which may be placed either vertically or horizontally, and is essentially a fixed frame designed to hold the foundation threads, or warps, of the rug under tension in order to allow knotting. Its length and width together govern the size of the completed carpet; a wide loom can accommodate several weavers.

The horizontal loom, or ground loom, has two bars lying parallel to each other which are held in position by stakes which have been firmly driven into the ground at each end. This type of loom is preferred by the nomadic tribes as it can be easily dismantled and carried around. The weavers working on it sit side by side on top of the completed woven pile as they progress along the warp. This explains why tribal rugs do not always lie flat, due to the varying tension created by the weavers' weights.

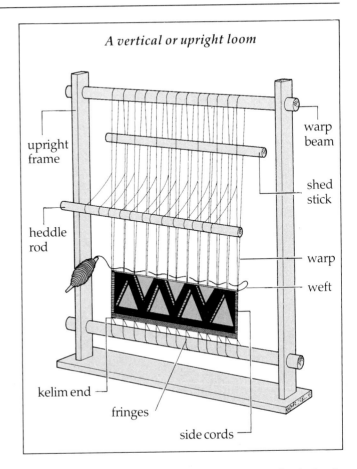

A vertical or upright loom

upright frame

heddle rod

kelim end

fringes

side cords

warp beam

shed stick

warp

weft

The vertical loom, or upright loom, is similar in basic construction to the ground loom, but it is held upright by two posts placed at either side of the beams, which make it much harder to transport. The weaver sits on a plank directly in front of the area of the carpet on which she is working. She weaves from the bottom up, and as the work progresses the plank is raised higher to the appropriate position.

For the weaving of very long carpets a variation on this latter loom, known as the vertical roller beam loom, is used. The warp threads are secured to the bottom beam and then wound around the top beam as many times as is necessary to accommodate the complete length of the required carpet. As the weaving progresses the completed section is rolled up around the bottom beam whilst the warps are unwound from the upper beam.

Pile knotting

All oriental pile rugs are hand-knotted on foundation threads known as the warp. This consists of parallel vertical threads held under tension by the loom. The number of warp threads used determines the fineness of the rug weave, and the finer the rug the more warp threads it has. To form the pile, short lengths of yarn are knotted to each pair of warp threads across the width of the carpet. When a row of knots is complete the weft is added to hold the pile in position. This is a continuous length of yarn that runs over and under alternate warps; it may be made up of one or more strands of yarn of the same, or different, thickness and texture.

When the weft has been inserted, the row is beaten down tightly against the preceding rows with a heavy comb-like hammer before the next row of pile is woven. Any excess of pile yarn is then cut off with a knife in one swift continuous movement after each knot is tied, and then trimmed with scissors after the completion of each row. In some cases, depending on local tradition, the pile may be trimmed to the required height after completion.

It is in the knotting process that the design is formed – by arranging the different coloured knotted yarns in various positions. The nomadic weaver works from memory, often to a design which has been handed down through many generations, but she – or, less often, he – may add small variations of her own, perhaps to celebrate a happening in the family, or possibly even just at whim. The weaver in a town or village, working in a more organized way, usually uses a pattern copying it from a design drawn on squared paper – a cartoon – where each square represents a single knot. Weavers in India often copy designs from written instructions.

A hand-knotted oriental rug showing the complex design formed by knotting various coloured yarns.

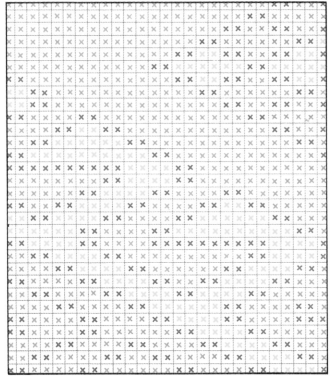

Detail of the pattern design, or cartoon, of the rug (left) with each square representing a knot.

Knots

The knots in a pile rug may be tied to the warp threads in different ways. In hand-made oriental rugs the two most common types are the symmetrical Turkish or Ghiordes knot, and asymmetrical Persian or Senneh knot. Both of these are tied around two warp threads. If the weaver wishes to proceed more quickly or make a much coarser rug she may use a Jufti knot, which may be either Persian or Turkish in type but is tied around four warp threads instead of two. There is also a knot which is tied around one warp only – the Spanish knot. This knot is tied to alternate warps in the same horizontal row and then staggered in the following rows.

The four types of knot

1 Turkish/Ghiordes knot *2 Senneh/Persian knot*

3 Turkish Jufti knot *4 Spanish knot*

Turkish and Persian knots

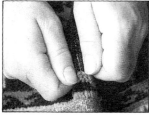 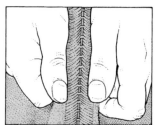

1 To determine the design of the knot, bend the rug back from the knots on both sides.

 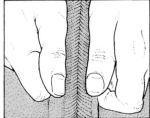

2 If you can part the two end threads and the warp is visible, (left) the knot is asymmetrical (Persian).

The type of knot used has little practical significance although the Turkish knot may be somewhat more secure while the Persian knot is more easily adapted to a closely woven and denser pile. As its name indicates the Turkish knot is used primarily in Turkey, and also in western Iran and in the Caucasus, while the Persian knot is generally used in central and eastern Iran, India and China. There are some exceptions, however, and in areas of Iran where the people are of Turkish descent the Turkish knot will almost certainly be used.

In order to determine whether a rug has been woven with Turkish or Persian knots, first find a line of knots where the design is only one knot wide and also runs parallel with the warp threads. Bend the rug back from the rows of knots on both sides and see if you can part the two end threads of the knot. If you are unable to, the knot is symmetrical (Turkish); if you can and the warp is visible, the knot is asymmetrical (Persian).

A pile carpet will have a massive number of knots, so speed of operation is essential. An experienced weaver can tie between 5,000 and 10,000 knots per day, depending on the fineness of the weave and the complexity of the design.

Kelim ends, fringes and side cords

At each end of the rug, the interweaving of the weft through the warp strands is used to form the foundation of what are called 'kelim ends'. These have both a protective and often decorative purpose and are made by weaving weft threads in and out of the warp and then beating them down with a metal comb. This technique is known as flat weaving. It is often used to weave entire rugs, which are then called kelims (see below). The kelim end is, however, found on pile rugs.

The depth of the kelim end can vary from 12mm (½in.) to 25mm (1in.), depending on the origin of the rug. Some tribal rugs, however, have kelim ends of 150mm (6in.) or more.

The warp threads continuing after the kelim ends form the fringes or tassels. Some rugs have the cut warp woven into a complicated braided band at one end and the more normal cut fringe at the other.

The sides of the rug, on the other hand, are usually secured by 'side cords', also known as selvedges. These are composed of one or more warp threads (in the latter case twisted together) bound by the weft threads. Alternatively, wefts are woven in and out in a figure-of-eight through several pairs of warps.

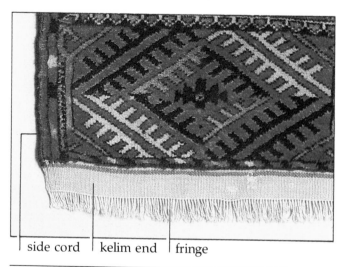

| side cord | kelim end | fringe |

Flat weaving

A kelim (the Turkish term) or gelim (in Persian) is a flat blanket-like fabric which is created by passing the weft threads in front of and behind alternate warps without any knotted pile. They are often woven on fairly narrow looms and may be constructed from two or more pieces.

The design is formed by the use of different coloured weft threads being carried backwards and forwards across the warps, not from one side of the rug to the other as a continuous thread but only as far as the pattern colour dictates. Where various colours of the design meet, a small split is formed between the two warps.

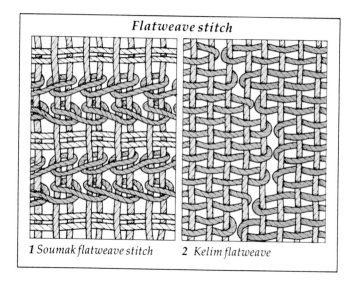

Flatweave stitch

1 Soumak flatweave stitch   *2 Kelim flatweave*

Soumak or weft wrapping is also a flatweave technique but in this case the weft is passed over and under two or four warps and then back again over two warps before being carried forward, so forming a continuous chain structure. Unlike the kelim weave, in which the pattern is usually equally clear on both sides, soumak is single-sided with the loose weft threads showing on the back. Soumaks originate from North-Eastern Iran and the Caucasus.

Kelims and soumaks are usually made of wool although they are sometimes made of silk, sometimes partially of cotton or all cotton.

Distinguishing a hand-woven pile rug from a machine-made copy

Now that you have some familiarity with the knotting techniques of an oriental rug and how the warp and weft are arranged to form the rug foundation, it should be possible for you to distinguish between hand-woven and machine-made rugs.

Machine-made copies can be impressive and at first sight one can easily be mistaken for a hand-woven original, but don't jump to conclusions until you have considered the following points.

Firstly, examine the back of the rug. If the rug is machine-made, the warp and weft will lie in perfect straight lines. Furthermore, only on hand-woven rugs is the pile actually the result of knotting on to warps. On a machine-made rug, each individual tuft can be removed from the front of the rug with a pair of tweezers.

The fringe on hand-woven rugs, as we have seen, is a continuation of the warp threads. On a machine-made rug the fringe is generally oversewn on to the rug.

Finally, the selvedge side on a machine-made rug has the overcast wool secured to the edge with a separate cotton thread similar to a line of sewing-machine stitches; the hand-woven rug has the overcast wool sewn directly between the warp threads in one continuous strand.

Remember that even the finest and most expensive of hand-woven rugs will show irregularities; it is these irregularities which make the rugs charming and unique.

A hand-woven Turkish rug. The fringe is integral, the cord oversewn unevenly, and the pile individually knotted.

The fringe and cord of this machine-made rug are secured with a machined chain stitch, and the pile is unknotted.

Dyes

Natural dyes

The aesthetic appeal of any rug depends in large part on its colours and these are achieved through dyeing. Originally all dyes were made from natural vegetable or animal substances: madder red, for example, came from the root of the madder plant; cochineal red from the cochineal insect; yellow from the weld plant, vine leaves or pomegranate peel; brown from walnut shells or oak bark; orange from henna leaves; blue from the indigo plant, and green from a combination of weld and indigo.

Vegetable dyeing has always been a very delicate and complicated process besides being very time-consuming. It is therefore understandable that in more modern times dyers have sought new and quicker methods to produce a more commercial product.

Synthetic dyes

In 1856 aniline dye was discovered in England by William Henry Perkin. The first colour was violet, or Fuchsine, and was soon followed by many others. Being inexpensive and easy to use it was imported into Persia and Turkey in vast amounts by the late 1860s. Unfortunately, the first aniline dyes were very unstable: blues turned to brownish greys, red faded to mauve, and yellows became greenish browns. The reputation of the oriental rug became seriously affected and people ceased to buy them. In 1903 the use of aniline dye was banned in Persia with very severe penalties being imposed on those who ignored the ruling.

In the 1920s and 1930s a new synthetic chromatic dye was developed in Europe. The quality of this new chrome dye was extremely good; in fact, it was more reliable and permanent than many of the original dyes and it became widely used in all of the rug-producing countries.

Natural dyes are now used only rarely in the production of rugs. However, nomadic weavers generally dyed their own yarn using natural dyes, and they continue to use natural dyes today in some areas. A current project in Turkey – the Dobag Project – actively encourages all weavers to use vegetable dyes as they produce a much more subtle colour than synthetic ones.

Left: *Careful selection of the right colours for restoration is often more important than the quality of the repair.*

Tools and equipment

1 Fringe; 2 Wools; 3 Fine
wire brush for ageing new
wool; 4 Dressmaking shears;
5 Trimming knife with spare
blades; 6,7,8 Various
weights of sewing thread and
cotton for warp and weft;
9 Pile scissors with flat
edge; 10 Fine pliers;
11 Bradawl; 12 Thimbles;
13 Tweezers; 14 Steel
pins; 15 Selection of
various needles; 16 Beeswax.

Most of the tools required for rug restoration can be found in a household needlework box or around the house. Always keep your tools clean and sharp. A blunt blade, besides causing damage by tearing at the fibres, is dangerous. It is the sharpness of the blade that should do the work, not force.

All the materials used must be of pure natural fibre only. Do not use synthetic substitutes however good the colour match, or this will, without doubt, devalue your rug. Repairs must also be carried out by using exactly the same type and thickness of fibre as the original. If the rug has a cotton warp and wool weft then those are the materials you must use. Do not improvise, even as a temporary measure. Thread should always be waxed before use to prevent unwanted knotting. On very fine rugs, if the needle point is pressed into beeswax before each stitch it will make penetration through the knot in the base of the rug much easier.

Linen sewing thread, size 18 for coarse rugs; size 35–60 for finer pieces

Beeswax, which may be purchased in blocks from a chemist, good hardware shop or wood craft shop

Sewing needles all have names and size numbers. You will find the following types and sizes the most useful: Tapestry – sizes 20 and 22; Straws – sizes 2, 6 and 8; Sharps – sizes 6 and 8

Metal thimble to be used on the middle finger. Thimbles are sold in all sizes and are an absolute must for all repairs

Tweezers with square ends

Pliers which must be small, and of good quality to be able to grip a fine needle without slipping

Scissors, either dressmaking 200mm (8in.) straight, curved pile or curved nail scissors

Wire brush of fine brass

Knife, a sharp craft knife or one with a safety blade

Cotton for warp and weft threads. You will need various sizes and colours of bulky fibre

Wool, tapestry and crewel

Small bradawl

Steel pins, 25mm (1in.)

Fringes

There are a number of ways in which a fringe or kelim end can become damaged, not least of which is the stretching and eventual breakage of the fibres caused by being constantly walked on. The first signs of damage to look out for are the untwisting and weakening of the warp threads and the breaking of the weft fibres at the ends of the rug. Should the weft threads in a kelim end actually break away, then the knots themselves are threatened, and if this is not attended to quickly, you can find that your rug is in serious danger of dilapidation.

The method of treating the repair is similar for both fringe and kelim end. There are, in fact, various methods available, and which one you follow depends on your expertise as a repairer and on the finish you are trying to achieve.

All fringes can be secured to stop further fraying by using an oversewing or blanket stitch, as in methods B and C on the following pages, but although both these methods will prevent further deterioration they will not always create an aesthetically acceptable finish. The alternative methods described here may take more time and care but they will enhance the beauty and value of your rug and increase its useful life.

However, it is important to decide on the most appropriate choice for your particular rug from the methods described, before starting any work. The main problem is, of course, how to eliminate the type of restoration which may be undesirable and then have the knowledge of how to make the correct choice of repair without causing any loss of value or detriment to the rug. This will certainly come more easily with experience but to the uninitiated it may at first seem a daunting task to reach a final decision. There are no straightforward rules, but you should not go wrong if you examine the state of the rug carefully and then read through all the alternatives with your rug in mind.

It will be found that most decisions will be simply made by using common sense. For instance, if only one small corner is missing of a rug which is otherwise perfectly sound, it would not be expedient to level the entire end by fraying out one inch of pile across the complete width, thereby losing part of the border just to eliminate the damaged area, when a small reweave of the corner would have sufficed. This adds to the value

Left: *Bokhara rug, before and after repairing a badly frayed and damaged kelim end.*

133

of the rug, whereas losing part of the border would have the opposite effect.

The first priority is to preserve the value of the rug, so do not rush into a repair without careful consideration. When repairing fringes it is very important to test the strength of the existing warp threads by checking to see if they are weak or damaged. It would be totally impractical, for example, to secure the ends by using Method A if the warps are weak, as within a few weeks you would find that they had disintegrated.

Remember, finally, that if after looking at all the methods in relation to your rug you feel that you do not have the skill to carry out the right one, then seek professional advice. No one wants to find they have frayed out a large proportion of border quite unnecessarily.

Removing frayed weft and loose knots

Whichever method you choose for securing the warp threads to stop further fraying you must first ensure that the final row of weft is in a continuous unbroken line across the end of the rug. If several rows of weft have become loose or frayed and the knots on them are either missing or falling out, then they must be removed completely before any securing method can be undertaken on the rug.

Using a blunt needle or bradawl and working from the back of the rug beginning at one edge, very carefully unpick the first line of weft thread which has become loose. If the weft is still secured at both ends cut it with scissors, being careful not to damage the warp threads. Remove the rows of loose knots and weft threads until you reach the last row of damaged knots. At this stage, start picking out each individual knot in turn with tweezers, being very careful not to disturb the next line of weft. Continue until the complete line across the rug is level. Always remove only as many rows as is absolutely necessary, taking account of what the finished work will look like and the balance of the design from one end of the rug to the other.

Method A: Tying with a simple knot

Fringes over 40mm (1½in.) in length can be tied with a simple knot to secure the weft. Even on many new loosely woven rugs it may be found necessary to prevent fraying by using this method where the weaver has failed permanently to secure the final weft. Knotting three or four warps together as described below will prevent any of the loose wefts from gradually sliding beyond the end of the fringe and becoming damaged.

Lay the rug on a flat surface or table, face up, folded in such a way that the fringe is easily accessible and pointing towards you. Twist three or four warp threads together at a time, fold them into a loop, pulling the ends through to form a simple knot. Secure the knot as tight and as close to the weft thread as possible.

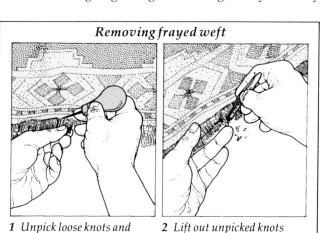

Removing frayed weft

1 Unpick loose knots and weft with a bradawl.

2 Lift out unpicked knots with tweezers.

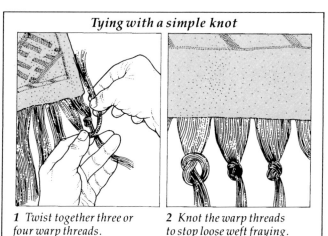

Tying with a simple knot

1 Twist together three or four warp threads.

2 Knot the warp threads to stop loose weft fraying.

Method B: Securing the weft with a simple oversewing stitch

This is probably the easiest stitch for the beginner and is very strong, although it is not the best-looking.

When using Method A it is not possible to secure the knotted warps very tightly against the weft threads and in time this will allow some slight movement. By comparison, Method B will make a very secure and permanent repair by not allowing any misplacement of the weft threads, although in some cases the final finish at the ends of the rug may appear to be incomplete.

Remove the frayed weft and loose knots as described on p. 134. Then lay the rug face downwards with the fringe running away from you. Use a double thickness of strong waxed thread to suit the fineness of the rug and tie a knot in the end. Hold the fringe end in your left hand (if you are right-handed) so as to be able to see the needle point coming out of the rug. Then sew sloping stitches from right to left, pushing the needle away from you, sufficiently deep to be able to catch the line of weft with

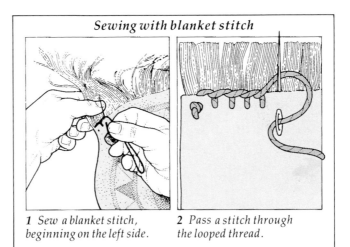

Simple oversewing stitch

1 *Oversew the weft using an even, sloping stitch.* **2** *Pull the thread tightly to depress the weft slightly.*

each stitch and shallow enough not to show through the height of the pile on the front side. Space the stitches about 10mm (³/₈in.) down from the weft and between every three or four warp threads. Pull the thread as tight as is necessary to depress the weft very slightly.

In some cases you may find that you need to use pliers to ease the needle in and out of the fabric.

Method C: Securing the weft with a blanket stitch

Lay the rug face down with the fringe running away from you. Work from left to right with a size 18 waxed thread of a colour to match either the fringe or pile, according to which looks better. Pass the needle through the kelim end parallel to the warps and just under the first weft. Hold a loop of thread down with your left thumb and pass the second stitch in line with the first and through the top of the looped thread. Do not pull too tightly. Continue in this way spacing the stitches evenly between every four or five strands of warp.

Sewing with blanket stitch

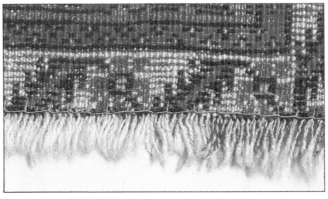

1 *Sew a blanket stitch, beginning on the left side.* **2** *Pass a stitch through the looped thread.*

Turkish rug that was missing part of the end borders. It is being secured with a blanket stitch.

Method D: Chain stitching

This method is probably the most widely used way of joining the warps together, but is more effective on silk or cotton fringes than woollen ones because silk and cotton threads can be pulled more tightly than is usually advisable with the woollen thread. The advantage of this method over the two previous ones is that besides being very secure it will give the rug a more ornate and professional-looking finish. The disadvantage is that if it is not done tightly enough, or if the thread has not been sufficiently waxed, the complete chain can slide off the ends of the warps, especially if it is abused during normal use, such as if it gets caught up in the vacuum cleaner

during cleaning or if it is too vigorously brushed.

Unpick the damaged wefts and knots in the usual way and place the rug pile upwards with the fringe running away from you. Use a single cotton/silk thread, waxed and proportional in thickness to that of the fringe. To secure the end, run the first stitch towards you from the right-hand edge and underneath the overcast wool on the side cord for about 50mm (2in.) and then back again at a slight angle. Pull the thread tightly enough so that the end cannot be seen on the surface. This is better than making a knot which would leave an unsightly lump under the side cord.

The chain stitches are formed by knitting every two warp strands together with the cotton/silk thread, in the following way, butting the knots tightly against the row of weft: pass the thread across the front of each pair of warps and hold it in place with the thumb of the left hand approximately 6mm (¼in.) above the weft. Then pass the needle behind the same two warps from right to left and through the loop held firmly in the left hand, pull to the right, parallel to the weft, to tighten.

Continue knotting each pair of warps across the complete width of the rug ensuring that all stitches are level and of equal tension. Finally, secure the thread as tightly as possible in the left-hand side cord.

Method E: Oversewing with wool

This method gives an excellent finish to a rug, particularly when part of the end border is missing and an extra line of contrasting colour is needed to complete the edge of the original design. It also gives a very strong finish to the end of the rug, particularly on short-piled pieces.

On your first attempt it will probably be found easier to begin from the top end of the rug (i.e. with the pile running down towards you, the knot being above the pair of loose ends) as when working on long-piled rugs it may be difficult, at first, to keep the ends of the tufts from being caught under the oversewn wool. It may also be found necessary to increase the bulk of the continuous strands which are placed across the base of the fringe at the lower end of the rug if part of the end border is missing and a definite contrasting line is needed to complete the finish of the rug. If the bulk is not increased the lay of the pile will cover the sharpness of the new line.

Choose a colour to match the side cord or, if the design is unbroken and it seems more appropriate, the exact

Chain stitching

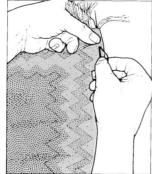

1 Secure the side cord with two stitches.

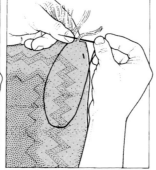

2 Take first loop behind not more than two warp threads.

3 Pull the thread tightly but with even tension.

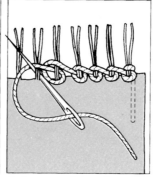

4 Ensure each knot is pressed tightly against a row of weft.

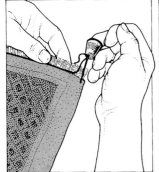

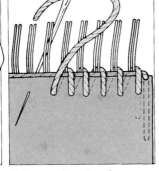

1 *Secure the overlaying wool into side cord.*

2 *Secure the pairs of warp threads with sloped stitches.*

colour of the original. You will need one or more strands of woollen thread to lay across the end of your rug as a new 'weft' and further woollen thread for stitching. Lay the rug face up with the fringe running away from you. Using a tapestry needle pass the 'weft' wool under the side cord to secure the end, and lay it across the complete width of the rug and on top of the fringe, in one continuous strand. Now wax a single wool thread of the same colour and secure this into the side cord as before. Use a simple oversewing stitch to sew each pair of warp threads together along with the overlaid wool, just below the first row of knots.

Method F: Weaving new warp threads for missing fringes

This method is quite a difficult one and is perhaps best avoided by people who do not have any experience of rug restoration.

On coarse rugs with Turkish knots and wool warps this method is not usually difficult, although on the medium to fine pieces with cotton or silk warps and Persian knots it can be extremely tough, especially on the hands, and at times it is very awkward to pull the eye of the needle through the base of the knots. As far as the value of the rug is concerned this system is certainly the best, as even an expert will not be likely to spot the repair, but it does take a great deal of practice to become proficient in it.

First, clean up the damaged warps by cutting off the loose ends, as close as possible to the knotted pile, with a sharp pair of scissors. Only prepare an inch or two at a time in order to avoid further damage during handling. Then, choose a thread which is of the same fibre and colour as the original and is also of the same physical size and texture. Place the rug face downwards with the fringe lying away from you, and using a needle appropriate to the fineness of the rug, pass the thread through one side of the first knot just above and parallel to the existing warp at least 12mm (½in.) down from the end. Return the needle parallel to the first stitch, just above the second existing warp around which the first knot is tied. Leave the new warps slightly longer than the existing warps (25-40mm/1-1½in.) and trim them when the work is completed.

Continue to insert the new warps in the same manner, remembering to make sure the thread is passed through each loop of the knots and not in between. When you have finished making new warps you should secure the fringe as explained in Methods B and D, i.e. by oversewing or with a chain stitch (pp. 135 and 136).

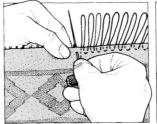

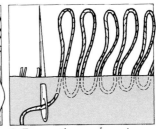

1 *Begin three or four rows below the exposed weft.*

2 *Ensure the new warp is parallel with the original.*

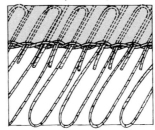

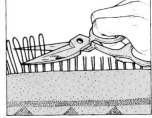

3 *Position the new warp just above the original.*

4 *Trim off the loops to match the existing fringe.*

Side cords

Introduction

Methods for binding and securing side cords vary from region to region. Isfahan rugs, for instance, have a single binding, some Caucasian rugs a double binding in the form of a figure-of-eight, while some Kurdish rugs have three or more bindings.

Side cords, like fringes and kelim ends, are designed to protect the rug. They are formed by binding one or more warp threads with weft threads. Most rugs also have an additional wool binding, or overcasting, as well as the weft threads.

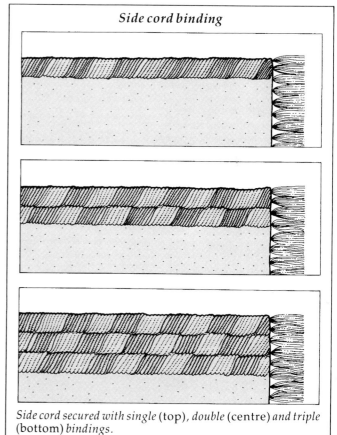

Side cord binding

Side cord secured with single (top), double (centre) and triple (bottom) bindings.

Left: *An Afshar rug whose side cord has been restored in the same two colours as the original.*

Simple rewooling

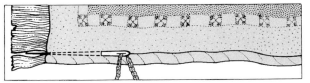

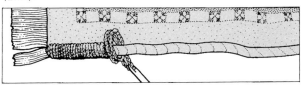

1 Secure the end of the wool into the side cord for about 50mm (2in.).

2 Oversew the cord with several strands of wool keeping the stitches close.

For simple rewooling where the edges are worn but unbroken, use a tapestry needle and colour-matching wool with a single or double strand, depending on the fineness of the rug.

Lay the rug pile side uppermost, with the edge facing towards you and, working from left to right, secure the end of the wool by running it through the side cord, parallel to the edge, for about 50mm (2in.). Then working from the front, simply overcast the cord, keeping the stitches close together to avoid unsightly gaps.

Replacing broken warps and wefts

If the actual warps of the side cord are broken they will have to be replaced before you can start on the job of replacing the wool.

First, trim the ends of the broken warps with a sharp pair of scissors to leave a clean cut.

Select a fibre of equal thickness and strength to the original warp and bridge the gap between the two broken ends of the same warp. Do not pull the new length of warp too tightly or leave it too slack as this will cause unevenness when the work is completed. Secure the thread at least 25-50mm (1-2in.) into the existing warp at both ends. It may be difficult to pull the new warp

through and you may need to use pliers. Replace all the damaged warps in this way. When all the warps have been replaced the new weft threads should be added. To add weft threads to a single cord, working from the back and starting about 50mm (2in.) in from the side, run stitches along the existing weft below the pile and round the new warps of the side cord. Be sure the stitching does not alter the tension of the warps or show through on the front. With a double or treble cord the wool has to be woven over and under each band in a figure-of-eight stitch.

Now overcast the new cords, using thread that matches the original side cord as nearly as possible and closely following the stitching of the original work.

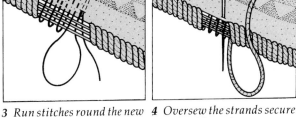

Replacing broken warps and wefts

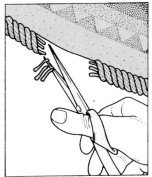

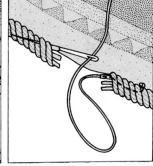

1 Trim off the loose ends with scissors.

2 Sew in a new fibre of warp to match the original.

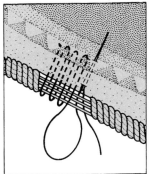

3 Run stitches round the new warps and into the weft.

4 Oversew the strands secure into the side cord.

Making a separate cord

Where several feet of side cord are damaged it is best to make up a separate cord and then sew it on.

Single cord Obtain a piece of upholstery piping cord of the same diameter as the original side cord. Cut off a length 75-100mm (3-4in.) longer than the rug and stretch between two fixed hooks. After selecting the appropriate wool, wrap three or four strands around the cord. When you reach the end of each strand of wool tie off by passing back under the overcast wool. This will avoid lumps in the cord. Begin the next length in the same way.

Double cord A double or treble cord is usually flat; it is therefore necessary to bind together three or four warp strands in each band. It is not practical to stretch the warps over a long length, so use a small, square frame which will hold the warps tight for you, leaving your hands free for overcasting the wool.

Hammer in six fine nails opposite one another in the top and bottom of your frame, spaced to fit the width of the new cord. Then cut off a sufficient number of warp threads for the complete length required. Loop these over the bottom nails and tie them off on the opposite nails at the top. The threads should be pulled taut in each case, but be careful not to stretch the yarn. Overcast the wool as explained on p. 136, working from the bottom upwards packing the strands tightly together.

When you have covered the full extent of the warps exposed, remove the nails from the bottom of the frame. Untie the warps from the nails at the top of the frame and move the completed section of cord downwards. Then hammer the nails back into the same place, passing through the completed cord, one or two strands down from the top. Ensure that the nails pass between the strands and do not pierce them. Tie the loose end at the top again, and proceed this way until the required length is done.

Sewing on the new cord

First trim off all the offending edge with sharp scissors by working from the front of the rug and folding back the edge to expose the gap between the knots.

Lay the rug face downwards with the edge away from you. Starting from the right-hand side allow 25mm (1in.) of the new cord to extend beyond the end of the rug. Hold the cord along the edge and sew it to the rug using a fine needle and size 35 thread in the following way: pass the first stitch away from you just under the base of the knots, parallel with the weft, then through the centre of the cord and draw together. Return the needle back through the same spot but at a slight angle to the first stitch and then again into the base of the knots. Continue this zig-zag stitch until complete. Always take the first stitch *away* from you at *right angles* to the edge and the return stitch at approximately 45°.

Unravel the wool from the surplus cord and thread it back through the overcasting to secure it. Cut off the surplus cord level with the pile at the end of the rug. Select a yarn to match the fringe and sew it in and out of the new cord parallel to the edge to finish off the end.

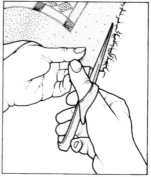

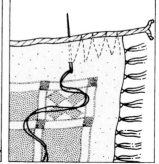

Sewing on a new side cord

1 Trim off the damaged area; cut between rows of knots.

2 Secure cord with zig-zag stitches kept closely together.

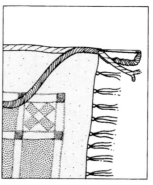

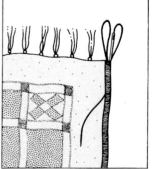

3 Unravel the loose wool and secure it into the cord.

4 Insert new warps into the trimmed off warps.

Curling edges

Sewing and binding

In general, the more tightly an oriental rug has been woven, the more probable it is that it will curl.

When rugs curl they turn underneath at the edge. This immediately makes them look shabby, destroying the pleasing appearance that comes from an attractive pattern lying flat on the floor. Also, apart from its unaesthetic appearance, curling should be dealt with promptly as the curled edges can form ridges in the rug, and these can quickly wear and create marks and patches.

There are two basic ways of dealing with this problem. The easiest one is to sew a narrowish tape under the offending edge, being careful to ensure that the stitches are not visible on the piled surface. This method reduces the curling but it may not remove it entirely. The other procedure is much more difficult, but will keep the rug flat almost indefinitely.

When the curling is only slight, you can iron it out with a hot iron and a damp cloth. However, this is only a temporary solution, and is of no use if the curling is at all stubborn.

If you do not feel sufficiently confident to tackle either of the two remedies detailed below, then try to put your rug in a room where it will not receive heavy wear. Excessive 'traffic' on it will make the ridges worse.

Remedies to avoid

There are several other ways to try to cure curling edges – but none of them is entirely satisfactory. Because they are encountered so often, however, it is worth noting them here.

Sewing a binding strip to the inside of the edge is acceptable but not always successful, depending on the type of rug. However tempted you might be, do not try to save time by gluing a strip in place. The glue will not hold indefinitely, and you will have done more harm to the condition (and value) of your rug.

Similarly, never try to attach your rug to the floor in any way to eliminate curling.

Left: A fine Kashan rug. This type of rug will invariably curl at the edges. Attaching tape to the edge will not improve its condition, so this rug was restored with a strong waxed thread sewn in a zig-zag manner. A fine needle and pliers were essential to penetrate the backing.

Method A

For this you will need a strip of vinyl or leather 40-50mm (1½-2in.) wide by 2mm (¹⁄₁₆in.) thick cut to the exact length of the piled section of the rug (that is, excluding the fringes). Work with the edge away from you.

Lay the rug face upwards, and turn the edge back, then sew on the strip using a size 2 straw needle and size 18 thread. Work from right to left. Hold the strip in position with your left hand and with the thread knotted and waxed pass the needle directly through the strip and then through the back and pile of the rug. Return the needle in almost exactly the same spot and pull tightly. You are now ready to herringbone stitch the strip to the carpet back. Keep the stitches close enough together so that they will not be visible from the front, but make sure you do not catch down the pile when pulling the thread tight. Continue along the rug in herringbone fashion.

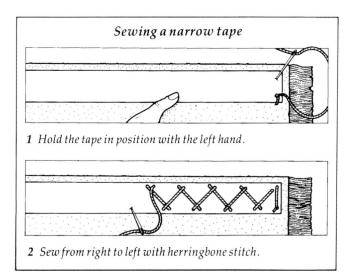

Sewing a narrow tape

1 *Hold the tape in position with the left hand.*

2 *Sew from right to left with herringbone stitch.*

Method B

This method is hard work, but is well worth the pain. Be prepared to spend two or three hours over a 2m (6ft) length.

Use a long fine needle (size 8 straw) and a double thickness of waxed size 35 thread. The finer the needle the easier it will be to use, but extreme care must be taken to push the needle in straight or it will break or bend.

Lay the rug face downwards with the edge away from you. Start from the right-hand side, uncurling the edge with the left hand. Push the needle in about 25mm (1in.) down from the edge parallel with and between the weft threads and pass it through the centre of the side cord.

Pull out the needle (with a pair of pliers if necessary) and return it back through the same spot but at a slight angle, pull the thread just tightly enough to keep the curled edge flat; if it is pulled too tightly it will have a tendency to curl in the opposite direction. Continue along the rug using a zig-zag stitch until complete. It will make it easier for the needle to penetrate the backing if you push the point into a block of beeswax before each stitch.

Sewing out a curled edge

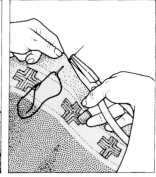

1 *Uncurl edge with the left hand and push needle in.*

2 *Pull out the needle, with pliers if necessary.*

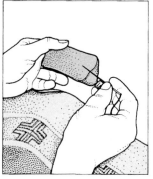
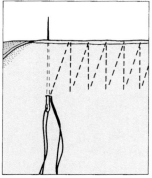

3 *Press needle into beeswax for easier penetration.*

4 *Make zig-zag stitches 25mm (1in.) below the edge.*

Repiling

Knots are susceptible to damage from a variety of common household features – wear and tear from their being walked on, cigarette burns, sparks from open fires, moths, and overzealous attempts to remove sticky liquids dropped on them. When the knots get damaged or worn away they have to be replaced, in a process known as repiling. This can be a difficult and time-consuming task for the amateur, particularly if the damaged area is of any size, but it can also be a highly satisfying job.

Repiling can only be done if the warp and weft are still sound. If they are also worn through or otherwise weak, you will have to reweave the area completely, or get professional advice on cutting the rug down.

A primary consideration in repiling is ensuring that the new wool is of the same texture as the original, and matches it in colour. If you cannot find exactly the right colours it may be necessary to mix various coloured strands of yarn together to obtain the right effect.

Always match colours in daylight as artificial light always has a colour bias, and this will distort the colours you are looking at. It is also important to bear in mind that the rug should be clean, or else you will be matching clean yarn to dirty, and the colour match will then be lost when the new pile gets worn or the rug is cleaned.

Before any work can commence, unpick the damaged portions of old wool. This is usually best done with tweezers. The warps and weft threads should be left clean and tidy.

Above: *The Melaz rug that has been repiled. The pile is being trimmed with a pair of scissors as the last stage of the job.*

Left: *A Melaz rug before and after repiling.*

Repiling with a Turkish knot

Lay the rug face upwards with the lay of the pile running towards you, i.e. when the pile is folded back parallel with the weft the knot is above the open end of the tuft. Begin at the left of the bottom row and make sure that the new knots are in line with the original ones.

You need a tapestry needle for this and length of the selected yarn about 450-600mm (18-24in.) long. Pass the point of the needle down between the first and second strands of warp threads, then under and around the left-hand warp and pull through, leaving 40mm (1½in.) of yarn projecting above the height of the pile. Hold down the end of the yarn with the thumb of your left hand and pass the point of the needle from right to left under and around the right-hand warp thread, below the loop of yarn, following the formation of the Turkish knot (see below). Pull up tightly between the first and second warps before moving right to the next pair of warps, changing colour as necessary.

Repeat this knotting procedure leaving the loops of pile uncut, about 40mm (1½in.) long.

When the area for repiling has been completed trim off the surplus pile with curved scissors, cutting in lines parallel to the weft. Cut down the height gradually. Remember that it is very easy to cut down, but 4mm (⅛in.) too far means another job of repiling, so be careful.

Finally, wire brush the tips of the pile in the direction of the lay, and hammer lightly to give age to the new work.

Repiling with a Persian knot

Repiling with a Persian knot is not quite as easy as with the Turkish knot because it is necessary to use the needle first in one hand, then the other.

Before you start you will need to work out whether your carpet has a right-hand or left-hand lay, but this can quickly be decided if you smooth down the carpet with the pile running towards you; you will find the pile has a definite lay either to right or left.

For a right-hand lay Begin in the same left-hand position as with the Turkish knot, passing the yarn under and around the left-hand warp thread as before. Then change the needle to the left hand. Study the illustration of a Persian knot and imitate this, passing the needle back over the first warp, under the second, and up again between the second and third warps. Pull tightly, and again, as with the Turkish knot, leave loops about 40mm (1½in.) long.

Repeat until complete and then trim the surface pile in the same way as with the Turkish knot.

For a left-hand lay Begin from the right-hand corner of the bottom row. Pass the yarn under the first warp thread from the left to right and pull up between the knotted row to its right. Change the needle over to the right hand and pass the needle back over the first warp, under the second, and up again through the second and third warps and pull tightly.

Sewing a Turkish knot

1 Pass the needle between the first and second warps.

2 Turkish knot, worked from left to right.

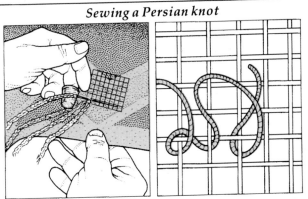

Sewing a Persian knot

1 Right-hand lay, inserting the needle with the left hand.

2 Persian knot for a rug with a right-hand lay.

Reweaving

Reweaving becomes necessary when knot damage or loss has progressed to actual damage or loss of the warp and/or weft. While reweaving can be undertaken at home it is inadvisable when the holes are particularly large, or if you are dealing with a fine antique rug.

Preliminary stages

First, examine the old warps and wefts to determine what fibre or fibres have been used – usually cotton or wool or mixtures of these. Now proceed as follows.

Lay the rug face downwards with the weft running from left to right. Clean up the loose pile on both sides of the hole by cutting through the back in a straight line between the knots and parallel with the warp threads for the complete length of the hole. Make sure the cleaned hole is angular, not curved.

Picking out the loose weft and warp of a Beluchistan rug prior to reweaving.

Left: *A fine Hamadan. This single wefted rug has been rewoven to match the original.*

Making the new warp threads

Select a suitable needle and yarn for the new warp which is exactly the same thickness and strength as the original. Still working from the back, begin at the bottom right-hand corner. Wax and knot the thread and weave in the new warp by passing the needle through the back of the right-hand loop of the original knots from three or four rows below the edge of the hole and out again just below the first row. (The first row of the original knots and wefts at the bottom and top of the hole will be removed at a later stage, so it is important that you do not run any of your new warp threads through them while you are stitching.)

Run the thread over the hole, keeping parallel with the original warps, making sure that the next stitch is above the first row of knots on the other side of the hole, and into the back of the second row of knots directly in line with the first stitch. Keep the needle below the surface until the fourth row. Return through the left-hand loops, remembering that for each knot you will make you must have two warp threads. Pull the thread through until it is secure.

Continue in this way, keeping each new warp below and above the surface at exactly the same point. Keep the tension firm but not overtight or you may cause distortion. Continue until all the new warps have been completed.

Making new warp threads

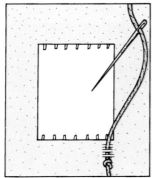

1 Pass thread through knot next to corner of hole.

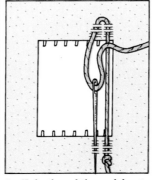

2 Take thread through knot on far side.

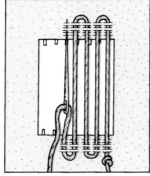

3 Continue sewing from right to left side.

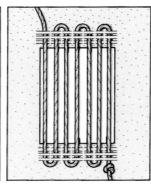

4 The hole with new warps completed.

Picking out the knots and wefts

It is now time to remove the first row of knots and wefts at the top and bottom of the new weaving. This row is removed after the insertion of the new warps rather than before, because it is virtually impossible not to loosen or disturb the original knot whilst pulling through the new warp thread. Pick out each individual knot very carefully with a bradawl or tweezers. Now cut the ends of the weft and remove carefully, making sure you do not disturb the next row of knots. Turn the rug over to the front side and cut each old protruding warp thread as close to the knot as possible.

Picking out knots

1 Pick out knots from top and bottom rows.

2 With rug face up, trim old warp threads.

Attaching the rug to a frame

To ensure that the rug stays in a firm and flat condition during weaving, it is necessary to attach the rug to a small square wooden frame, like the one used to make up double cord (see p. 140). Proceed as follows.

Lay the rug face upwards over the frame with the warp threads running from top to bottom and perfectly square with the sides. Position the hole in the centre of the frame. With 20mm (¾in.) long carpet tacks fix the rug to the frame by nailing it onto the bottom rung, spacing the nails about 12mm (½in.) apart. Make sure the rug has a firm but even tension throughout the length of the warps by stretching it over the top bar of the frame and then nailing it into position as before. Be careful that you do not overstretch or distort the area around the hole as the newly weaved area will not then fit properly when the rug is taken from the frame.

Making the new pile

Select a suitable yarn for the weft, and with a tapestry needle build up each row to match the original by passing the yarn over and under alternate warp threads. At this stage do not cut or secure the new wefts at the side of the weaving to the original but just wrap them around the end warp and pass back again at the completion of each row; the splits along the sides can be sewn together on the back when the weaving is complete.

Choose the required colours for the pile carefully and matching the design as you work, insert the pile as described under repiling (pp. 143–4). Pack down the new wefts tightly after each row with a comb or needle making sure they are exactly in line with the original. Continue weaving alternate rows of pile and weft until complete. You can then untack the rug from the frame and, using waxed thread, sew the splits on each side of the weaving with an invisible zig-zag stitch.

Trimming and finishing

Now that you have inserted the knots, the final stage is to trim the pile to the correct height, as described on p. 144. You will find that, however well executed, the new weaving will be slightly lumpy. To eliminate this problem press on the back of the newly piled area with a hot iron and damp cloth for several minutes.

Making new pile

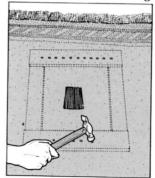

1 Tack rug to frame at 12mm (½in.) intervals.

2 Pass new weft threads around end warp.

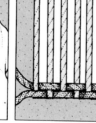

3 Tightly pack down new wefts with needle/comb.

4 Continue interweaving wefts until complete.

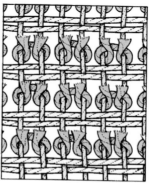
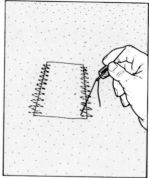

5 Repile in line with original knots.

6 Unfix rug and sew up side splits with zig-zag stitch.

Patching

Reweaving and repiling becomes impracticable once a hole exceeds certain dimensions – at least for the non-professional. The only solutions remaining are to patch, or have the rug professionally reduced in size.

Whilst patching itself is not difficult when compared with reweaving and repiling, finding the appropriate patch which matches, if only approximately, the design of your rug can be difficult. Ideally the patch should come from a rug from a similar region to your own, as well as be similar in design, colour and age. This may be the occasion to consult a professional dealer or repairer to see if he has suitable patching material.

It is not possible to patch a round hole because the knots will be incomplete and, therefore, impossible to secure correctly; to make a satisfactory job all the sides of the patch have to be straight. The more proficient one gets the more complicated can be the geometry of the patch, but to begin with avoid anything other than a simple square or oblong hole.

Left: *With this Beluchistan rug, the only possible repair is to insert a patch; the damaged area must be removed* (above) *before patching.*

Preparing the hole

Select a suitable patch slightly larger than the hole, bearing in mind that the pile of the patch will need to run in the same direction as the pile on your rug.

Lay the rug face down on a flat surface and with a strong knife or blade cut both sides of the damaged area parallel with the warps, cutting between the rows of knots, as described in the previous section on p. 145. Next, carefully unpick the rows of damaged knots and wefts along the top and bottom of the hole until they are level, cutting the ends of each weft cleanly.

Do not cut the warps at this stage.

Preparing the patch

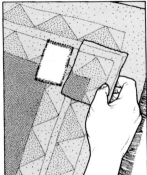

1 Check patch against hole for size and pile direction.

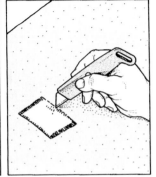

2 Cut two straight sides to hole through wefts.

3 Unpick damaged wefts and knots with needle/tweezers.

4 The prepared hole with warps uncut.

Above: *More time was spent finding a suitable patch for this Hamadan rug than actually repairing the hole.*

Fitting the patch

Having prepared the hole you need to prepare one side of the patch, cutting a straight line between two warp threads. Cut from the front with scissors, folding back the edge to expose the knots. Be careful that you cut between the knots and not through the centre of any of them.

With the pile running in the same direction as in the rug, lay the patch into the hole, pressing the straight newly-cut edge of the patch along one of the straight edges of the hole. Measure across the width and cut to size once again making sure you cut between the knots. Since the patch is unlikely to have exactly the same knot count as the original, it will obviously not line up row for row, and it is better to cut the patch a knot wider than the hole rather than narrower.

Your next step is to fray out the first two rows of knots and wefts along the top row of the patch (see p. 146). Take out the last weft very carefully so as not to disturb the next line of knots. The warps will not be protruding. Cut them off as close to the knots as possible, and cut off the ones, too, that you left in the top row of the hole.

Using a fine needle and knotted waxed thread, hold the patch firmly between the thumb and forefinger and push the needle with great care through the back of the knots parallel with the warp about three rows down. Pull the needle out between the fingers carefully so as not to disturb the knots.

Place the rug over a bottle or hard tube for support and sew in the patch in the same zig-zag fashion as already described, keeping the first stitch in a shallow line just below the back of the knot and returning the next stitch at an angle as deep as possible without showing on the front side.

Pull the thread tightly, keeping the stitches close enough together so that when the join is folded back it does not open up along the back. If the stitches are not alternated, one deep and one shallow, the patch will fray at the edges from wear. Removing the weft and sewing two rows of knots together, although more difficult, ensures a good clean join on the front side.

When this line of stitching is complete, fray out the bottom edge of the patch to the required length and cut the warps as previously described. Sew in position. Finish off by sewing both sides. If necessary you can then press the patched area with a hot iron and damp cloth.

Inserting the patch

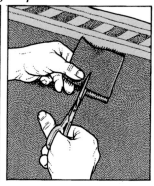

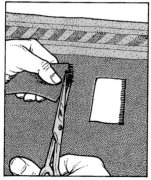

1 Fold back to expose knots; cut between knots.

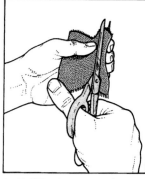

2 Cut patch one knot wider than hole.

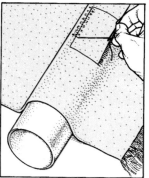

3 Trim warps at top of both patch and hole.

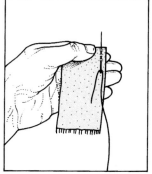

4 Insert needle through knots three rows from top.

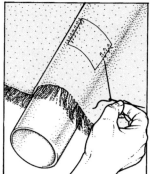

5 Sew patch into hole with zig-zag stitch.

6 Sew side splits with zig-zag stitch.

Splits and tears

Splits and tears can be caused in many varying ways but in all cases the repair must be attended to as soon as possible. If they are neglected for any length of time they get much worse and extensive reweaving then becomes necessary. Moreover, once the main foundation of the rug has become damaged (i.e. the warp or weft) the knots will inevitably loosen and come out if they are disturbed in any way.

Straight unfrayed cuts

Providing the tears run parallel with either the warp or weft, they can easily be resewn together from the back with a waxed thread in a zig-zag manner.

However, any loose threads must be trimmed away as close to the break as possible to obtain a good clean finish. Even repairs to the most simple of tears can look quite unsightly, particularly from the front, if the loose strands are not cleaned away carefully before sewing starts – and you cannot remove them after the sewing has been done.

Frayed cuts

If several of the warp or weft threads have been severed but the knots have remained in their original position the foundation (i.e. the warp and weft) can be strengthened with a strong waxed thread.

The first stage is to replace the damaged warp fibres without disturbing the knots. In previous sections it has been emphasized that all foundation repairs should be repaired with the original fibre. Unfortunately, in the case of tears the main object is to avoid any further unnecessary damage, so a new fibre (waxed thread) must be used.

After trimming all of the loose fibres with sharp scissors, knot the end of the thread and begin about 12mm (½in.) below the weak area where it should be possible to get a good firm hold. Working from the back of the rug pass the needle through one side of the knot, parallel with the warp, just below the surface. Continue through the weak area for a further 12mm (½in.), again looking for a good firm hold.

When passing the needle through each side of the

Left: *This Indian carpet was badly cut* (inset) *but has been re-sewn with only a slight loss of its design.*

Frayed tears

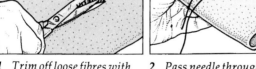

1 Trim off loose fibres with scissors.

2 Pass needle through back of knots on both sides.

---

knots you have to be very careful not to disturb their position in the rug. The longer and finer the needle you use the easier this will be. Hold each knot in place firmly between the thumb and first finger while pushing or pulling the needle through. If the damaged area is in the centre of the piece, the knots can only be held between the fingers by folding the rug face to face just below the weak section while supporting the rug in the palm of the same hand.

Continue across the damaged area running each stitch parallel with the warps and pulling the thread tightly enough to draw the area together but at the same time being very careful not to cause any puckering in the pieces of the rug. Finally, strengthen all of the weft threads in the same manner, but this time keeping the stitches between the rows of knots and not sewing through them.

Tears in coarsely woven rugs

In certain cases where a tear is in either the edge or end of a coarsely woven rug and there are two or three lines of pile missing, it is possible to mend it without reweaving the whole damaged area. To do this you have to extend the length of the damaged section and then rejoin the raw edges by sewing them together. The length of the cut you have to make is determined by the width of the missing pile.

Working from the back of the rug cut a straight line, parallel with the weft, to just beyond the damaged area. Pull the two sides of the damaged areas together, laying the newly-cut straight edge over the uncut frayed section until the torn portion is completely hidden. If there is a

Mending tears

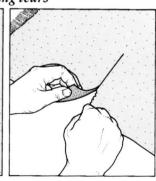

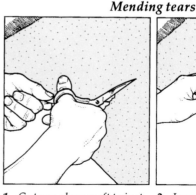

1 Cut rug along weft to just beyond tear.

2 Lay cut edge over frayed edge to cover damage.

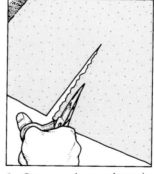

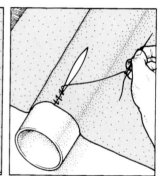

3 Cut away damaged area in a straight line.

4 Lay cut on tube. Sew up with zigzag stitch.

---

bump or fullness at the point of the inner angle, extend the length of the cut until it disappears. Draw a line from the end of the cut to the outside edge of the rug at an angle and then from this position cut away the damaged section.

Place the split section over a tube for support and sew together with thread in a zig-zag fashion. Begin from the outside edge to the centre remembering to make the alternate stitches first shallow and then deep. Even greater care than normal has to be taken not to fray out the raw edges when handling the rug because the angled cut has also cut some of the knots through the centre. Continue back again in the opposite direction to add further strength. Press with a hot iron and damp cloth to flatten any remaining distortion.

Repair of kelims

Not all the repairs that can be done to piled rugs can be produced on kelims. The problem is that a kelim does not have a layer of knots to hide stitches and joins. Any work done on a kelim is therefore more exposed. However, some of the repairs described previously in this section can be done, notably repairing fringes and edges and reweaving, but it is difficult to mend tears or patch a kelim without producing highly noticeable results.

Fringes

In most cases the fringes can be repaired as described in chapter 1. If the end of the rug is found to be very weak and fragile it may be best to secure the damaged section firmly with either an oversewing or blanket stitch as described for repairs to Fringes, Method B or Method C (p. 135).

Repairing edges

This is normally a simple job of re-inserting the broken wefts and wrapping them around the warps of the side cords in the same manner as described for repairing the edges of piled rugs in chapter 2 (p. 139).

Reweaving a hole

Although the technique of kelim-weaving is simple it is very difficult to carry out a completely invisible repair. The main reason for this is that there is very little fibre to cover any loose threads. However, if you are willing to accept that the repair will show to some extent, you can reweave a section, by working as follows.

Clean up the damaged area by trimming off all the loose ends. Re-insert the missing warps as described in Reweaving (p. 146) and attach to a small frame as on p. 147. Pass the new weft threads over and under alternate warp threads, returning back again in the opposite direction at every change of colour or design (see kelim-weaving, p. 129). It may be necessary to weave in a few extra wefts to give added firmness and strength to the area. Continue the new wefts well into the undamaged area to make sure the new work is well secured.

Left: *The hole in this kelim cut across two of the colours* (inset) *but nevertheless it was possible to reweave it completely with just about perfect results on both sides.*

6

ANTIQUE METALWARE

Although there are many metal objects within the home they tend to be replaced rather than repaired once they become damaged. This is not so with antiques or decorative objects, which is why the particular pieces illustrated in this section of the book, rather than articles in everyday use, were chosen. There is no reason why more metal-working should not be undertaken by the amateur providing it is approached in a sympathetic way.

The average person treats metal as a totally alien material. It can, however, do most things if treated in the correct fashion. The main thing to remember is that any action you take against it tends to be fairly permanent. The approach to metalworking, therefore, has to be thorough and methodical. That is not to say there is only one way to achieve your objective. The projects here are meant to guide and encourage you to explore your own potential on the material and your own skill. Hopefully, after reading through them, you will be able to restore your own pieces with an added degree of confidence.

Tools

Special tools for metalwork tend to be very expensive, but if they are looked after they will last for decades and will prove to have been an excellent investment. It is said that a bad workman always blames his tools but nothing makes a job easier than having the correct tool that is in good condition. Many repairs can, however, be undertaken with a very basic toolkit and it is possible to modify some of the more common items to perform a specialist function.

Building up a comprehensive toolkit can literally take a lifetime but you do not have to spend a fortune on equipment to achieve good results. A toolkit comprising the following basic items will allow you to carry out many of the more straightforward repairs, and you can add specialist tools as and when the need arises.

Basic tools

A small vice (vise) is ideal for holding a piece securely while it is being repaired. Vices come in all price ranges and can be either dismountable or permanently fixed to the bench. The type which has a swivel head is a great help in getting at awkward angles. Make sure that the type you choose is fitted with soft jaws which will not damage the work.

A gas torch is invaluable as a source of heat for soldering, and for loosening jammed parts. If more than the occasional repair is to be attempted, a torch with a separate gas tank will prove to be an excellent investment. Always get a torch or heat supply with a greater capacity than you initially think you need. Reserve capacity, when soldering for example, makes for speedy and efficient working. Remember you can always reduce the amount of heat but you cannot increase it if the equipment is unable to supply the demand. Larger torches have the added advantage of being able to provide varying sizes of jet so that flame shape and size can be changed as necessary.

Miscellaneous tools such as the following are recommended: a hacksaw (full-size or junior), pliers of various sizes, tin-snips, screwdrivers, a wooden mallet, a ball peen hammer, marking-out equipment (scriber, centre punch, square and dividers), an assortment of files, an electric soldering iron and a jeweller's frame saw, which is probably the most important of metal-cutting tools. Be sure it is of good quality; the most convenient type has an adjustable frame.

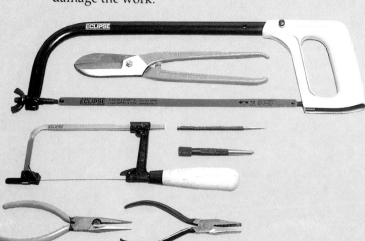

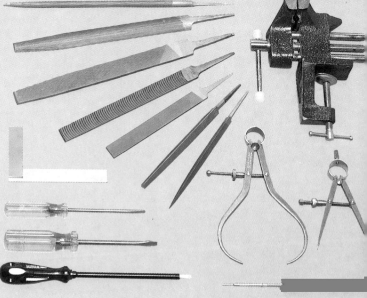

1 Hacksaw; 2 tin-snips; 3 piercing saw; 4 scriber; 5 centre punch; 6 pliers;   *7 files; 8 square; 9 screwdrivers; 10 vice; 11 dividers; 12 soldering iron.*

Specialist tools

A planishing hammer is a good investment, although a standard carpentry hammer can be used. Planishing hammers come in various weights but a general-purpose hammer would be between 140g (5oz.) and 280g (10oz.). They must be kept highly polished and protected when not in use.

Clamps can be made of metal or wood and usually have a simple closing system of a metal slide or wedge. They are used for holding small pieces of work while you are filing or polishing and are used in conjunction with the bench pin.

The bench pin is a hardwood V-shaped tool used to hold irregular items when piercing with a saw or filing to shape.

The pin vice is ideal for working on wires or pieces which have slender shanks. They come in various sizes and can also be used to hold very small drills.

The scraper is ideal for taking burrs off metal edges before soldering or taking material off the surface of the work piece. Most useful to the metalworker is the three square hollow ground type. It is important to keep it well honed.

The burnisher is used to smooth and consolidate the surface of the metal into a high polish. It is made from hardened and tempered high-carbon steel.

Mallets: four main types are used – round boxwood, rawhide, bossing and soft-faced.

A scoring tool is made from high-carbon steel which has been hardened and tempered. It is used to cut a groove of specified angle in sheet material. The sheet can then be folded up and soldered in place.

Needle files are used for fine intricate work with the minimum of material removal. Each file has a handle and there are a variety of sizes. They should be purchased individually and not in a pack. The most useful shapes are the hand, warding, three square, half round and round; there are eight other shapes. The cuts range from 00 which is the coarsest to 8, the finest.

Swiss files are slightly different from files normally purchased in the UK or the United States. They are made from chrome steel for durability and hardness. They

have a range of shapes which is a little different from their British and American counterparts and, in addition, they have slightly more taper. They are designed for precision work and should be treated with great care.

Rifler files come in many shapes. They are used to file in areas which would otherwise be inaccessible. Both ends of any one tool have the same shape.

File care is vital. Files used on non-ferrous metals should not be used on steel. If you are working very soft alloys (e.g. aluminium-based or lead-based), keep separate files for this. Particles of lead transferred by file to a piece of silver can cause untold damage. Good files should be kept separated and not allowed to clank together. Do not use oil on files as this impedes the clearance of material. Files should be cleaned using a piece of copper which is worked obliquely across the surface to remove the small, hard pieces of compacted waste material known as 'pinning'.

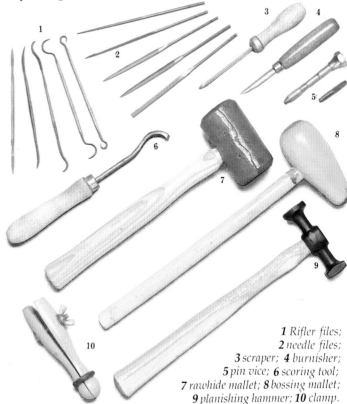

1 Rifler files;
2 needle files;
3 scraper; 4 burnisher;
5 pin vice; 6 scoring tool;
7 rawhide mallet; 8 bossing mallet;
9 planishing hammer; 10 clamp.

Materials

Emery cloth is a natural abrasive, blue/black in colour, mounted on cloth and used for cleaning and polishing. Several grades are available. Do not use on silver, because it can burrow into the surface.

Steel wool can be used with a little oil to clean a corroded surface or to give a matt finish to an article.

Crocus papers are used for fine polishing by hand, several grades being available. They provide an alternative to Water of Ayr (Scotch) stone for fine scratch removal and will produce a high polish.

Methylated spirits (wood alcohol) is useful for cleaning surfaces before soldering. It is also mixed with fire-stain inhibiter (see Argo-Tec below).

Paraffin (kerosene) is a general-purpose cleanser. Used with steel wool, it will clean badly corroded surfaces.

Beeswax is used in block form as a lubricant for piercing saw blades. Mixed with turpentine it will protect freshly cleaned ferrous surfaces against rust.

Thrumming thread is used in hand polishing and is charged with tripoli or rouge. Tripoli is used in hand or machine buffing for surface scratch removal before using rouge. Rouge is used in powder or bar form for the final polish.

Pumice powder is mixed with water or oil to make a controllable slurry which can be used to clean metals before polishing or after heat treatment.

Water of Ayr (Scotch) stone is a very fine, slate-like material used in the removal of small scratches. It should always be used with plenty of water and with care, as it can very easily form a hollow on the metal.

Fluxes used for soft soldering include zinc chloride which is an active (corrosive) flux and any residue must be cleaned off after use. It must not be used on electrical work. Ammonium chloride in petroleum jelly is also classed as an active flux. Again, any residue must be removed. Tallow and resin are 'safe' fluxes for soft solders, but will leave a greasy deposit. Active fluxes are usually more effective as their slight acid action helps to clean the metal. It is important that any residue of active flux is removed after soldering as it is so corrosive.

For hard soldering, borax can be used as a flux for most silver soldering but there are proprietary fluxes available which are sometimes more suitable as they are made to be used with a specific solder grade; Argo-Tec is a powder used for the prevention of fire stain when hard soldering silver. It is mixed with methylated spirits to form a creamy paste.

1 Selection of emery paper; 2 rouge; 3 thrumming thread; 4 borax cone; 5 beeswax; 6 Water of Ayr stone; 7 steel wool; 8 methylated spirits; 9 paraffin; 10 solder.

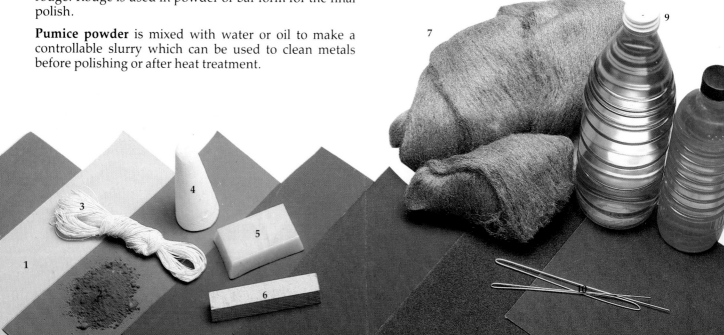

Basic techniques

Fluxing and soldering

The heat required for soldering would normally cause oxides to form on the metal. As oxides prevent solder from adhering, you must protect the surface by applying flux (see p. 158) to the areas to be joined. Flux breaks down any thin surface oxide, prevents further contamination, and reduces the surface tension of the solder and assists its flow along the joint.

Flux can be purchased as a powder, a liquid or in cone form. A thin, creamy paste can be made by dissolving the powder in a little water or by rubbing the cone in water in an unglazed dish.

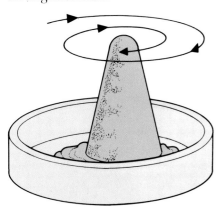

Rubbing the borax cone in a little water in an unglazed dish produces a thin, creamy paste flux.

Paint the flux on the joint. The heavier the pieces to be soldered the thicker the flux required. Too thin a deposit will burn out before the solder melts. Too much will cause the solder to spread over the surface rather than along the route of a joint.

Once the piece has been fluxed and secured, heating can take place. Remember to raise the objects off the hearth slightly to enable the flame to heat all parts evenly.

As the temperature rises, the flux will bubble. Watch carefully and make sure that the bubbling has not displaced any parts. With additional heating the bubbling will subside and the flux will form a jam-like deposit over the joint. This prevents air from reaching the joint and forming an oxide. Heating continues and eventually the flux will melt and run across the surface and into the joint. It is at this stage that the solder is

Soldering

1 *Scratch the grade on the solder sticks.*

2 *Solder sticks are reduced in width when 'fed' in.*

3 *Paillons are made by piercing small sections.*

4 *Place paillons on the joint with tweezers.*

introduced. This sudden change of state of the flux is a perfect indication of the required temperature and should be looked for. The solder can be fed into the joint as a stick or pre-placed along the joint as paillons panels, which are small pieces of solder cut from the strip. If you use these small chips, you will find it easier if the job is first heated just enough to let the flux bubble up and die down. Coat the chips with wet flux and place them in position with tweezers. The flux on them immediately dries and holds the chips in position.

Only the minimal amount of solder should be used. If it does not flow, it is because you have failed to give it the correct conditions for movement. Make sure that both parts of the job are at the same temperature or the solder will be attracted to the hotter one. Try to get the solder to melt by using the heat transferred through the job rather than by playing the flame on the joint. Excessive heating of the solder will make the zinc in the alloy vaporize and cause pin-holes in the joint.

Finally let the job cool before pickling or quenching. Premature quenching only puts stress on the joint.

Polishing and finishing

Polishing and finishing are the last stages in the repair and restoration of any article. The surface may be left matt or worked to a high polish.

The principle of polishing is to start by dealing with the worst marks using the coarsest abrasive; follow successively with finer abrasives until the finest is reached. Excess solder and deep scratches will probably need a file or emery cloth to remove them. Fine scratches are then removed with Water of Ayr (Scotch) stone or paper-backed abrasives.

Once any residue has been washed away, the surface should be perfectly matt. Jeweller's rouge can be used for the final polish. This can be in cake form (bound with hard grease) or in powder form which is mixed with water to form a paste. The rouge can be applied with a stiff brush or chamois leather. Any pierced work can be polished by thrumming thread. A few short lengths of thread are tied to a hook at the bench front and pulled taut. Wipe the rouge along them, pass them through the pierced work and rub the piece back and forth. Threads will quickly cut a groove so make sure to work over the whole surface evenly. Finally, wash the piece in warm water with a little added detergent.

Quicker results can be achieved by using a polishing motor and buffing wheels. These vary in diameter, thickness and composition. When used in conjunction with the correct polishing compound, each wheel will give a different effect, the general rule being that the harder the wheel the coarser will be the finish obtained. It is important that wheels are kept for use with one grade of polish and do not become contaminated by a different grade. The type of abrasive used can be marked on the mop side. After polishing with one type, make sure that the article is cleaned before moving on to the next wheel and abrasive grade.

Motors for polishing have one fixed speed, around 3,500 r.p.m. Polishing speed will depend upon the diameter of the buffing wheel, which is expressed in surface feet per minute (s.f.p.m.).

The recommended s.f.p.m. will depend upon the metal being finished, the kind of wheel, the type of abrasive and the finish required. What is important is that there are no short cuts to a good finish. Good preparation of each component will repay the time spent many times over. When buffing, keep the work on the move constantly otherwise surface damage can occur. This is especially true in the case of hard wheels, which are normally used for flat surfaces and to prevent blurring square edges, but they must be used with care.

Soft wheels are used where the surface is irregular and it is not intended to have fast metal removal.

Care of buffing wheels

From time to time it is necessary to clean the mops as they become clogged with unused abrasive and removed metal. This can be done by holding against the wheels a length of wood with protruding nails. Alternatively use a long-handled, stiff-wired brush. Do not try to wash the wheels as this can break them up and reduce their effectiveness.

Wheel types

Below is a short list of wheel types and abrasives. Always use the utmost care when polishing. Make sure that any loose clothing or long hair is kept confined. Finger rings, if worn, should be removed if possible or taped over to prevent snagging.

Soft wool (for soft metals) gives a fine finish; use with rouge.

Flannel and cotton types have a nap on the fabric. When used with rouge, they will not scratch.

Muslin wheels vary between light, loose discs of fabric to closely woven, heavy starched canvas. They are either unsewn or can be stitched in a variety of geometric patterns. A number of compounds can be used with them; tripoli is the most common.

Canvas is used for the hardest cloth wheels for fast metal removal. The canvas can be cemented together and produces a harder wheel than stitching. Use with tripoli.

Pressed felt wheels come in grades ranging from soft to rock-hard, some wheels being pre-shaped for access to awkward areas.

Bristle brushes are used with greaseless brushing compounds to create a matt surface.

The three most common types of abrasives are tripoli (the coarsest), crocus (intermediate) and rouge (for the final polish). There are many types of each of these.

Project 1: Scales

First impressions

On first inspection these scales appear to be incomplete. They do not have a stand of any kind and comprise solely the balance beam with pointer and the pans. However, there is no provision made for any additional pieces and it would appear that they are to be hand-held, probably from the finger inserted through the top ring. Alternatively, they could have been suspended from a hook although the amount of wear on the ring is minimal.

The quality also is better than a cursory glance would indicate. The pans, although they appear to be rather thin and cheap, in fact are on the heavy side for their size. This is due to the manner in which they have been made. They have been made out of a sheet of copper (in itself unusual, as most scale pans are of brass). The material apart, the manner of their forming is out of the ordinary. They have been raised from the sheet. This process is now only used on very good-quality hollow-ware, and is an aid to putting a date on an otherwise common everyday object. If they had been made within the last century there would be a good chance that the pans would have been made by some semi-automated process: either by stamping or possibly by spinning. Also the bowls are quite deep in relation to their diameter. This would indicate their use as a commodity balance rather than a weighing scale.

The beam is also an indication as to the age and quality of the item. It is made from wrought iron and has been forged in one piece. When cleaned, it shows the water pattern markings common to this material.

Order of work

Although generally in a reasonable condition, one of the scale pans has quite a severe dent in it which will have to be removed. Before this can be attempted, however, the chains must be removed to facilitate access to the pans, and the pans must be cleaned. These scales have been lacquered at some time in their life and this must be removed before hammering begins.

Once the pans have been restored, the chains can be cleaned and polished, and the balance beam cleaned of rust.

Left: *The damaged scales, with the pans dented and creased; and restored and reassembled* (top).

Hollowing and sinking

There are several ways to make a hollow vessel out of non-ferrous material by hand. The technique used depends upon the depth and diameter of the object and also the quality.

The first method 'hollowing' (or blocking) is used for making bowl shapes. It can be done with a wooden mallet or metal blocking hammer. The metal is shaped by hammering it into a depression in either a wooden block or sand bag. It is gradually worked into the depression by regular hammer blows starting from the outside edge and spiralling into the centre, each successive row being the width of one hammer blow.

If the vessel is to have a flat rim the hammering will commence at a distance in from the edge determined by the rim width. This is referred to as sinking.

The main difficulty with this technique is in trying to keep the base of the article flat.

Raising

Most items are too narrow and deep to be made just by blocking alone and these will have to be raised. Both in sinking and blocking the object is hammered from the inside; in raising it takes place on the outside of the form. The process requires the use of a metal bar or stake against which the metal disc is worked. Starting from the base the metal is hammered in concentric circles pushing it on to the stake. Raising makes a characteristic rectangular flat mark on the metal which is later removed by planishing. With this process the metal would need to be softened (or 'annealed') several times before a vessel is in the desired shape. Although a long process, raising has the advantage of being able to produce shapes which are not necessarily round but can be used if need be to produce a complete sphere.

Whatever technique has been used, work-hardening will have been aggravated by damage.

Hollowing and sinking

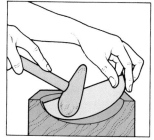

1 Start at the rim to hollow a bowl.

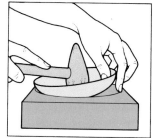

2 Support the back rim with your fingers.

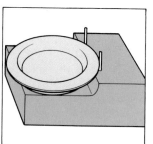

3 Sinking is similar to hollowing.

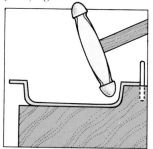

4 Rotate the work as hammering progresses.

Raising

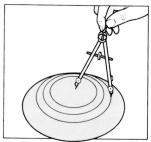

1 Draw circular pencil guidelines on the bowl.

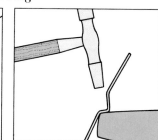

2 Place smallest circle on the stake edge; hammer metal.

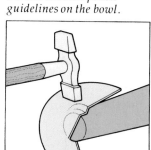

3 Turn work 12mm (½in.) for next blow. Repeat.

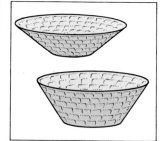

4 Raising should take place in gradual stages.

Removing the chains

The first job here is to remove the support chains. This must be carried out with care, so as not to distort the jump-ring. Take the ring in two sets of smooth-faced pliers and twist. The chains may now be slipped off the bowl, but first note each chain's position. The pans must now be thoroughly cleaned before any major amount of hammering takes place. Before doing so, however, you must consider whether the loss of any major area of patination will be detrimental to the value of the object. In the case of the scales the surface is clearly not good, having at some time been lacquered. This lacquer is now disintegrating.

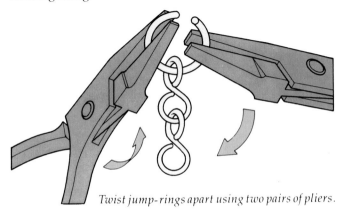

Twist jump-rings apart using two pairs of pliers.

Removing the lacquer

The lacquer can be removed by using a solvent and by working with a wet rag and pumice powder. The pumice powder should also remove most of the oxides on the inside surface of the pans. If it proves stubborn, immerse the pans in a pickling solution of approximately ten parts water to one part sulphuric acid. This should be in a broad-based 'Pyrex' type dish or plastic container preferably with a lid. It is also possible to purchase 'safety pickling' in small quantities for those people who do not wish to handle acids or have them around the house. As a useful addition copper and its alloys plus silver can be cleaned using citric acid (present in citrus fruits) and acetic acid (as found in vinegar) mixed with common salt. Dip a rag into the solution and swab the surface liberally. Whatever you choose make sure the object is well rinsed and dried before you move on to the next stage.

Removing dents

In order to remove the dent a bossing mallet is needed. This is a mallet that has an egg-shaped end. They can be made quite easily or a piece of wood with a domed end can be used. The work is held upon a sand bag or a wooden block which has a hollow gouged out of it. Sand bags are usually made of leather but an adequate substitute can be stitched up by using several layers of calico.

Hold the work firmly on a sand bag and mallet the bump from the inside. If the dent has a sharp crease line it will be necessary to push the surface out further than the original hollow. For sharp dents the use of a wooden punch is recommended.

The pan can now be reversed and placed over a mushroom-headed stake. Commercial stakes are very expensive but a good substitute can be made from a mild steel bar. For small work spare hammer heads held in the vice can be used to good effect. Stakes should be of slightly smaller radius than the work and need to have a very well finished surface. Any blemish on the stake will become impressed upon the inside of the pan. Using a cylindrical mallet, tap any raised bumps on the surface of the pan back flush with the surface. The pan should be manoeuvred over the stake head while the mallet is used to strike in the centre of the stake. The rim of the pan must also be tapped true. In order to keep forms regular it is important to tap gently around all the rim and not just where any imperfections are.

Removing dents

1 *Push dents out from inside with the bossing mallet.*

2 *True up over a stake using a flat-faced mallet.*

Planishing and polishing

We must now decide whether it is necessary to re-planish the form. Planishing has the effect of work hardening the form but it will also slightly flatten the form and thin the metal. If the metal has any severe creases, planishing will almost certainly be needed.

Planishing requires a special metal-faced hammer which is highly polished. As with the stakes, any imperfections in the hammer face will be imparted to the surface of the job. This is usually a finishing technique which will take out any ridges after hollowing or raising and will impart small regular facets to the surface.

Start by placing the dish on the stake and lightly tap the metal. Move the metal slightly until a clear ringing note is heard. This indicates that the metal is in contact with the stake below. Tap the metal, beginning at the centre, and

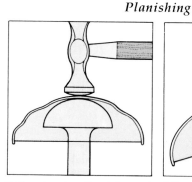
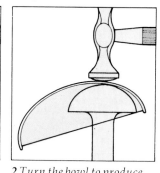

Planishing

1 Place bowl on the stake, and tap the metal.

2 Turn the bowl to produce concentric rings of facets.

The repaired and polished scales are laid out ready for inspection and checking before final assembly.

make sure the hammer strikes constantly over the same spot on the stake. Turn the metal to produce concentric rings of overlapping facets. Take care not to stretch the metal when getting near to the edge. The marks left after planishing should be slight and must not be confused with the coarse dimpling which appears on reproduction copperware at times. While planishing produces a finished surface, its primary use is to harden the piece and remove the raising or hollowing marks.

Providing the final planishing has been well done, the polishing of the surface should be relatively straightforward if a polishing motor and mops are available. If not, the pieces may be polished by hand.

Initially any scratches that are not too deep can be removed by using a Water of Ayr (Scotch) stone (see p. 158). Make sure no flats or grooves are cut by the stone and always use plenty of water. There is also a range of jeweller's abrasive papers which are much less aggressive than emery cloth. The finest grades will produce a very satisfactory shine on their own. Final polishing can be done using jeweller's rouge and a chamois leather or soft cloth. Alternatively the rouge can be mixed into a paste and used with a stiff brush. For controlled polishing of individual areas either wrap a stick approximately 250 × 25 × 5mm (10 × 1 × ¼in.) in felt or cloth and apply the rouge with this. Lastly clean off all traces of rouge with a degreasing agent. There are very good commercial metal polishes on the market which will easily maintain the shine you have achieved. If they are in use they will quickly obtain a

Hand polishing

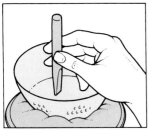

1 Punch out sharp dents with a shaped wood tool.

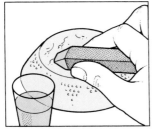

2 Use Water of Ayr stone and water for scratches.

3 Brush in pumice and water, then rouge powder and oil.

4 Remove oxide with citric and acetic acids, and salt.

which can get snatched by the mop head of the machine.

The balance beam is iron and shows all the imperfections of being hand made. It has rust on it at present and this must be removed. On steel or iron items, brush off the surface dirt and try to assess the extent of cleaning required. Do not resort to the buffing wheel unless it is really necessary. There can be a real danger of destroying inscriptions, inlays, maker's marks, blueing, and so on.

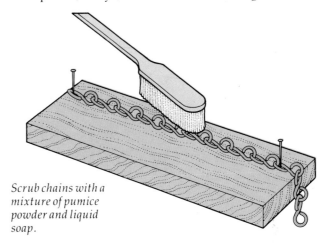

Scrub chains with a mixture of pumice powder and liquid soap.

pleasant patination but you may wish to lacquer the pieces at this stage. The lacquer will colour the metal and reduce its brilliance but against that you must balance the time you will spend cleaning.

Cleaning the chains

Now the bowls are finished, the chains can be removed from the balance arm and immersed in the cleaning solution. Leave them in the pickle for ten minutes, remove and wash thoroughly.

Take the chains and pin them to a piece of scrap wood. Now using a stiff brush, pumice and liquid soap, scrub them until all the oxides are removed, then rinse well. They should now have a fine matt finish. This will look quite acceptable but if you want a bright lustre, repeat the scrubbing using jeweller's rouge in paste form or a liquid polish. Chains can be buffed on a polishing motor but take care. They can be wrapped around a wooden strip and offered up to a small-diameter buffing wheel but make sure that there are no loose ends of chain or slack

Treatment for rust

There are basically two types of rust you will come across, the reddish brown, light surface coating and the more damaging hard blackish crust which pits the surface. Always use the minimum amount of abrasion required for its removal. A lot of effort can be saved by soaking the worst off by brushing in a paraffin (kerosene) and oil mix which is left to soak. There are a number of good rust removers on the market but make sure they are not used for too long otherwise they will etch the surface being cleaned. Always make sure you read the instructions as some rust removers have a surface priming action also. Abrasion of the rust can be carried out using steel wool, varying grades of emery cloth and, finally, polishing papers. If paraffin is used, make certain that any residue is rinsed away because otherwise it will cause rusting due to its high water content.

The finished surface can be lacquered or sealed using a wax polish. The balance can then be re-assembled, the bolt rings being held in two pliers once again and twisted closed. The balance is now ready for use or display.

Project 2: Policeman's lamp

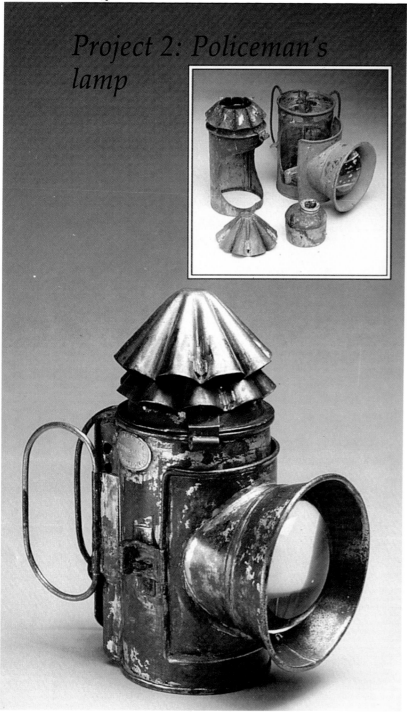

The collecting of oil lamps has been popular for some time, although generally they have been of the domestic variety. With the recent upsurge of interest in all things from the past it has become increasingly difficult to find unspoilt examples of domestic lamps, consequently the collecting and display of commercial and industrial articles has become more widespread. This lamp is a good case in point. Articles connected with police work have always held a fascination for a small group of collectors. Now that interest has outgrown supply, all manner of police paraphernalia is being sought out. Things like helmets and painted truncheons have been fetching high prices on the open market.

The bull's-eye lamp

This lamp was made about 1880 in Bishopsgate, London, by Joyce and Son and still carries their brass plaque under the grime. It is a particularly nice piece as the bull's-eye lens is in very good condition and the body of the lamp itself is complete. Inside it carries the original burner which, strangely, has no adjustment. The wick would be set and lit at the beginning of the patrol and then left. The lamp gives off a very good beam of light. But there is a world of difference between sitting testing it in a darkened living room and trying to get it to penetrate the gloom of some fog-shrouded riverside alley. The lamp was designed to be either hand-held or clipped to the officer's belt. The bodywork is of tin plate and has been very well made as befits government-issue equipment. The component parts of the lamp have been cleverly designed so that the piece obtains maximum strength for little weight, the bull's-eye lens being set deep in the face of the lamp where it is well protected. The front casing is assembled around the lens and provides a watertight seal.

The general standard and skills exhibited in the original assembly of any piece should be carefully assessed. Any unusual technique should be noted and investigated further. The repair required for this lamp looks on first inspection to be a very simple affair. The chimney cap of the lamp is loose and must be removed, cleaned, trued up and resoldered.

Left: *The main components of the lamp were heavily contaminated with soot and grease. The lamp had to be taken apart* (top) *and all this removed before repairs could be carried out.*

Dismantling the lamp

Before attempting to unsolder the cap, it is necessary to take the central core of the lamp out of the casing. This is achieved by twisting the top cap and lifting. The burner, reflector and chimney sub-assembly should lift free of the main body. Now remove the burner casing and lift clear. If the burner is held by soot and grease, place it on top of a hot radiator until the grease becomes softened and allows the burner to be eased free. The top cap seems to be soldered and held on to the base cap with fixing tabs (see diagram below). By heating the area around the tabs the solder should melt and allow the tabs to be prised (pried) up with the end of an old screwdriver. Whilst doing this, support the lamp chimney assembly securely in a well-padded vice (vise). If, however, the sequence of making the lamp is considered, you will quickly realize that the tabs would have to be placed through fixing holes and soldered into position after the caps have been placed one on top of the other. This would mean that the tabs have also been fastened on the inside cap face (see diagram). On heating the areas concerned and removing the solder, the cap becomes looser but no nearer to coming free.

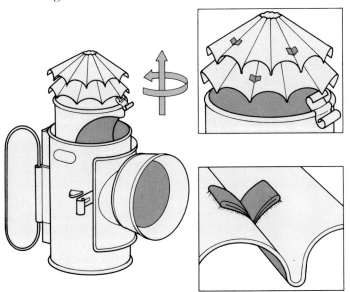

Remove the chimney from the body of the lamp by lifting and twisting (left). The top drawing shows the position of the soldered tabs, which are detailed above.

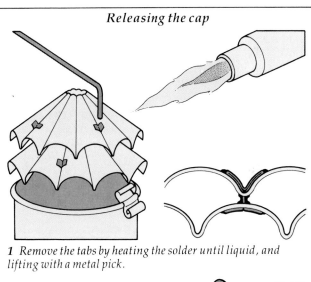

Releasing the cap

1 Remove the tabs by heating the solder until liquid, and lifting with a metal pick.

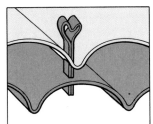

2 Prise up the tab centre and unfold the ends.

3 The straightened tab can now be lifted free.

On closer inspection of the fixing tabs they were found to be of a pattern which would prevent them releasing the cap even if they were very loose. The tabs were, in fact, hairpin-shaped. The two ends pushed through the caps and bent outwards. The loop left above the cap was pushed down in the middle, forming two narrow loops. These were then flattened and the cap sides and the whole assembly soldered.

Once this was discovered, it became comparatively easy to remove the cap. A large percentage of repairs call for the initial removal of component parts. It is essential that any would-be restorer tries to see the piece through the maker's eyes. Surprises will still occur, as in this case, but it should stop the frustration which may lead in turn to brute force and damage.

Cleaning

The lamp is now in several pieces: the top cap, the chimney, the burner and the lamp body. Most lamps of this age will be very dirty with dried oil and soot. Some will have heavy candle wax deposits inside.

If any solder repairs are required, the removal of grime is essential. First, place the parts of the lamp in a bowl of paraffin (kerosene). This part of the cleaning process can be speeded up by agitating the surface with a toothbrush or small brass scratch brush. When the majority of the dirt has been removed, transfer the parts to fresh paraffin to complete the process. Then wash the pieces in a solution of hot water, washing soda and a little washing-up (dishwashing) liquid. Take particular care in the cleaning of surface junctions; if necessary, clean these with a cotton-wool bud (Q-tip swab).

The article must now be thoroughly dried. The best way to do this is by placing all the pieces in a box of dry sawdust or alternatively, after initial drying, finish off with a hair drier.

Cleaning

 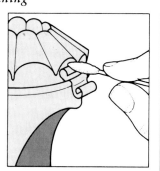

1 *Remove grime with paraffin on a small brush.*

2 *Use a cotton-wool bud for awkward places.*

Treating rust

If the surface is rusted, treat it with a proprietary rust remover. Choose one carefully – some commercial preparations leave a deposit which is a preparation for painting. Bear in mind, too, that any solutions left for long on the surface will etch the metal, possibly causing more damage than they cure. It might be possible to remove

Reaming with a wire drill

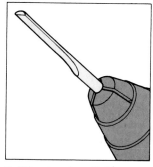 

1 *File wire of a suitable gauge on one side.*

2 *Feed it slowly into the blocked hole of the handle.*

the rust with abrasives alone. Some rust lies just on the surface and can easily be removed with steel wool and a little oil. More stubborn areas can be tackled with emery cloth or a paste of emery grit, pumice and oil.

Apart from the cap there are two small problems to be taken care of. First, the handle on one side of the lamp is so stiff that any attempt to move it is liable to tear the metal. It can be eased, however, by treating the affected area with penetrating oil. Leave the oil to soak in for a time and then try to move the handle gently. It may require several applications to free the handle completely; you can then take the handle out and remove any remaining rust.

Rust inside the handle retaining hole can be cleaned off by reaming with a piece of wire held in a hand-drill. Take a piece of high tensile wire (piano wire) of a suitable gauge and file one side flat. Cut the end to approximately 30° and place in the drill. Turning the drill as you do so, push the wire into the hole. Move the drive gently forward, turning continuously. This will remove the rust without increasing the bore size.

The same solution is also used to eliminate the other problem, that of the hinge pin. This has become rusted and is causing the door of the lamp to sag badly. The pin must be removed, the hole reamed and the pin replaced with a larger wire. The replacement should ideally be of nickel, which is tough and will not rust.

Reaming using a wire drill is also very useful for hinges which do not have the knuckles exactly in line. The wire drill is used to ease the path of the hinge pin.

Trueing up the cap

With the piece now clean and rust-free, the cap can be secured in place. First, however, it must be trued up. This can be achieved by taking a wooden block into which you cut a tapered groove, which is then held in the vice. The cap is placed with one of its ribs in the groove. Now, using a narrow-faced mallet, tap the metal down into the groove; do this with all the ribs in a regular pattern. This way the cap will remain circular, whereas an attempt to re-form odd ribs is liable to distort the overall shape. The making of this cap is similar to a method of raising where the circumference of the disc is reduced by just this technique.

Making a new cap

If caps need to be replaced, they can be made by cutting a tin-plate disc and marking the number of ridges required. Form the first ridge with the mallet, then its opposite number, followed by the intervening ridges. The disc will rapidly start to make a cone-like shape. The ridges can then be trued up by using the grooved block and a shaped wooden punch.

The cap has been trued up using a shaped wooden block and wedge mallet.

Making a new cap

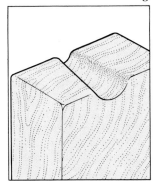
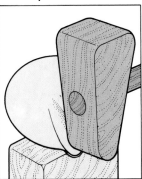

1 *Use a wooden block with a tapered groove, and make the first flute with a narrow wedge-shaped mallet.*

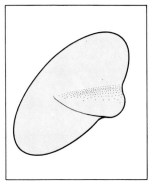
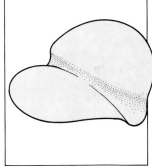

2 *The flute runs from the rim to the disc centre.*

3 *Position the second flute opposite the first.*

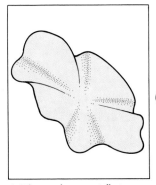
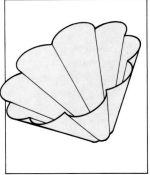

4 *Place subsequent flutes opposite each other.*

5 *The disc gradually forms a cone.*

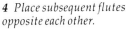

Soft soldering

Once you are satisfied with the re-formed shape of the top cap, it can be resoldered on to the chimney. New retaining tabs can be cut from a sheet of tin plate. These tabs are approximately 25mm (1in.) long and 6mm (¼in.) wide. Bend them around a piece of dowel to form a hairpin shape. The cap is placed and the retaining tabs fed into position. Allow the tabs to pass through the lower cap by about 6mm (¼in.). With an orange stick smear non-corrosive flux on the tab ends.

Bend the tabs up underneath the lower cap, then gently heat the area and solder the tabs into position. The heating can be done with either a small flame from a gas torch or a soldering iron (the soldering iron is more convenient and safer). You can use either an electrically heated iron or one which requires preheating in a gas flame. If the latter type is used, heat until a green flame appears. This indicates that the iron is at the required temperature. The iron will need to be tinned before use. When it is hot enough, lightly file the surface to remove any oxides. Now dip the tip into the selected flux and touch on the solder. This should immediately coat the tip of the soldering iron. It is now tinned and ready to use.

Electric soldering irons are usually slimmer, as they have a constant heat source and do not rely on having a large hot mass to retain enough heat for the job. If a gas torch is used, it is important to ensure that over-heating does not take place. Most of these lamps were heavily tinned on the surfaces prior to painting and we do not want this to be damaged. If a flame is used, therefore, it must be kept constantly on the move. Once the tabs are soldered into position underneath, the top loop can be made in the upper tabs. The middle loop is pushed down with a screwdriver, forming two flatter loops. These are then burnished flat to the curved sides on the top of the cap. Paint these with flux and solder into position then remove any flux residue.

This particular lamp retains large patches of the original paint-work, but it also has areas of pitting by rust. You really need to decide for yourself whether to repaint and add a new surface to the objects in your care. There is no doubt, however, that an old damaged but original surface is valued higher in the auction rooms. Surfaces can nevertheless be treated with care and with consideration for patination and original colour without detracting too much from their value.

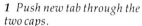

Fixing the cap

1 Push new tab through the two caps.

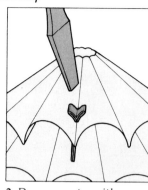

2 Depress centre with a screwdriver.

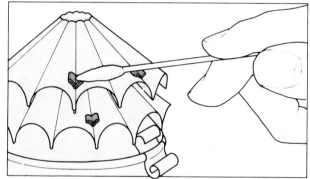

3 Fold ends underneath the lower cap, and add flux to the top and bottom of tab.

4 Heat the area with a soldering iron.

5 Solder tab in position with soft solder.

Although this item is relatively modern, the techniques and the problems involved in the repair of silver remain constant regardless of age.

The manufacture of silver has not changed for many hundreds of years. It is rather in the production and preparation of the raw materials that advances in technology have helped the silversmith. Silver has to be alloyed with other metal to make it hard enough for domestic use. By the end of the 12th century the alloying of silver and copper to the sterling standard was usual in the United Kingdom. Sterling silver is made up of 925 parts pure silver to 75 parts copper and this standard is still recognized in the UK.

The silver standard

Each item of silver made in the UK must conform to this standard and is tested at one of the assay offices situated around the country to make sure it does so. Scrapings are taken, analysed and if proved to be satisfactory, the piece is stamped (hallmarked). Each item must carry four stamps: a maker's mark, assay-office mark, standard mark and a year letter.

There is one other standard acceptable in the UK and that is of 958 parts per thousand silver and is known as Britannia silver. On no account should this be mixed with Britannia metal as this is pewter with a tin base. It was used briefly in the 17th century to discourage the melting down of the coinage. The standard was abolished in 1719 but can still be used for special items and receives a mark depicting the figure of Britannia.

In the United States hallmarking started in 1814 and manufacturers are personally responsible for marking their goods. The 'sterling' stamp is applied for 92.5% silver and 'coin' for 90%.

It is necessary to understand how important those marks are if you are undertaking any repair to silver. Any major replacement of material would invalidate the hallmark. In addition, there are many pieces which have a value out of all proportion to their material content because they bear the mark of a particular maker. It is vital that these marks are not erased or damaged.

If any repair is liable to interfere with the hallmark, obtain expert advice as to its effect.

Left: *The stem of this goblet was bent, and the base almost torn free – it had to be removed completely* (inset) *before repairs began.*

Repairs required

Repairs to this goblet, however, will not interfere in any way with the hallmarking. The goblet has suffered from bad packaging during moving house. The base has been squashed and has nearly been torn free of the item.

The piece is made in three parts, the bowl, the stem and the base. The bowl and the base have been made by spinning. This is a process in which a thin revolving disc of metal is shaped on a lathe over a metal or wooden former by using smooth, blunt tools. The disc which is in a softened state is held against the former and pressed down by the hand-held tool.

The stem has been cast and then soldered to both the bowl and the base. The joint at the point where the stem meets the base has been almost torn free, the base being distorted slightly in the process. The first job will be to separate the stem and base by heating with a gas torch until the solder flows, allowing the base to drop off.

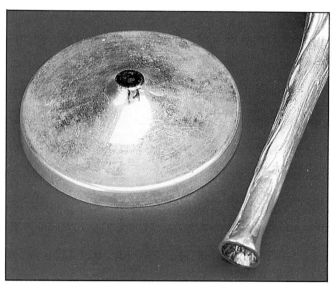

The start of a delicate soldering job – the stem must be straightened and cleaned, then a new location found on the base.

Problems and precautions

Before the base and stem are separated, however, there are several things to be considered. We cannot be sure, if the item is heated overall, that the base will separate from the stem before the bowl does. This could be rather inconvenient as we will then have two repairs to do.

The goblet will have to be placed in the refractory material in such a manner as to deflect most of the heat from the bowl. On silver objects there is usually more than one grade of silver solder used. The temperatures at which these melt can vary between 630°C (1166°F) and 830°C (1526°F). Even at the lowest temperatures copper oxide or fire stain will form on the exposed surface. When heated, silver, which is an alloy, will separate into pure silver on the surface under which is a layer of oxide. On subsequent polishing the thin silver layer is stripped, leaving this much harder oxide which is seen as a grey shadow. A lot of time and effort is then needed to remove it, usually by pickling but if the layer is thick it has to be removed by abrasives.

In order to prevent the oxides forming it will be necessary to exclude the air from the surface. This can be done by painting the whole piece, inside and out, with a borax-based flux. There are also powders sold commercially which are specially designed to do this; one of these is Argo-Tec.

The Argo-Tec is mixed into a paste using methylated spirits (wood alcohol) and painted over the job. The spirits are ignited (make sure the surrounding area is safe) and driven off. This leaves a white powdery deposit which will melt and fuse on subsequent heating. If we were soldering, the job would be heated until the fusing of the Argo-Tec took place, then left to cool. Joint areas would be cleaned off, fluxed and then placed in their positions before the final soldering.

Using Argo-Tec

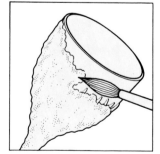

1 Paint on Argo-Tec and methylated spirits.

2 Ignite meths and allow to burn out.

Removing the base

For the present, heat the Argo-Tec until it fuses and then let it cool to a comfortable handling temperature. Make sure all the surface is covered, especially the edges, and place fire-bricks around the vessel to support it and to shield the cup. Heat up the base joint and gently pull off the base when the solder is flowing by using long tweezers or tongs. The surface coating is now removed by using boiling water.

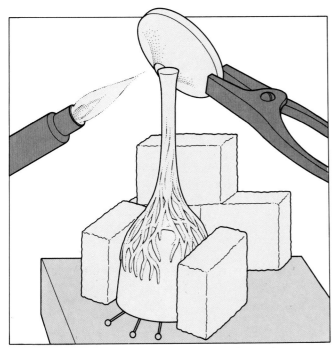

Heat solder joining stem and base, then remove base using tongs.

Repairing the base

Take the distorted base and, supporting it on the bench pin, file off any unwanted solder. The base at this stage can be carefully coaxed back into shape with a mallet and wooden former. Avoid using metal tools as they will stretch the material. Cut the profile of the base out of a piece of hard wood, and hold this in the vice (vise) as a support for the base plate while you are working on the base plate.

Repairing the base

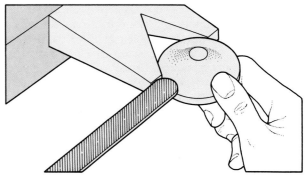

1 Support the base on the bench pin and file the stem contact area flat.

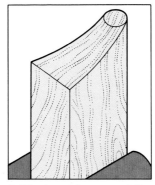

2 Wooden stakes support the base during remodelling.

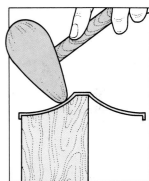

3 Correct distortions using a small mallet.

4 True up the rim on the edge of a metal bar with a boxwood mallet.

Repairing the stem

The base of the stem should also be filed free of old solder and generally cleaned up. Check that the stem is not bent. If any distortion has occurred, now is the time to correct it. To do so hold the vessel by the cup and support the stem on a wooden block. Turn the cup in your hand and watch the gap between the block and the stem. Any variation will indicate the amount of bend that must be removed. Continue revolving the cup and gently tap the stem onto the wood with a leather mallet. When you are satisfied that all is well, re-assembly can begin.

Mix fresh fire-stain inhibitor and liberally coat both parts of the vessel inside and out. Prepare as previously described and cool. Scrape the two areas where the base and stem touch and paint with flux. We will be using an extra easy grade of silver solder which melts at approximately 680-700°C (1256-1292°F). It is the lowest melting point of silver solder and should form a joint before the solder that is holding the cup to the stem melts.

Wiring up

When soldering, one of the main problems is how to hold the components in place long enough to allow the joining to occur. For any pieces other than the smallest this can be achieved by using soft iron binding wire (the type used by florists in floral decoration). This wire is almost pure iron and is virtually free from spring. When heated it has a minimal amount of movement. As this is rather an awkward shape to wire, it is easier to use two small pieces of welding metal mesh. These will provide legs which the wire can be attached to and give the added benefit of raising the job clear of the fire-bricks. This will ensure that the base becomes heated quicker than if it was standing flat on the brick. The binding wires are cut to approximate length and a loop is made at each end. Next twist the wire about half-way along to provide a third loop. This will be used to tighten the wires. Now with the mesh in place top and bottom slip on the retaining wire, tightening each one using pliers. Make sure the goblet remains upright during this time and be careful not to over-tighten the wires. The object is to hold the goblet secure but if the wires are too tight, damage will occur as it tries to expand on heating. When you are satisfied that everything is as it should be, soldering can begin.

Preparation for soldering

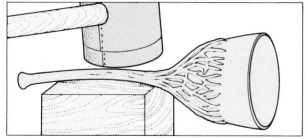

1 The stem can be straightened with a mallet. Rest stem on a wooden stake while you work.

2 Remove Argo-Tec from contact area with a file.

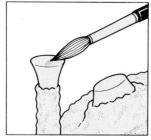

3 Apply fresh flux to both parts to be joined.

Wiring up

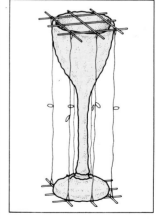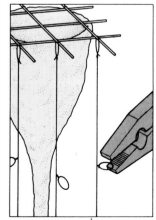

1 Use soft iron wire to hold pieces together.

2 Twist loops with pliers to tighten wires.

Soldering

Position the refractory material around the goblet so it will heat up quickly. The faster soldering occurs, once started, the better.

Begin with a soft, gentle flame, play it over the whole piece so that it warms up gradually and evenly. Any uneven heating may give rise to distortion. Watch the flux as it will bubble as the moisture is driven off, and make sure that this has not caused any movement in the joint. If everything is all right, increase the flame and bring the metal to the soldering temperature. Ideally

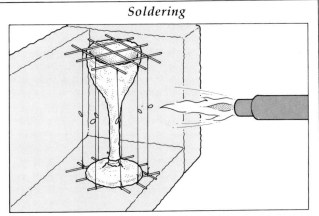

Soldering

1 Surround the object with fire-bricks and heat the whole piece with a gas torch.

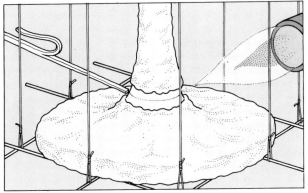

2 When the flux flows as a liquid in the joint, introduce the solder.

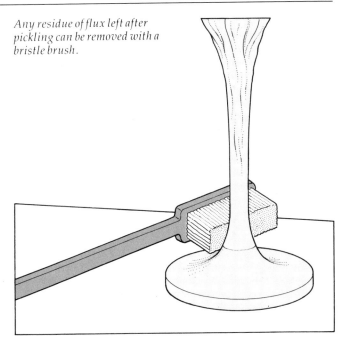

Any residue of flux left after pickling can be removed with a bristle brush.

soldering should be done in subdued light so that you will see the metal become a very dull, dark red. At this point the flux will flow as liquid – a very good indicator as to when to apply the solder. Feed the stick into the joint and it will 'flush' right around as a very bright silver streak. Reduce the flame immediately but do not withdraw it until you are satisfied that the solder has indeed flowed all the way round. Allow the vessel to cool and remove all the wires. Wash in very hot water, then place in the pickling solution to remove any remaining residues. Leave immersed for ten minutes then remove and wash thoroughly under running water. The areas of heavy texture can be brushed with a brass-bristled scratch brush. This should break up any particles of scale inhibitor remaining.

Polishing

It should now be possible to polish the piece using a commercial polishing cloth or liquid polish. Always try the polish on an easily cleaned area first and avoid polishes which leave a dark residue as this will be very awkward to remove from any crevices.

The repair is now complete.

Project 4: Copper kettle, trivet and burner

The base and burner

Copper's malleability – which makes it easy to form the material into almost any shape – and its ability to transfer heat, make it a natural choice for items like this kettle.

The piece we will be working on comes in four parts. First there is a trivet-like base, which supports the other components. This is made from perforated mild-steel plate held by wrought-iron 'c' scrolls. The overall condition of this piece is good to perfect and it should only require cleaning then refinishing as desired.

The lower part of the trivet holds the methylated-spirit (wood alcohol) burner. This is made from copper and brass and, apart from slight surface damage, is also in good condition. It has been machine-made but is of good quality because it has been made from a thick gauge of metal. Fortunately it has well-defined maker's registration marks and serial numbers in the base. These make it possible to date the piece very accurately.

The burner should require only slight cleaning in order to bring it back to its former condition.

The top plate

The third part of this set is placed on top of the trivet and acts as a hot plate for the kettle. When the burner is lit the heat would normally discolour a copper plate set over it but in this instance the top plate is double-skinned. As well as copper being decorative, it also holds heat very well – hence its use in soldering irons. Therefore this double skinning does not affect the heating of the kettle but prevents buckling of the top plate due to the direct application of heat. The top surface of the plate has been decorated by regular hammering which has caused concentric rings of dimples where the hammer has struck. This hammering, although primarily for decoration, also performs several other functions. The dimpling stiffens the sheet and helps prevent heat distortion. It also disguises surface damage due to the kettle sliding over it. Thirdly it helps prevent accidental movement of the kettle by creating a heavily textured surface. This top plate is very dirty underneath and will require a long soak to remove the oxides and grease, but there seems to be no major damage.

Left: *Although the kettle is covered in a light patination of small scratches and dents, there is one large dent* (top) *which must be removed before final cleaning and polishing.*

The kettle

The polished and restored kettle.

The last component of this set is the kettle which is made mainly from copper and copper alloys. All the parts have been machine-made apart from the spout of the kettle, which has been seamed and hand-formed.

The kettle handle is in direct contact with the body of the vessel and has no form of insulation. In use it must become extremely hot. On some sets of this kind, the kettle is held in a cradle which is tilted to pour water. This piece, however, has no such luxuries. The set is intended for use and not merely for decoration as the inside surfaces have been heavily tinned. The kettle is our major problem. Allowing for its age and the softness of the material the condition of the kettle appears to be good. There are, however, two large dents plus one small one on the same side. One of the dents is creased. The damage adds nothing to the general texture of the kettle and appears recent.

The handle has been riveted to the main body and is loose on one side. This will require tightening, or possibly replacing.

The base of the kettle is very lumpy and looks as though it has been hit on many occasions, possibly in an attempt to remove swelling caused by the heat. With the type of burner used, good surface contact would be necessary to produce any significant rise in temperature in a reasonable time.

Removing the dents

With the dents positioned as they are, the main problem is one of access. While working on the scales (see p. 163), it was possible to hammer the dents out from the inside of the bowls. Here that is not the case.

There are two main ways of removing dents from an enclosed container: the level of difficulty determines the chosen method. How difficult it is will really be decided by the position of the dent in relation to the other features on the vessel. Any dent that is hard against the base or a rim wire will prove awkward, as will dents in spouts or at the junction of spout and body. All these positions prevent ease of access to the tools required. The shape of the dent is also of significance. If the impact has caused a sharp crease line to form, this always makes removal that much more difficult.

There is no sign of this unsightly dent on the restored item.

The snarling tool

If the dent cannot be reached with a hammer as in this case, it will be necessary to make up a snarling tool. This consists of a tapering bar which is cranked at both ends. One end is held tightly in the vice (vise) while the other end passes through the lid hole of the kettle and is cranked to an angle where it can touch the inside of the dent. The head of the tool should be polished and shaped to suit the dent being worked on. If the dent is sharp and narrow, file the head of the iron so it has a small area of impact. Keep the face of the snarling tool as smooth as possible because while it is pushing out the dent it will also be imparting a smooth internal finish. In the case of the kettle a well-finished surface will prevent damage to the tinned interior.

To use the iron hold it securely in the vice and rest the kettle on the other end. Move the kettle around until the head contacts the dent. Hold the kettle into your body with one hand and keep it as steady as possible. With your free hand holding an old hammer or piece of heavy wood strike the arm of the iron. This will cause the snarling iron to flex and rebound, striking the inside of the vessel. It is most important that it is held steady otherwise it will just get pushed out of the way and have little effect on the dent. Keep repeating this action until it has pushed the dent just past the surface, so there is a small lump rather than a dent. This lump is just the merest feature and should not be at all pronounced.

It is now possible to planish the area back level with the surrounding material. Sometimes the job can be rested on the head of the snarling iron when planishing. It must be remembered, however, that the iron has been especially made to vibrate so it is not very easy. If facilities for making a metal snarling tool are not available, it can be made from a piece of suitably springy timber. The same also applies to the stake on which to planish.

While working with a snarling tool as described above, it is possible to hold a piece of hard wood on the outside of the vessel against the point of contact inside. This stops the material getting pushed past the surface level and so minimizes planishing afterwards. Better results are achieved if, instead of wood, a piece of polished steel plate is used, because the quality of finish is improved.

If the area is to be planished, this must be carried out gently – the last thing that is wanted is excess stretching of the material and a consequent bulge.

Using the snarling iron

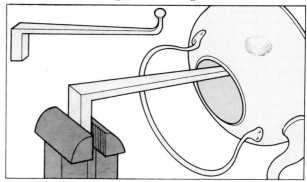

1 The snarling iron has a long springy neck. Set the kettle in position on the head of the tool.

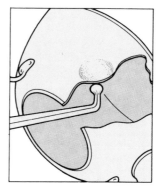

2 Position polished head of stake under dent.

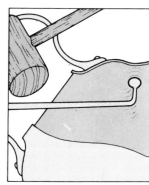

3 Strike iron so that vibrating head hits the dent.

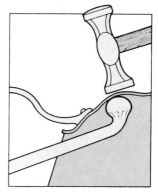

4 Material pushed clear can be planished later.

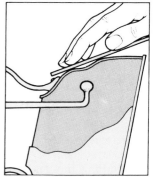

5 Polished steel behind the dent prevents excess raising.

Flattening the base

The base of the kettle should be tackled next. There are a large number of lumps and bumps to be removed and the main problem will be how to get to them. Initially they seem to be easy but the handle will get in the way of most of them. The excess material in the bulge must be eased away by stretching the surrounding metal. It is pointless just hammering the bulge as it will only appear somewhere else. However, we are not concerned with obtaining a dead flat surface on this particular object, merely to remove most of the unsightly bumps and obtain the maximum amount of contact with the hot plate that can reasonably be expected.

The method of doing this is to stretch the surrounding metal so that the bumps are pulled flat. Obviously there is a limit to how far the area around the bump can be stretched as it is defined by the 'dome' of the kettle.

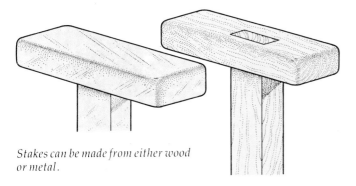

Stakes can be made from either wood or metal.

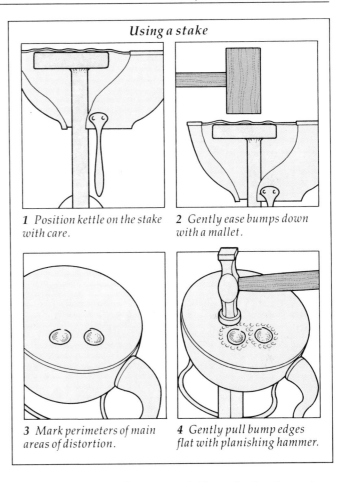

Using a stake

1 Position kettle on the stake with care.

2 Gently ease bumps down with a mallet.

3 Mark perimeters of main areas of distortion.

4 Gently pull bump edges flat with planishing hammer.

Using a stake

Before starting any hammer work several stakes will be required. These can be purchased but they are expensive if they will only be needed for the odd job; fortunately, suitable substitutes can be made. The stakes required need to be in the shape of a 'T' but with the top bar slightly off-set (see diagram above). It is usually possible to persuade the local garage or repair shop to weld a couple of pieces of scrap steel bar together for a small fee. Alternatively some home arc-welders will do the job very well.

A stake can, as a last resort, be made from a hardwood such as beech or maple. Care must be taken, however, in constructing the joint of the junction as it will have to take a lot of pressure.

Set the stake in the vice and place the kettle on top. Now using a boxwood or rawhide mallet gently go over the base of the kettle to even out the bumps. It may be that this will be sufficient to give an acceptable surface. If not, the next stage is to identify the main areas of damage and mark these out with a felt pen. Anywhere on the surface within these boundaries is now left alone.

Using either a planishing hammer or one which you have shaped and polished, begin to tap gently around the perimeter of the areas marked. Ensure that the area being hammered is well supported on the stake or more harm than good will result. Continue with the planishing until the rim of the bumps becomes stretched and pulls the raised area flat. This can be encouraged with careful use of the mallet or wooden block.

Sharp indentations

In cases where there are small, sharp indentations it is often possible to push these out from the inside by using shaped wooden or metal punches and a hammer.

Place the object on which you are working on to a flat base which will give slightly under impact. This can be linoleum, a lead sheet or a wooden block with the end grain uppermost or anything that moves away from the point of contact. Support the punch just above the surface to be worked on, making sure that your hand is supported on the rim of the vessel or any convenient spot. Strike the punch with a light rhythmic action: the intention is to apply many rapid blows to the punch as you move it across the damaged surface. Watch the area of the job around where you are working and not the end of the punch which you are hitting. The force of the blow is controlled by keeping a close watch on the results of previous blows and appropriate force should be applied with action of the wrist rather than the arm. You will find just using the wrist less tiring and self-limiting in the amount of impact you can apply. You should be able to produce good results after a little practice.

Sharp indentations can be pushed out with a wooden punch.

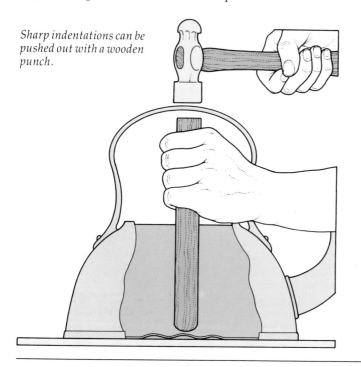

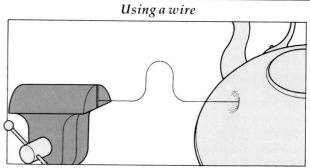

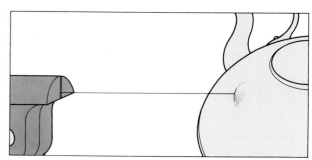

Using a wire

1 *Solder the wire to the dent. Hold the other end of wire in the vice and pull sharply.*

2 *The wire will pull the dent proud of the surface. Several jerks may be needed.*

Using a wire

There is an additional method of dent removal which can be used in extreme cases. It may not always be possible to get a snarling iron in contact with a dent because of its position. This is usually when it is hard up against a rim or protected by an overhanging feature. In this instance a wire is hard-soldered to the middle of the dent on the outside. The wire should be positioned so it is at right angles to the surface. The loose end of the wire is clamped firmly in a vice, while the object soldered to the other end is supported. Holding the vessel securely in both hands jerk the wire taut. This will pull the dent level. Several attempts might be needed before the level of the surrounding metal is reached. Ideally, the dent should be pulled just proud of the surface. The wire is then removed and the solder cleaned off with files. The area can be planished back to its original shape.

Air pressure used in planishing

It might not be possible to get a planishing stake behind the damaged area. In this case the vessel should be made airtight by putting on the lid and taping or closing the holes by using card and tape. The piece can now be held in the crook of your arm and *gently* planished using the air pressure inside for support.

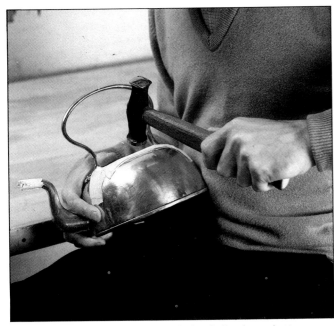

Tape the spout and lid, then hold the kettle firmly against your body to planish raised areas flush.

The handle

The handle of the kettle is rather loose on one side and ideally should be tightened. If it is not possible to make the rivet secure it will have to be drilled out and replaced. On this type of item that would be rather awkward as the rivet has been tinned on the inside of the kettle. This effectively has soldered it into place. Its removal would not be easy and of course the new rivet would need tinning if the kettle were to be used. As the inside head of the rivet is so secure there is a good chance of being able to expand the rivet on the outside so the handle is gripped.

Tightening the handle

1 Position head of rivet firmly on the stake.

2 Using a centre punch strike rivet head.

3 Expanding the rivet head takes up the slack.

4 Use a ball peen hammer to re-form dome.

Place a cranked piece of metal that can support the kettle on the internal rivet head in the vice. Hold the kettle against your chest and place a tapering round-headed punch on the middle of the loose rivet. Make sure that your hand is well braced against the kettle. Strike the punch smartly so as to create a small dimple in the middle of the rivet. Hopefully, this will push the metal of the rivet outwards to grip the handle. Repeat as necessary. Now using a ball peen hammer gently re-form the domed rivet head, making sure that the kettle is still well supported and no damage is caused to the handle.

All that now remains is to clean and re-polish the surface of the kettle. Follow the advice given on pp. 164-5 for the best ways to clean and polish copper.

Project 5: Nineteenth-century percussion musket

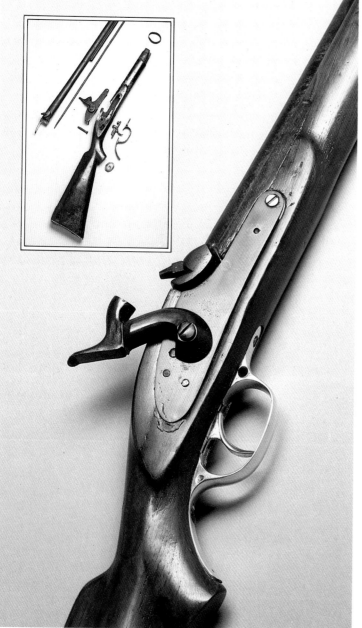

Restoring antique weapons

The repair and restoration of an antique weapon can cause more problems than most items. The main theme behind any work should be the restoration of the weapon to its original condition. It would not, however, be desirable to add or embellish any part or decoration which would not have initially been there.

Collectors, however, might not agree on the extent of repairs the amateur restorer should undertake. The individual skill of the restorer will of course play an important part in the decision as to what should or should not be tackled. With a muzzle-loading weapon such as the musket, a check should always be made to ensure it is unloaded. It is not at all unusual to find weapons with an undischarged load. When checking, the easiest method is to push a piece of dowel down the barrel and compare the length reached with the outside length of the barrel.

Should a charge be found, withdraw the load with great care and wash the barrel out with warm water. Dry it thoroughly. And *never* attempt to fire the musket, even when it is restored.

Stripping down

The first job will be to strip down the weapon. Remove the lock first, this can be achieved by undoing one or two screws which pass through the lock. If they are stubborn or rusty, placing a hot soldering iron on the end for a few minutes will usually loosen them.

The barrel can be removed by releasing the fixing screw in the tang and releasing any barrel bands. On some models retaining pins will also secure the barrel.

To remove the trigger assembly release retaining pins and extract any screws. As with many antique items much damage can be done by overcleaning. Armourer's marks and dates should be treated with great care.

By looking at things such as the retaining screws it is possible to judge whether the object has been repaired recently. Old screw threads are completely different from their modern counterparts, and usually far coarser in pitch. As the weapon is stripped down make notes so that you can re-assemble it in the correct order.

Left: *This musket is a major repair* (inset). *The lock is here returned to the partially restored stock.*

Dismantling the lock

Since the lock contains a number of springs, extra care is needed when taking it apart. Never release a screw until you are sure that the part it retains is relaxed. If you are at all unsure, place the lock in a plastic bag while releasing the screws. This will allow you to see what is happening but the bag will contain any sprung pieces which might fly off.

The particular musket pictured is in very bad condition. It will also be necessary to do a good deal of investigation about the piece as it appears to be made from several weapons which have been modified and married together. The lock is based upon that of a military musket but it has probably been manufactured in India. Possibly some pieces such as the lock plate are original and have had locally made parts added. The stock is based upon a European sporting arm and has had the military furniture such as the trigger guard modified to suit. To restore this piece completely would involve a lot of repair to the wooden stock.

As this will be such a major repair, the following section will deal with specific jobs which would be likely to be found when dealing with antique weapons.

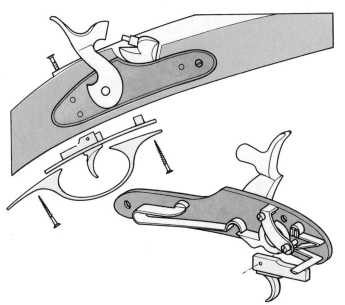

To remove the trigger assembly, first remove the guard retaining screws. Take care when releasing the springs of the lock.

Trigger guard

The end of the guard has snapped off. This can be repaired by hard soldering on a new piece. The main problem will be trying to hold the guard steady during soldering. For this reason it will be easier if the piece to be added is left over-size to allow for any movement.

Clean up both ends to be soldered and make sure they are filed square and well fitting. Flux each end and support both pieces on fire-bricks. Keep them clear of the surface by laying them on split pins which have been opened out to a V-shape. Heat both parts, but remember to build up the heat in the large piece first. When the flux fuses apply the solder. It will be better to use a stick rather than a small chip. Sometimes if heating and subsequent soldering is not immediate, the solder can be bled from the chip leaving the skin or husk remaining. Any attempt to continue heating in the hope of melting the husk and getting it to flow usually ends up with over-heating the job and a depression occurs on the surface where the chip was.

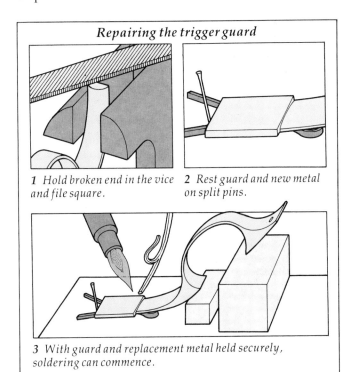

Repairing the trigger guard

1 Hold broken end in the vice and file square.

2 Rest guard and new metal on split pins.

3 With guard and replacement metal held securely, soldering can commence.

Finishing the trigger guard

After cleaning off the flux residue and oxide, the trigger guard can be filed to shape. Any adjustment to the curved form can be done at this stage by tapping the guard with a mallet while supporting it over a steel bar. Final finishing and polishing can be achieved with abrasive papers and rouge.

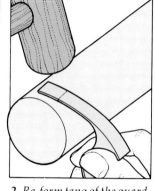

Forming the guard

1 *File off excess material with a piercing saw.*

2 *Re-form tang of the guard with a mallet.*

Barrel ramrod pipe

The barrel of this weapon is very heavily pitted especially around the area of the nipple. This is only to be expected due to the corrosive qualities of the firing charge. The nipple needs to be removed but this should only be attempted following prolonged soaking in a penetrating oil. Even then it should be undertaken with care to prevent the screw shearing off in the breedle plug.

Before any further action is taken the heavy rust on the ramrod pipe and barrel needs to be killed. This can be done using a proprietary rust remover. Make sure that the muzzle is blocked and also the nipple hole is plugged before applying the anti-rust agent.

Further cleaning of the barrel can be undertaken with steel wool and oil or, if necessary, by using emery cloth. Because the barrel is so badly corroded, it would be unwise to try and reach a finish which would enable reblueing to take place as this will require a lot of material

removal to obtain the high polish required. Providing the rust has stopped and any loose material has been removed, the surface will look satisfactory if it is finished with fine steel wool and beeswax. This can be burnished to a high lustre.

Before that takes place, however, there are several large dents in the ramrod pipe which must be removed.

Removing rust

1 *Soak corroded pieces in penetrating oil.*

2 *Brush on rust remover to kill any rust.*

Take a steel rod at least three quarters the pipe length and fractionally less than the internal diameter. This should have one rounded end. Take the rod and gently tap it into the pipe in order to push out the dent. Do not hammer too hard as there is, of course, a danger of getting it jammed. Tap the rod in a little at a time and then withdraw. Grease pushed into the bore will assist its withdrawal. Keep moving forward each time you enter and gradually ease the depression out. If the walls of the pipe are too resistant it might be necessary to heat them.

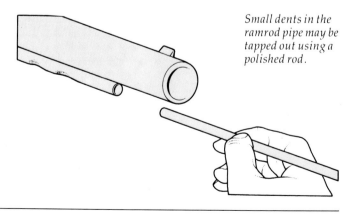

Small dents in the ramrod pipe may be tapped out using a polished rod.

Heating the barrel

Place the barrel in a vice (vise) and, using a gas torch, heat up the ramrod pipe at the dent. As the pipe has probably been soldered to the barrel you will have to prevent the rest of the pipe from getting hot. This can be done by wrapping the remaining area in wet bandages. When the dent area is hot, try tapping the rod into the pipe. This will need to be undertaken quite quickly as the rod can become trapped by the cooling metal. When all dents have been satisfactorily removed complete the final finishing of the barrel.

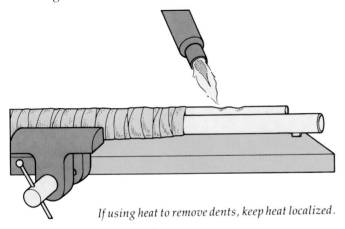

If using heat to remove dents, keep heat localized.

Hammer

The hammer on this lock is also very badly corroded. The striking face of the hammer has been virtually eaten away over the years. The hammer tail has been worn smooth and shows hardly any chequering marks.

The body of the hammer has been crudely modified to suit the weapon. It has been filed very thin and exhibits nothing of the full, well-rounded form of its contemporaries. This has been done so that the hammer could be riveted in place rather than held by a screw. It will be necessary to cut the rivet in order to free the hammer. Once this has been done any surface corrosion must be removed either chemically or mechanically.

Use a home arc-welder to deposit fresh material around the nose and flank of the hammer. (Alternatively, ask a local workshop to do this for you.) Then, file back the excess to form the desired profile. It may be that this has to occur several times before a satisfactory surface is

Repairing the hammer

1 Build up hammer around the head and body.

2 Add fresh material to the hammer by welding.

3 File new material to the correct profile.

4 Cut fresh chequering with a knife edge needle file.

achieved. The recess for the nipple can be drilled out by using a very shallow ground drill bit, the base of the hole being almost flat. The chequering on the tail can be cut using a three square or knife edge needle file. There are special files for chequering but they do tend to be expensive. As the hammer is in such a bad state it is important that research into hammer profiles is carried out before final assembly of the lock.

The lock itself must be cleaned to remove any corrosion and the parts which interact polished to a high finish.

Remember that it is far better to have an item which, when clean, still exhibits elements of its age and history rather than being over-cleaned and lacking any period feel or crispness.

Index

Figures in italic refer to
illustrations

Kayseri (Turkish) rugs 126, *135*
'kelim ends' 129, *129*, 133, *133*,
  135, 138
kelims (gelim) 126, 129, 153, *153*
knee joints 31, *31*
'knock-down' frames 44
knots 128, *128*, 137
knotted blanket stitch 66
knotted-pile rugs 126
Kurdish rugs 138

L

lacquers: metal 163, 164
  wood 70, 75, 76, 85, 90
'lap' 21
lashing (cording) 43, *43*, 54, 55,
  55, 60
lathers 14, *14*, 31, *31*
leather, replacing 11
legs, chair, making on lathe 14, *14*
  turned, repair 31, *31*
lids, repair 24
linings, removal 23
linseed oil 87
linter felt 41, *41*, 56, 59, 60, 62,
  66, 67
looms 126, *126*
lustre finishes 101

M

mahogany crystals *85*
mallets, boxwood *173*
marquetry 78
Martin brothers 89
Melaz rugs *143*
mercerising 126
metal dippers 119, 120, 121
metal staples, removal of 105
methylene chloride 76
mouldings, replacement 23, *23*,
  28, *28*
moulds 98, 114–115
muntins (stiles) 26, *26*

O

oil finishes (wood) 70, 87–8,
  87
'oil-resin' finish 88
'orange' polish 90
overcasting 130, 138
  wood 139, *139*, 140
oversewing stitch 133, 135, *135*,
  136
oxalic acid 86

P

paillons 159, *159*
paint 106, 116, 117, 120
  123, 124
paint stripper (water soluble) 97,
  104, 105
patching: rugs 148–50
  wood 78, *78*
pattern design (cartoons) 127, *127*
penetrating stains *83*, 84
Pennsylvania Dutch furniture 33,
  33
Perkin, William Henry 131
Persian (Senneh) knots 128, *128*,
  137
petroleum jelly 115, 123
pickling solutions 163, 165, *165*,
  175
pigmented stains ('wiping stains')
  83, *83*
pigments and paints 118, *118*
pile 126
pile knotting 126, 127–8, *127*
  128
pile rugs, distinguishing hand-
  woven from machine-made 130,
  130
pinning (skewering):
  calico 58, *58*, 59, 66
  scrim 64
piping (welting) 42, 53
planishing 164, *164*, 178–9, *178–9*,
  181, *181*
planishing hammers 157, *157*, 164,
  164, *178*, *179*, *179*
plaster of Paris 76
polishing: metal 160, 164, *165*, 175
  wood 29, *29*
polishing motors 160, 165
polythene sheeting 74
potassium bichromate 85, *85*
potassium permanganate 85, *85*
pry-bars (flooring bolsters) 19, *19*
punches 180, *180*
PVA (wood glue) 122, 124

Q

Q-tip swabs (cotton wool buds)
  98, 114, 115, *115*

R

raising 162, *162*
reamalgamation 75, 80, *80*
reaming 168, *168*

Regency Period 30
regulators 40, 50, 52, 58, 66, *66*
repairs, planning 25
repiling 143–4, *143–4*
reweaving 145–7, *145–7*
rivets, tightening 181, *181*
rubbers 91, *91*
runners 27, *27*
rust 165, 168

S

sabre leg chairs 30–32, *30–32*
safety 74, 76, 96
sand bags 163, *163*
sanding 71, *71*, 81, *81*
scratch brushes, brass-bristled
  175
scratch stocks 8, 23, *23*
screwholes, renovation 36
scroll arms 57–9, *57–9*, 66
scrollwork 33, 34, *34*
sections, wood, insertion 10, 24,
  24, 28, *28*, 31–2, *31–2*, 34, *34*,
  36, *36*
selvedges *see* side cords
Senneh (Persian) knots 30, *128*,
  137
shellac 9, 75, 89, 90
shellac sticks 79, *79*
shoe polish, as wood stain 84
show wood frames 44, 49, 50, 52
  63, 64, 65, 67
side cords (selvedges) 129, *129*, 130
  136, 138–40, *138–40*
silicon carbide wet and dry paper
  117
silicon waxes 87
single cord 140
sink stitches *see* blind stitches
sinking 162, *162*
skewering (pinning):
  calico 58, *58*, 59, 66
  scrim 64
skin wadding *see* wadding
'skinning in' ('fadding') 92
slip stitching 62, 63
slipping (buttoning) thread 42,
  59, 62
snarling irons 178, *178*
soldering 159, *159*
  silver 172–5, *172–5*
  soft 170, *170*
soldering irons 170, *170*
soumaks (weft wrapping) 126, 129,
  129
Spanish knots 128, *128*

spinning metals 172
spiriting off 92, *92*
splits: rugs 151–2
  wood 10, 16, 20
springs 42, *42*, 43, *43*, 54–5, *54–5*,
  60
sprung seats 54
spun sheep's wool 126
stains: rugs 154, *154*
  wood 29, 70, 82–6, 83–4, *83*
stakes 162, *162*, 163, *163*, 179, *179*
stay (stuffing) rails 44, *44*, 53,
  56, 57, *57*, 60, 64, 66
steaming wood 78, *78*
sterling silver 171
'stiffing' 93, 96
stiles (muntins) 26, *26*
stitches: blanket 133, 135, *135*
  blind (sink) 43, *43*, 51, *51*, 56, 58,
  60, 64
  chain 136, *136*, 137
  herringbone 142, *142*
  joining (knotted blanket) 59, *59*
  looped running 47
  oversewing 133, 135, *135*,
  136–7
  roll 56
  running 50
  slip 62
stitching 49, 51, 56, 64, 66
stoving enamels 108, 119, *119*
strapping, ceramics repair 105,
  105
strengthening methods 10, *10*
'striking through' ('bleeding') 84
stripping: wood 18, *18*, 75–6, *76*
  upholstery 44, *44*, 49, 53, 63
stuck mouldings 28
stuffing (stay) rails 44, *44*, 53,
  56, 57, *57*, 60, 64, 66
stuffing ties 50, *50*, 51, 56, 57
  60
stuffings: first 43, *43*, 49, 50,
  50, 53, 55–6, 57, *57*, 59, 60
  second 43, *43*, 49, 51, 53, 56, 59,
  60, 67
stuffover frames 44
symmetrical knots 128

T

tabs, retaining 167, *167*, 170, *170*
'tack rags' 81
tail vices 10
tapestry-type (flat-woven) rugs
  126, 129, *129*
tassels 129

Acknowledgements

Swallow Books wish to acknowledge the assistance given to them in the preparation of the *Craftsman's Guides* series by:

David Allen, E. Amette and Co, Graham Bingham, Jon Bouchier, Fanny Campbell, Michael Carter, Steve Cross, Del and Co, Liz Eddison, Glynis Edwards, Hussein Hussein, Victoria Keller, Aziz Khan, The London College of Furniture, Maureen Maddren, Nick Maddren, Ray Martin, Su Martin, Coral Mula, Elaine Partington, Stuart Perry, Nick Russel, Tom Seavey, Rob Shone, Eric Smith, Sylvia Tate, Catherine Tilley, Barry Walsh, Jackie Wedgwood, John Woodcock, Anne Yelland.

The following individuals and organizations kindly supplied photographs: The American Museum in Britain 33, 34, 36; Derek Balfour 54, 61I, 64B; The Bridgeman Art Library 11, 43CR, 87T, 90, 93, 111; Eldridge London 67B; Henry Flack (1860) Ltd 5, 91; International Paint 70L, 70R, 82, 83C; Michael Holford 110, 112R, 113; Jaycee Furniture 22; Ronseal 17B, 18, 70CL, 70CR, 75, 79, 83B, 87B, 88; Jessica Strang 17T, 22, 86; Elizabeth Whiting and Associates – photographer Tom Leighton 67T.